Form 178 rev. 01-07

British Film Music and Film Musicals

British Film Music and Film Musicals

K.J. Donnelly
University of Aberystwyth

First published 2007 by
PALGRAVE MACMILLAN
Houndmills, Basingstoke, Hampshire RG21 6XS and
175 Fifth Avenue, New York, N.Y. 10010
Companies and representatives throughout the world

PALGRAVE MACMILLAN is the global academic imprint of the Palgrave
Macmillan division of St. Martin's Press, LLC and of Palgrave Macmillan Ltd.
Macmillan® is a registered trademark in the United States, United Kingdom
and other countries. Palgrave is a registered trademark in the European
Union and other countries.

ISBN-13: 978–1–4039–9673–2 hardback
ISBN-10: 1–4039–9673–3 hardback

This book is printed on paper suitable for recycling and made from fully
managed and sustained forest sources. Logging, pulping and manufacturing
processes are expected to conform to the environmental regulations of the
country of origin.

A catalogue record for this book is available from the British Library.

Library of Congress Cataloging-in-Publication Data
Donnelly, K. J. (Kevin J.)
    British film music and film musicals / K.J. Donnelly.
        p.   cm.
    Includes bibliographical references and indexes.
    ISBN-13: 978-1–4039–9673–2 (cloth)
    ISBN-10: 1–4039–9673–3 (cloth)
    1. Motion picture music—Great Britain—History and criticism.
    2. Musical films—Great Britain—History and criticism.
    3. Musicals—Great Britain—History and criticism.   I. Title.
    ML2075.D66 2007
    781.5′420941—dc22   2007060065

10   9   8   7   6   5   4   3   2   1
16   15   14   13   12   11   10   09   08   07

Printed and bound in Great Britain by
Antony Rowe Ltd, Chippenham and Eastbourne

Contents

Acknowledgements

I would like to pay tribute to the variety of hardware upon which this book was written over the years, including my cousin's antique Atari ST, Warren's prehistoric word processor, a cybercafé in south Belfast and (under a pseudonym) the workstations at Imperial College London's branch at Wye.

I would like to thank everyone who has helped and encouraged me in thinking and writing about British cinema. At UEA, Glen Creeber, Jason Jacobs, Miles Booy, Jon Burrows, Bob Neaverson, Janet McCabe, Charles Barr, Mike Allen, Warren Buckland, Tim Bergfelder, John Street, Andrew Higson, Peter Kramer, Dimitris Politakis, Pam Cook, John Cook, Steve Pain and Richard Deswarte. At Staffordshire, Lez Cooke, Victor Horboken, Alan Lovell, Christine Gledhill, John Manuel, Martin Shingler, Ulrike Sieglohr, Barbara Kennedy and Derek Longhurst. At Aberystwyth, Jamie Sexton, Jamie Medhurst, Catrin Prys, Ernest Mathijs, Martin Barker, Mikel Koven and Kate Woodward. Some people have had more of an input than others. Some read and commented upon drafts, others merely discussed matters with me, while others still simply nurtured my energy for the subject. Thanks to all, as much as you all deserve (and to any I forgot to mention).

My parents, Joan and Robert Donnelly, infused in me the desire for knowledge as well as interest in both film and music. My mother deserves particular thanks, for having tried hard to convince an often ungrateful child about the virtues of British cinema and musicals. Mandy was always supportive and furnished false identities for me when required.

An earlier version of "Wicked Sounds and Magic Melodies: Music in Gainsborough Melodramas" appeared in Pam Cook, ed., *Gainsborough Pictures* (London: Cassell, 1997), pp.155–169. Republished by permission of Continuum. An earlier version of some of the material in "Pop Music Culture, Synergy and Songs in Films: Hardware (1990) and Trainspotting (1996)" was published in "Constructing the Future through Music of the Past: the Software in Hardware" in Ian Ingis, ed., *Popular Music and Film* (London: Wallflower, (2003), pp.131–147. Material republished by permission of Wallflower. An earlier version of "The Perpetual Busman's Holiday: Sir Cliff Richard and British Pop

Musicals" was published in *Journal of Popular Film and Television*, vol. 25, no. 4, Winter 1998, pp.146–154. This was last reprinted with permission of the Helen Dwight Reid Educational Foundation, Heldref Publications, 1319 18th Street, NW, Washington, DC 20036-1802. (c) 1997.

1
Introduction

In the introduction to James Park's book *Learning to Dream*, he states that "...the history of British cinema is one of unparalleled mediocrity." [1] I would beg to differ and perhaps this book, a historical consideration of British film music and film musicals, might be taken as some evidence to the contrary. Britain not only has produced a range of outstanding films over the years, but has also highly created extraordinary material at the intersection of the film and music industries. Since World War I, the British film industry has worked in the shadow of its richer and more successful American relation. Yet despite American films proving overwhelmingly popular in Britain, British films often have retained a sense of their own distinct character, even in the face of the increasingly international status of film industries over the last half century. The British film industry lacked the rationalized production line that characterized American film production from the 1930s to the 1950s, which exerted a prescriptive effect on the music in British films. Rather than being a standardized element that was produced communally and to a strong blueprint, British film music often was more modest in sound and scale and was produced by a system that was altogether more artisanal in its methods. Composers and musicians worked only part-time in the film industry and in the vast majority of cases plied their trade primarily in other areas of musical culture. In the 1930s and 1940s, many film scores were not written to fit the precise momentary dynamics of film activity on screen. By necessity, there was more "autonomy" to music as it often was not composed to fit a rough cut of the finished film, as was (and largely still is) the case in Hollywood. While many films may have aspired to sound like the high aural standards set by Hollywood films, British cinema's budgets could rarely afford the attention to music allowed by the Hollywood studio system. Perhaps because of this, music could become "semi-detached", as a featured aspect in film rather than simply being conceived as an insignificant support for the images.

Composer Maurice Jaubert famously noted, "We do not go to the cinema to hear music. We require it to deepen and prolong in us the screen's visual impressions..."[2] Of course, in some cases we do: most notably in film musicals, rock concert or rockumentary films, this whole expanded genre being premised upon an audience going to the cinema wanting to hear music. However, beyond this, arguably some films conceive that audiences will to some degree be attracted by a film's incidental music. Art music composers writing for films might think their music important and not merely subordinated to the requirements of the images and dialogue. A good example of how such music could be a "featured" aspect of a film is Ralph Vaughan Williams's credit appearing as one of the first and occupying the whole screen at the inauguration of *49th Parallel* (1941).

Despite a handful of exceptions, films have always included a musical dimension. Silent films were accompanied whenever possible and synchronized song films predated the coming of the "talkies" by a couple of decades. The music industry had been involved intimately with films since the 1930s at least,[3] but a further development took place when the selling of disc recordings superseded the selling of sheet music. The development of the LP record market in the late 1950s bolstered the situation and allowed non-diegetic scores to be released as a commodity together with the title song. Music appears perhaps to have been the most successful tied-in product in the cinema. Between the early 1950s and early 1960s massive growth took place in the Disney merchandising division. *Kinematograph Weekly* pointed out that "It was once estimated that a song from a Disney picture was played somewhere in the world every three minutes of the day...[and now] top disc stars are being contracted to record the popular music, which has great hit potential."[4] Since that time, we have become used to film soundtracks as a commodity and advertisements for films. In Britain, there has been a strongly developing interest in music as a marketable heritage product. In recent years, this has manifested itself in films about The Beatles (*The Birth of the Beatles* [1979], *Hours and the Times* [1991], *Back Beat* [1994]) or films like *Velvet Goldmine* (1998 UK/US). There has also been a growing interest in the heritage of British film music, sadly not from scholars but from the point of view of radio and the availability and consumption of recordings. The two have gone hand in hand, both looking for accessible orchestral music, to sell or to fill the airwaves. At the turn of the millennium, the Chandos record label released a number of discs celebrating the work of British film music composers: Alan Rawsthorne, Richard Rodney Bennett, Malcolm Arnold, William Alwyn and Arthur Bliss.[5] The music in British films has been admired consistently, perhaps more abroad than in Britain, and while British film history might be conceived as a catalogue of high quality musical scores, these have never received the critical attention they deserve. As of 2006, British films have received 10 Oscars from Hollywood for best original score (*The Red Shoes* in 1948, *The Bridge on the River Kwai* in 1957, *Lawrence of Arabia* in 1962, *Tom Jones* in 1963, *The Lion in Winter* in 1968, *Midnight Express* in 1978, *Chariots of Fire* in 1981, *A Passage to India* in 1984, *The Full Monty* in 1997 [as a comedy score], and *Shakespeare in Love* in 1998 [as a comedy score]). British film music has been praised in its primary context of the film and additionally has often had a life of its own outside the cinema as concert pieces and recordings. While scores have been landmarks for differing reasons, either being conferred the status of "serious" music, becoming popular pieces outside the context of the film, or influencing the use of music in subsequent cinema, music in British films has a history of richness that may have been unmatched throughout world cinema.

Any consideration of film music, or even British music more generally, would not fail to note William Walton's outstanding score for Olivier's *Henry V* (1944) and Malcolm Arnold's music for *The Bridge on the River Kwai* (1957). Yet often these fail to be mentioned in the kind of scholarly books and histories produced in the domain of "British cinema" studies. I would like this book to help begin setting this to right. It addresses music in British films, both as musical scores (in the first half of the book) and as British film musicals (the second half). British cinema has an undiscovered history that has begun fitfully to be charted over the last 15 years or so. A crucial part of this is British film music and the British film musical. As Alan Lovell notes, British cinema, what he once termed "the unknown cinema" is now all-too well known.[6] However, British film musicals remain a "lost continent" of British cinema, as Julian Petley once referred to another British film genre ignored by scholarship.[7] Here we often find a very different world from "quality" British cinema that habitually is celebrated by writers, critics and historians. On many occasions, in the deep past, we find something that often involves third-rate performers and unfunny comics making bawdy jokes, matched to low-rent songs and singers. Many of the film musicals from the 1930s and 1940s look cheap and nasty to modern eyes: in many cases they are and as such they constitute a highly fascinating object of scrutiny. At times, the British film musical seems to constitute something of an underbelly of the "respectable" British cinema, which has been the focus of the overwhelming majority of scholarly attention.[8] While I must be careful not to overstate the case, the British film musical marks a film tradition that has heretofore received patchy and very little attention, despite – or perhaps because of – having proven eminently popular with the British public in the past. Indeed, during the 1930s, British-made musicals, starring actors such as George Formby and Gracie Fields, were among the most popular films seen (and heard) by British audiences.[9]

It is perplexing as to why musicals have been marginalized in critical and historical commentaries about British cinema. One likely reason for this is that they have represented a most obvious manifestation of "low culture" in the face of an unacknowledged project to "legitimize" British cinema, presenting it as "art", some way above the products of Hollywood, or perhaps connecting it in some way with the Heritage industry's hawking of a Britain of "class" and old world opulence.[10] Film musicals are only sometimes discussed, and on the occasions when they are addressed, they are often not addressed as film musicals. Marcia Landy's survey of British film genres notes: "The British commercial cinema from the 1930s to the 1960s can be characterized as working within the genre system. The dominant British genres of the 1930s were melodramas, historical films, musicals, comedies and films of empire."[11] Yet she then proceeds to discuss film musicals under the rubric of "comedies" rather than specifically as film musicals ("... the comedian comedies of Gracie Fields and George Formby feature regional and working-class characters and situations").[12] Similarly, Justine Ashby and Andrew Higson's edited collection *British Cinema: Past and Present*, while containing two chapters with discussion about *Band Waggon* (1940) and *Radio Parade of 1935* (1934), calls them "popular entertainment" but fails to use the term "musical". While both films include much that is not musical, they include song and musical sequences, which receive little explicit attention.[13]

Perhaps one of the reasons why film musicals have been neglected is their "uncinematic" character and relationship with other media. Musicals have had a close relationship not only with the (downmarket part of the) stage, but also with radio and television. Musicals are habitually "uncinematic" in formal terms. Music makes them an impure format that is not true to the nature of film, as it has been theorized over the years. Adrian Wootton dismissed Led Zeppelin's concert film *The Song Remains the Same* (1975) as "uncinematic",[14] while Geoffrey Nowell-Smith's verdict on The Beatles's *A Hard Day's Night* (1964) was as follows: "It can hardly be called well directed, unless you believe that the rapid gyrations of a hand-held camera are intrinsically more cinematic than the usual methods, which is patently not true."[15] These appraisals fail to register that film musicals are not only "cinematic" but also "musical": the visuals about which commentators have been negative are a product of the image reflecting and pursuing the excitement and the primacy of the music. Reviewing *Help!* (1965) Peter Harcourt noted: "What is the effect of all this endless running and jumping, this refusal to stand still? Up to a point, it seems an attempt to render in visual terms some of the energy of the Beatles's music..."[16] As Rick Altman noted, during song or dance sequences in film musicals the image ceases to follow its usual diegetic and narrative-inspired patterns and becomes a reflection of the music.[17]

Perhaps another reason for neglect might be a question mark over how indigenous British film musicals might be, particularly when approached in the light of the overwhelming international success of the Hollywood musical. This inevitably has been a key influence upon developments. Yet on the other hand, there has also been an indigenous influence from the British tradition of music hall and the London West End stage. The early years of the British film musical, in the 1930s, demonstrate what might be construed as an indigenous model, adapted from music hall traditions and around stars like, for example, George Formby, a product of the northern English music hall and clubs circuit. With the advent of very successful American musicals on stage and screen in the 1930s, Britain began to follow American style more openly, with American songwriters producing material for Jessie Matthews's films.[18] By the 1950s, rock'n'roll was imported to British films, with many seeming like poor copies of the American originals, while by the early 1960s some American singers like Gene Vincent were featured in British films. The beat boom in 1960s and the success of The Beatles led to a more British style of pop musical, although by the next decade transatlantic (mid-Atlantic?) culture and international co-productions destroyed any solid sense of an indigenous British musical. Despite the setting of Ken Russell's *Tommy* (1975) (Portsmouth locations, holiday camps, terraced houses, etc.), the film in many ways was international, not least in that it followed a successful stage show that had been a hit on Broadway. By the end of the twentieth century, despite musicals using an obvious British setting like *Absolute Beginners* (1985), *Little Voice* (1998) and *Julie and the Cadillacs* (1999), a much more successful musical film *The Commitments* (1991) was shot in Ireland with an Irish cast, using American songs and directed by Englishman Alan Parker, and was a British–American–Irish co-production. Yet over the years, there have been some specifically British feed-ins: art music, indigenous pop and rock music in the wake of The Beatles, the West End theatre and the "middlebrow",[19] and a sense of cultural ambiguity that derives from a fundamental difference between British and American culture. This is that in Britain, commerce has never managed to become the sole arbiter of taste and yardstick of success. A sense of cultural value beyond box office and supermarket-sized sales have been retained from (strained, perhaps residual) connections with high art and the persistence of relatively strong class and culture divides in Britain.

Since synchronized sound films came into being, there has been a reciprocal relationship between music and films. Initially, this involved the mutual promotion of films and sheet music, and later cross-promotion between films and musical recordings.[20] Consequently, film musicals should likely be conceived less as musical accompaniment to images and narrative, but more as image and narrative emanations from or embellishments to the songs. Perhaps the key is to think of film musicals less in relation to general cinematic traditions than in relation to the music industry and popular music traditions. Music defines the whole genre – indeed, films were regularly built around it.

While film musicals may have been marginalized by "serious" film culture and scholarship in Britain, the opposite might be noted in relation to orchestral incidental music in many British films of the 1930s and 1940s. As part of a "campaign" to project Britain as upmarket, and films as a step away (if that) from art, film scores were procured from respected art music composers for British films[21] – indeed, from some of the most respectable of British art music composers. Music has proved to be a good way to sell films, and vice versa. Yet this has been particularly true of popular music, and is testified to by the success of songs from musicals *outside* the film, be it as sheet music or as recordings.

The history of British film music can broadly be seen to follow waves and trends that correspond with developments in the British film industry as a whole. The "Golden Age" of British cinema in the late 1940s, the boom of the British film industry in the mid-1960s and the "renaissance" of the early 1980s all evince noteworthy film music. Music often has an intimate link with the concept of "quality" cinema, a particularly potent category for film export.[22] The production values of a film are perhaps embodied most clearly by its musical score. Expensively produced music sounds expensive and regularly adds another dimension to films. So while there have been cheaply made films with outstanding music, the most sumptuous and boldest music was reserved for films that could afford it.

For the purposes of this study, British films were taken to be films that were registered in the UK, including co-productions. Films that are made in Britain, films made with British personnel, films featuring a British cast or directed by British director, or films set in Britain are not enough to be considered British for the purposes of this study. While in the vast majority of cases, these are relevant factors; they are not here seen as definingly "British". Debates surrounding British cinema largely have been concerned with, on the one hand, the notion of British cinema as crucial indigenous national culture and, on the other, the notion of British cinema as an industry, lacking in political substance perhaps, but one with massive possibilities for successful export.[23] Films as manifestation of indigenous culture have something of a communal function, emanating from and being largely aimed at the consumption of a distinct community while dealing with themes and representations relevant to that community.[24] That description does not seem very apt to the film industry, where there have – in the overwhelming majority of cases – been attempts to sell products overseas. In numerous cases, this has been the major concern of production. The "national cinema" debate, which at times has been the principal debate surrounding British films, primarily has been interested in how films function for the national good and how this might be corralled into a kind of civics (of national pride, consensus and unity) by the state – in functionalist terms, how it allows for the representation of society and its concerns.

Incidental music in British films

Non-diegetic music (also known as "non-source music", underscore, background or incidental music) appears in the film as if from nowhere, emanating from outside the diegetic world constructed by the film. Non-diegetic music occupies a unique position within any mainstream film, in that unlike all the other elements of the film, it is "outside" the film's world. This allows it to form a musical discourse that is coherent in itself, not simply chained to the conventional demands of the diegesis. Consequently, the non-diegetic music of classical and mainstream dramatic cinema evolved a highly particular form and functional role in films: to comment on, articulate, energize and aestheticize the screen action, and to encourage particular emotional responses. The music in mainstream dramatic films has tended to follow the principle of using non-diegetic music as a parallel and support to screen action and narrative development. The role of the non-diegetic underscore has been to comment upon and articulate the action while diegetic music regularly functioned as a "realistic" guarantor of the diegetic world.

Scores for feature films traditionally are written by a single composer (sometimes with help from assistants or orchestrators). It is usually written to the precise requirements of a nearly finished "rough cut" of the film.[25] British films saved money and time on production by often including music that had not been written to match the precise dynamic requirements of the momentary development of the film (was written "blind"), which was a contrast with the norms of Hollywood. This mode of film music production was somewhere between the most expensive Hollywood feature film, where large amounts of music were written especially to fit the exigencies of film dynamics, and the low-budget film method of using existing library music that would make a rough fit to the film's development (or the film would be cut with the music in mind). British film nevertheless followed the traditional blueprint of the "Classical film score",[26] as established by the dominant Hollywood film industry. Indeed, in terms of overall sound and function, incidental music in British films often appeared superficially similar to that in Hollywood films.[27]

Film music is not a self-contained process. Britain, lacking the large-scale film industry manifested by Hollywood, always lacked the rosters of composers that would specialize in film music. Instead, composers were compelled to write music for different things, be it orchestral concert hall music, "easy listening" orchestral music, or popular music. Consequently, these other forms of music have had a paramount influence upon music in British films. In the 1930s and 1940s, music written for films included some very prominent music written by respected art music composers, who largely remained true to their concert hall origin. Similarly, from the 1960s onwards there were an increasing number of composers from a pop music background who provided music for British films. In both cases, the influences they brought to bear on film music from their respective fields were significant, and arguably had more effect than in Hollywood where the studio institutions had to some degree standardized the practice of film music.

Indeed, this sometime semi-independent relationship of film and accompanying music in Britain became particularly suited to the increasing development from the 1960s onwards of using pre-existing songs as incidental music in films. *The Graduate* (1967 US) is a good example of a film utilizing a "song score",[28] while the increased use of "compilation scores" of diverse songs has caused the concomitant rise of music supervisors, who are responsible one way or another for the use of pop songs in films.[29]

The nature of pop music is very different from traditional underscore, primarily in the way it matches the dynamics on screen if the images are cut to and staged around the music's dynamics. This is due to its own strong rhythmic and temporal schemes, which mean that it is often foregrounded when used as non-diegetic music in a sequence. So while pop songs work best in sequences of loose visual dynamics (e.g. long travelling shots) or fast rhythmic editing (montage sequences), the use of pop music as non-diegetic music regularly energizes the filmic narration. It provides kinetic forward movement for the image track, and in the absence of anchoring diegetic sound converts the image track to an energetic play of shape, texture and movement.

The half of the book concerned with British film music begins with a panoramic overview of the historical development of underscores in British films. It then goes on to provide a number of more precise studies of particular films or historical moments. Chapter 3 looks at the less celebrated area of workaday film music produced by one of the more successful but less prestigious British production companies of the 1940s. Chapter 4 is about the way that music coheres with a seemingly integrated system of sound to illustrate some ideas about Northern Ireland in *Odd Man Out* (1947) that are not immediately apparent. Chapter 5 documents a notable moment, where British films experimented with scores by pop musicians who were film music novices, generating highly individual results. Chapter 6 looks at the way that pre-existing pop songs can be utilized in recent films as a replacement for more traditional film music.

Musicals

The film musical's relationship to its elder cousin on the stage is significant.[30] The strategies of the screen musical often betray origins on the stage. Operas usually have sung dialogue in between the set piece songs (the recitative between the arias), yet so do some musicals, such as *Les Misérables*, which is "sung-through", as they say. Otherwise, musicals tend to have dialogue sections and songs that appear well demarcated. The film musical is premised upon the set-piece sequence which tends to break the film's development into episodes. The non-diegetic underscore in musicals has a similar function to that of Classical mainstream cinema, although it often provides a sense of continuity between songs and dances and the film's sections of dramatic development. According to Rick Altman, the divide between songs and the conventional film world is the single most defining aspect of the Classical Hollywood Musical genre.[31] Indeed, musicals are divided into two types based on how they deal with the divide between songs and the dramatic, narrative parts of the film. They are "integrated" if the songs and dances have a notable character function or help develop the narrative in some way. In many cases, particularly before the 1950s, they did not. During the 1930s, the "backstage" musical was in ascendancy, where songs were performed as part of a stage show in the story. While backstage musicals can also be integrated, the two forms have often proven distinct. In backstage musicals, the songs are attractions in themselves but function as a contrast to the backstage activities and relationships between the performers. Martin Sutton states: "There are basically two kinds of musicals when it comes to the relationship between plot and number. There are those which make clear separations between the two . . . and those which attempt to cement over the rift and present the number 'naturally' as part of the plot . . ."[32] Not only the divide between song and the rest of the film, but its join is also significant. Rick Altman describes the process of "audio dissolves" at the point where the song or dance starts in such integrated musicals. Here, the superimposition of the two distinct aural tracks signals a modulation of cinematic regimes, from that of the narrative to the song sequences, where from a conventional film style the images' actions reflect the music.[33]

In discussing pop music in British cinema, I used two terms to differentiate between means of visual accompaniment to a song or dance sequence in musicals.[34] I use the term "performance mode" to designate an attempt to express an ineluctable connection between images seen and sounds heard, and to indicate where images show the *production* of simultaneous sounds. Moving away from this, sometimes images show only some of the music's production. The clearest example of this would be the "bursting into song" of the integrated film musical, for which I used the term "lip-synch mode", deriving from the industrial process of matching the lips to a preexisting musical playback. Both the performance mode and the lip-synch mode offer a greater or lesser degree of the experience of the musicians performing the song or dance for the implied audience. The performance mode references a documenting of "the real", while the lip-synch mode tends to signify a hyperbolic move to "fantasy", the former being associated particularly with backstage musicals and the latter with integrated musicals such as *Seven Brides for Seven Brothers* (1954 US) or *South Pacific* (1958 US). The film of Andrew Lloyd Webber's *Phantom of the Opera* (2004 US-UK) mixes the two, with operatic arias sung in public at the opera house using the performance mode and song sung intimately between characters using the lip-synch mode. As this description suggests, the two modes often work in different manners, with the former more amenable to use in mainstream dramatic films while the latter tends to indicate the traditional integrated film musical.

A development in the tradition, pop musicals, used rock'n'roll songs yet followed the same means of rendering songs as traditional musicals. Rick Altman sees a continuity between the musicals of Hollywood's classical era and films that are based on pop music.[35] However, other commentators view pop music as providing a rupture with the traditional modes of musical film. Barry Keith Grant points to pop music as an emergent form that hastened the destruction of the classical musical form and musicals as a viable genre: "The rapid decline of musicals in the late 1950s seems to me more likely explained by the existence of an ever-widening gap between the music in the musicals the studios were making and the music an increasing percentage of the nation was actually listening to – rock'n'roll."[36] In the late 1950s, with Britain's films close behind, American films began to use rock'n'roll, either through featuring cameo appearances by groups in narrative films and backstage musicals or through building films around singing stars.

Overall, Britain's film musicals have been consistently overshadowed by Hollywood's. In terms of box-office success, production values, stars and innovations, Hollywood has always led the way. However, in one way perhaps it did not: in the decline of the film musical. According to Rick Altman, the number of musicals produced by Hollywood peaked in the late 1940s and early 1950s,[37] and peaked in terms of its creativity in the early and mid-1950s. Britain, on the other hand, made many musicals in the 1930s, which began tailing off in the late 1940s, with few being produced in the 1950s. The half of the book that is concerned with film musicals begins with a synoptic overview of the developments in the British musical film. It then goes on to discuss the relationship between musicals in the theatre and in cinema, in Chapter 8. After this, it looks at the career of one of the longest-serving British music professionals, in "Sir Cliff Richard and British Pop Musicals." It then looks at the innovative manner in which The Beatles re-invented the musical format in "The Musical Revolution: The Beatles in *A Hard Day's*

Night," while the final chapter investigates one of the most lavish of all British musicals, in "Musicalising Britain's Past: *Absolute Beginners."*

Conclusion

It might easily be argued that British cinema has always been reliant on developments elsewhere, and might also be argued that music in films and film musicals are more reliant than most areas of British cinema on other determinants than film. It is crucial, therefore, that Britain has proven itself very good at music: in terms of popular music, Britain has been a world-beater since the 1960s, consistently punching above its weight in the international pop music marketplace. Since the Beatles and British pop and rock in their wake, Britain has held its own and at times had a stranglehold in the international popular music market. Furthermore, in terms of orchestral film music, Britain still produces copious amounts of composers who are siphoned off to careers in Hollywood (the most recent examples include Edward Shearmur and Harry Gregson-Williams), while in terms of stage musicals, Andrew Lloyd Webber has dominated the world's musical stages for the last 20 or more years. Furthermore, it is notable that two of the most significant moments in British film production's international success have taken place concurrently with massive international successes of British popular music internationally.[38]

Arguably, there has been a convergence between incidental music in films (non-diegetic music) and the modes of the film musical. The musical may remain as a genre but its impetus, aesthetics and attractions now also exist in many mainstream films. Indeed, one could argue that such characteristics have always been there, most clearly in mainstream films that included a featured song or two. With the recession of the musical as a perennial film genre, its role of selling music has migrated to mainstream films, taking with it something of the aesthetics that film musicals derived from their dominance by music dynamics and requirements.

Despite their close relationship, film musicals and incidental music in film are most easily dealt with as separate entities. This is the way that the book approaches them, opening with a selection of chapters about British film musicals followed by a second half of chapters about incidental music in British films. Both British film music and British film musical here receive a panoramic survey history, covering a large period of time in a little space, after which there are subsequent chapters that provide detailed analysis of individual films or periods within the larger continuum. While the overall histories are detailed and systematic, the "close up" chapters can only provide detailed accounts of a few relevant instances. Thus, I am more than aware of what I have neglected or left out. The aim of the book is to provide coverage of some of the rich, engaging and interesting films and music that have been produced by the British cinema.

2
British Film Music

The non-diegetic music of the British counterpart to classical Hollywood cinema had a highly distinct trajectory from its American relation. Since the second decade of the twentieth century, the British film industry has been overshadowed by the more successful and more popular model supplied by Hollywood films. British film music lacked the fully industrialized basis that characterized its American counterpart from the 1930s to 1950s, and also lacked the concomitant tendency towards standardization of forms and functions. However, the continual influence of Hollywood films and their treatment of music held an enormous sway upon British film music, one which could never be disregarded and which was a perennial problem for British film production as a whole. The lack of stable studio employment meant that it was difficult for composers to become specialists. British cinema produced far less films than Hollywood and in the vast majority of cases they included less incidental music than their Hollywood counterparts. Consequently, British composers had to find work across a number of media, often mixing a career composing for the respectable concert hall with film and other less prestigious activities, and in many cases also managing a career teaching about music as well. British film music had a considerable influence from the languages of concert music and, from the 1960s, a quite direct input from popular music, which has differentiated it to some degree from the music in Hollywood films.[1]

Composers for British films commonly worked in the industry part-time, and were often sustained by other jobs. The lack of a Hollywood-style studio employee structure also meant that there was no real standardization of musical procedures.[2] One effect of this was that, certainly during the 1930s and 1940s, many scores were not written with the prime intention of fitting intimately the momentary dynamics of the film action. There was more "autonomy" to the music and it was less subordinated to the demands of the film than the majority of scores in classical Hollywood cinema. However, this is not to suggest that British film music was purely a case of music editors and directors fitting pre-existing music to films. Hubert Bath, writing music for films throughout the 1930s and half of the following decade, had a reputation for providing music that was unobtrusive, music that would never impinge on the diegetic effect or wrest the audience's attention away from the screen.[3] The use of non-diegetic foreground music, particularly that written by concert hall composers, demonstrated the possibility of music being a prominent element of the film experience. The prestige of using an eminent art music composer for a film project demanded that music would not be relegated to minor functions within the film, as it was an attraction in its own right. By the 1950s, composers like Malcolm Arnold were integrating music with narrative and action in much the same way as Hollywood films, and more specialist musicians like Arnold, William Alwyn and Philip Green were often more concerned with the craft of writing music for the cinema, and were thus happy to use music solidly subordinated to the other filmic elements.[4]

The 1930s

The coming of sound cinema to Britain caused a high degree of upheaval.[5] Hubert Bath pioneered the crossover to synchronized sound film scores, providing music for the semi-sound *Jessie* (1929) and Hitchcock's *Blackmail* (1929), with Henry Stafford, which was the first British feature film with full synchronized sound. It was adapted from the already finished silent film, and the musical score was simply compiled and recast from the compilation of music that had been written to accompany the silent film.[6] Louis Levy, another film music pioneer, progressed from a career as a musical director of a large cinema's silent showings to providing recorded scores and overseeing their production throughout the 1930s. He was the foremost musical director in Britain during the early years of the decade, working for Gaumont British (for more details see Chapter 3). However, the appointment of Muir Mathieson as musical director for Alexander Korda's London Films, succeeding Kurt Schroeder while still in his twenties, was to prove a decisive moment for film music in Britain.

Muir Mathieson's influence on British film music, from the 1930s to 1950s is difficult to overstate. His involvement in the production of film music on all levels – as musical director, eliciting music from composers, and conducting – enabled him to strive for the highest quality of music for British films. His preeminent position affected film music production as a whole. From 1934, Mathieson was the musical overseer for London Films at Denham studios as well as working as a freelance musical director, concurrent with the boom in British film production from 1933 to 1937. The Second World War elevated his position further, as he was appointed musical director for the Ministry of Information which controlled film production in Britain, and after the war he joined the bolstered Rank organization, the nearest Britain probably ever came to a Hollywood-style studio.[7]

Mathieson oversaw the foundation of a mode of film music production that was to become highly influential in British cinema.[8] This was established largely by the science fiction film *Things to Come* (1935), in which the music was wholly remarkable and has lost little of its impact. The project was undertaken by producer Alexander Korda, uniting respected concert hall composer Arthur Bliss with director William Cameron Menzies and author of the original story H.G. Wells. The music was conceived and composed as an integral element of the whole, and rather than being added to the finished visual product, a large amount of the music was completed before the visuals.[9] The film uses a memorable march that is not subordinate to the dynamics of any action, but occupies the foreground and articulates the visual proceedings. Bliss's style of music was highly suited to writing film music, the score manifesting arguably not only one of the landmark scores of the cinema, but one of Bliss's most interesting works. The march is perhaps slightly reminiscent of Elgar and recalls the Victorian tradition of celebrative martial music. The regular rhythm of the rousing march articulates the scenes of war, while the attack on the moon gun involves kinetic music based on the famous motto from Beethoven's *Fifth Symphony*. The pulse of the music in *Things to Come* often comes to dominate the erratic rhythm of the film's action, and significant sections allow the music its head, effacing dialogue or sound effects.

Although it was not the first film to have music written by a composer with a concert hall reputation, its success and acclaim led to a tendency which saw British films commission music from respected composers.[10] William Walton was one such composer, and he regularly peppered his scores with marches that were never fully subordinate to film dynamics. Musical forms such as marches never aimed to integrate with films through matching their momentary ebbs and flows. Consequently, film music like this could be written before the film had finished shooting, or indeed even before it had begun shooting. In some cases, composers from the art music world insisted on working in this manner to retain the "autonomous" aspects of their music. Film producers were still largely happy with their music, specifically with the level of "cultural distinction" that music from an art composer could bestow upon a film. This was essential in an international market where product differentiation and quality branding were essential for success.

Arthur Bliss persevered with film music, producing another high quality score for *Conquest of the Air* (1940), a dramatic reconstruction of the history of flight. It took 4 years for the film to eventually be released while the music had been finished in the early stages of production, the consequence being that Bliss's score felt the brunt of the recutting. However, Bliss had already seen the premiere of his suite from *Conquest of the Air* at the Proms in 1936. Film music made by such concert hall ("classical") composers in many cases had a double life: on the one hand being a functional score for a film, while on the other appearing as a concert piece. In a way, this distinction still holds for a zone of film production that uses successful pop groups to produce music that appears in films, the music having a double life both in the cinema and outside as a CD.

The decade of the 1930s saw a significant influx of foreign technicians to the British film industry, including a number of composers, some of whom used British cinema as a stopping-off point on the way to Hollywood. Composers who were working in the 1930s included Australian-born Arthur Benjamin, who scored *The Man Who Knew Too Much* (1934) for Hitchcock and *The Scarlet Pimpernel* (1935) at the behest of Mathieson, his ex-student. *The Man Who Knew Too Much* has virtually no underscore and Benjamin's main endeavour is the *Stormcloud Cantata*, which appears at the climactic assassination attempt at the Royal Albert Hall in London. This was written as a concert piece anyway, rather than as a piece of film underscore in the Hollywood sense. Yet some immigrant composers were more interested in film music as a specific technique and discipline. Miklos Rozsa arrived in Britain to work for Korda, scoring, among others, *The Four Feathers* (1939) and the Oscar-nominated *The Thief of Baghdad* (1940) before leaving for Hollywood with Korda and a subsequent career as one of the most prominent composers for the cinema. It is notable that film music in Britain appeared to have had less of a Viennese influence than its counterpart in Hollywood. There was, however, a significant continental influence, with the influx of personnel from the German film industry in the 1930s. Immigrants like Hans May, Allan Gray and Mischa Spoliansky not only added to the establishment of film music as a particular entity in Britain, but allowed something of an international style to take root in British films.

The documentary movement of the 1930s has found high acclaim as a pinnacle of British filmic achievement. It was correspondingly distinguished for its music, both in terms of quality and in terms of allowing scope for composers to investigate the possibilities of the new medium. Documentaries were among the first noted scores in British films,[11] John Greenwood's music for Robert Flaherty's *Man of Aran* (1934) and Walter Leigh's score for *Song of Ceylon* (1935), both conferring some degree of artistic legitimacy upon the writing of music for sound films. *Man of Aran* utilizes what must have been one of the first symphonic scores, while *Song of Ceylon* demonstrated experimentation as expedient, Leigh being the first composer working for the groundbreaking General Post Office (GPO) Film Unit and being forced to approach the sound design of the whole film rather than build a score to a finished film.[12] The opportunities for the integration of music with the film, as more than simply a secondary element, were manifested in Benjamin Britten's work on documentaries for the GPO Film Unit, which predated his establishment of a concert hall reputation. In *Night Mail* (1936) and *Coal Face* (1936), the music acts as an almost equal partner with the other elements. The former unites music and sound with both the image and W.H. Auden's poetic voice-over narration, while the latter has a narrating chorus and lone piano accompaniment. These were highly specific cases in cinema history, all of the elements of the film coalescing in a multi-media artwork along the lines of Wagner's conception of the *Gesamtkunstwerk*. Throughout the 1930s and 1940s, the documentary form allowed a number of British composers to work in the medium of film, many of whom gradually began scoring feature films. A good example was William Alwyn, who scored about forty short documentaries, mostly for Strand Films and Greenpark Films and provided the music for some of Paul Rotha's films before commencing a prolific career in feature films.

Wartime

The outbreak of the Second World War centralized and swelled the production of documentary films, providing the impetus for more composers to enter the field of scoring films as well as guaranteeing each one a certain measure of musical resources.[13] Probably the best example of the quality of music written for wartime documentaries is the drama-documentary *Western Approaches* (1944) (also known as *The Raiders*). This film about the endeavours to supply Britain across the Atlantic was produced by the Crown Film Unit, directed by Pat Jackson and scored by Clifton Parker. The music is all derived from one theme and the majestic *Seascape* is highly impressionistic and reminiscent of concert hall and popular instrumental music that aims to evoke the sea,[14] while the whole score concentrates primarily on the expressive possibilities offered by instrumental colour. The film was actually shot at sea, taking great pains to follow the men in a lifeboat, and utilized technicolour in order to be as impressive as possible. While the dramatic sea shots were achieved at great pains, Parker's music adds considerably to the film's effect and drama.[15]

The war effort demanded the production of melodramatic feature films too, and none contained more prominent or popular music than *Dangerous Moonlight* (1941), also known as *Suicide Squadron*, which incorporated the musical phenomenon of *The Warsaw Concerto*. In 1947, John Huntley called it "perhaps the most remarkable piece of film background music ever written...",[16] and indeed the music has far outlasted the film in popular memory. Although a British film, *Dangerous Moonlight* was produced by RKO and directed by Brian Desmond Hurst. The film reflects the cosmopolitanism of the European concert hall with Anton Walbrook's Polish concert pianist becoming a fighter pilot in wartime Britain and Richard Addinsell's pastiche of Rachmaninoff appears as underscore as well as played on screen by Walbrook. Indeed, the identifiable style of Rachmaninoff reappeared consistently in British film music throughout the 1940s, utilized for *Love Story* (1944) and *While I Live* (1947). *Brief Encounter* (1945) converted Rachmaninoff's *Piano Concerto no. 2* into a background score, and the same piece also surfaced in *The Seventh Veil* (1945). In *Dangerous Moonlight*, *The Warsaw Concerto* decidedly occupies the foreground, working for the narrative and as a central aspect of the film's cohesion. It has themes that reappear constantly and yet do not have finite functions, while the music was used primarily to articulate the film's romanticized tumult of war. The film was highly popular and may be almost forgotten now, yet the music has persisted in popularity, appearing in light orchestral concerts as well as the occasional materialization in the "legit" concert hall as well as on recordings. This case vividly underlines the fact that film music is not always subservient to the film in which it appears.

The co-ordination of Britain's cultural resources to serve the war effort also included the soliciting of film music from Britain's most respected concert hall composers, the best examples being the initiation of Arnold Bax and Ralph Vaughan Williams into writing music for documentary films. Bax composed the heroic music for the defence of Malta depicted in *Malta G.C.* (1943). Vaughan Williams's score for Michael Powell's

Canadian-set feature *49th Parallel* (1941) (US title: *The Invaders*) exhibits his trademark pastoral lyricism[17] and its prelude was swiftly made into a song. Mathieson had been instrumental in enticing Vaughan Williams into writing for the cinema,[18] but the composer, who was nearing 70, had an energy and enthusiasm for the new medium. The following year he provided another exceptional score, for *Coastal Command* (1942), a drama documentary about a flying boat. Both of these scores are as impressive as that of any wartime documentary, and the prestige of his reputation added to the growing legitimacy accorded to film music in Britain. Other scores by art music composers included *Merchant Seamen* (1940) by Constant Lambert, a number of documentary shorts for the Crown Film Unit by Elisabeth Lutyens and *Hotel Reserve* (1944) by Lennox Berkeley.

Laurence Olivier's production of *Henry V* (1945) proved a landmark for the perceived legitimacy of film music, a major achievement for both British cinema and film music generally. William Walton provided what is perhaps one of the most impressive and celebrated scores that cinema audiences have heard. Two years later, Hubert Clifford noted: "Judged by purely musical standards the best in this score nears comparison with Walton's own output for the concert platform. Judged as film music, it is one of the most distinguished and effective scores in recent times."[19] Walton was already well established as a concert composer at this point, having been acclaimed for *Façade* when only 21. By the mid-1940s he had already scored a number of feature films as well as wartime documentaries. Perhaps the most acclaimed of these was Leslie Howard's *First of the Few* (1942) (US: *Spitfire*), which relied on a principal theme which Walton varied upon each of its appearances. His first film score was for *Escape Me Never* (1935), and he went on to work on 20th Century Fox's *As You Like It* (1936), *Stolen Life* (1939), *Major Barbara* (1941) directed by Gabriel Pascal, and three Ealing films, *Next of Kin* (1942), *The Foreman Went to France* (1942) and *Went the Day Well?* (1942). Walton's score for *Henry V* tends towards utilizing music for particular action rather than repeating identifiable themes, includes some organum and plain-song, but predominantly uses a contemporary orchestral language. The music was praised upon release for its musical language containing "... a happy absence of the ersatz, the musical equivalent of Wardour Street Tudor."[20] The film opens with an overture that precedes the play, as the film visually establishes the location, time and performance of the play. Moving through some choral plainchant, the music then takes up a Tudor flavour as the film moves into the space of the theatre itself. The striking use of music during the battle sequence involves the music providing the acceleration for the action, with regular rhythmic pulses that speed up as the brass fanfare frame the charging French forces. At the height of the charge, diegetic sound is superseded by the momentum of the music, the stylization creating a fever pitch of battle.[21] Earlier in the film, Walton's use of a distinct musical form, a *passacaglia* for strings (a form of variations over a repeated musical framework), is testament to the possibilities of using art music forms within films. It starts with the *ostinato* (a repeated loop of notes) being stated by the 'cellos while the integrity of the *passacaglia* form unites an intercut sequence of the dying Falstaff and the announcement of his death to the king. *Henry V* undoubtedly and self-consciously set the quality standard to which film music more generally should aspire.[22] Composer Gerard Schurmann noted,

> I think the classical composers for want of a better label in England thought of film music as a kind of aid to making a living and enable you to write one's concert music without having to teach ... [We did it] in order to make money and to be able to experiment – that was the *marvellous* opportunity we had in those days, of trying out musical ideas in different shapes and forms and then having them played back instantly, that you could subsequently use in your concert music.[23]

Not all composers saw themselves as "moonlighting" from their vocation in the concert hall. Indeed, more prestigious film music was something of a contrast with the music that appeared in the more prevalent lower budget and less ambitious films of the 1930s and 1940s. Many of those writing music for such films had little or no "classical training" in the virtues of Western orchestral music for the concert hall. Louis Levy, one such notable figure and a pre-eminent musical supervisor, emphasized: "... it is appropriate to point out that not by any means all the great films have been 'made' by music specially composed by the important composers. ... It is bitterly true that often the small composer is nearer to the really essential things of life, and although his work may lack the initiative of greatness or the touch of genius, it may result in a composition better fitted to the mood of the film."[24]

Post-War feature films

The post-War cinema boom in the UK encouraged film production in Britain and higher budgets allowed British films an international status. Rank's position in the late 1940s echoed the command of resources wielded by Hollywood studios, and ensuing international acclaim and box-office success buoyed British film production.[25] Success in foreign (and especially American) markets was of primary importance to international prestige, and while some British films starred American actors, others played upon the particularities of British locations or the traditions of literature and the stage in Britain.

There was a cycle of literary adaptations of Charles Dickens's novels. *Great Expectations* (1946), *Nicholas Nickleby* (1947) and *Oliver Twist* (1948) were all prestige productions, with high budgets and a tendency to parade the quality of the production. Consequently, composers with concert hall reputations were elicited for the music, the famous aristocratic *dilettante* Lord Berners for *Nicholas Nickleby*, émigré Walter Goehr for *Great Expectations*, and Arnold Bax for *Oliver Twist*, the latter two both being directed by David Lean. *Great Expectations* has some visually striking moments, at times is played as pure gothic with an expressionistic set and low key lighting, although Goehr's music only occasionally tends to go beyond the conventional. Other notable scores from the post-War feature film boom include William Alwyn's playful music for *The Rake's Progress* (1945), a comedy starring Rex Harrison, the calypso music from which became popular in light concerts and on record. Richard Addinsell continued his distinguished career with the music for *Blithe Spirit* (1946), which was directed by David Lean and adapted from his own stage play by Noel Coward. The comic story of Rex Harrison being plagued by the ghost of his first wife required music to signify the supernatural, where using the resonant tones of the vibraphone proved effective, and the popular song-waltz *Always* functioned as a portal to the "Other Side".

Throughout the 1940s, Michael Powell and Emeric Pressburger had produced a strain of British cinema that was highly distinctive. The musical component largely had been provided by two composers: Brian Easdale and Allan Gray. Easdale was acclaimed for his music for *Black Narcissus* (1947) and won an academy award for the music for *The Red Shoes* (1948) which is celebrated for its prominent music for the ballet section within the film.[26] Émigré Gray (with the help of Walter Goehr and Robert Farnon) had produced an impressive Scottish-inflected score for *I Know Where I'm Going* (1945) but arguably his most memorable score is for *A Matter of Life and Death* (1946) (US: *Stairway to Heaven*). The narrative of a fighter pilot being pursued by the forces of the afterlife is perfectly counterpointed by Gray's score, with the love that blossoms between David Niven and Kim Hunter summoning a sweet romantic theme for strings. The other worldly aspects of the afterlife

are represented by a solemn ostinato, often on the piano, that discon-
certingly is sequenced downwards by semitones, creating a discon-
certing effect through the whole music dropping in pitch.[27] This motif
is precisely a device, foregrounded as one of the principal signifiers
of the supernatural, and makes itself most apparent, moving between
underscore and source music in the film, and cementing the association
between music and fantasy. *A Matter of Life and Death* was a prestige
film, chosen as entertainment for the Royal Family, in the first post-War
Royal Command Performance, and proved a pinnacle of British fantasy
cinema with a score that added considerably to the final product.

Vaughan Williams's continued willingness to be involved in films led
to a working relationship with Ealing Studios, and produced one of the
most famous scores in British cinema. *Scott of the Antarctic* (1948) was
directed by Charles Frend and starred John Mills as the eponymous hero.
Vaughan Williams's characteristic and impressive music appears in short
bursts, not solidly integrated with the film's action, having been written
before the film was completed and then fitted to the film.[28] This was
more common in British cinema of the time than might be expected,
with little of the intricate action-matching of Hollywood film music, and
many pieces of film music being integrated with the action by the sound
editor. However, Vaughan Williams's music played an important part
in the tale of British greatness and folly rolled into one, not least adding
prestige/art credibility to the project. Concert hall composers made only
occasional forays into film scoring and there were a growing number of
specialist composers working in the burgeoning field. Vaughan Williams
used the score as a basis for his *Sinfonia Antarctica*, as had become the
fashion for composers – re-using their film music in the concert hall.[29]

Film producer John Croydon sardonically declared: "Most really good
British composers are difficult to get for film work... Even when they
are able to spare the time to score a good British picture, they write
their music with one eye on concert hall receipts which may later accrue
from the score, and as a result, the unity of the film suffers."[30] There
is doubtless some truth here, which accounts for the hybrid nature of
much British film music written by composers who predominantly saw
their career in the orchestra concert hall. Of course, this charge might
also be brought to composers of light music and pop music in later years,
who in many cases desired the validity of their music in a context other
than merely that of the film. In Britain, the situation was that music
was often semi-outside films. Film music production often was closer
to the music industry than the film industry, with each being more
autonomous than was the case in the USA. Yet in the vast majority of

cases this led to something apart from "synergy", in that both industries wanted profit on their own terms rather than having a more concerted attempt at co-ordinating for publicity purposes. Films in a number of cases undeniably appeared to be showcases for music, much like film musicals.

In the wake of the success of both *Dangerous Moonlight* and its corresponding music, *The Warsaw Concerto*, a number of films surfaced that followed a similar format. The decade of the 1940s saw a series of romantic melodramas that included what was sometimes referred to as a "tabloid concerto". The success of the *Warsaw Concerto* set the format, although it was predated by *The Case of the Frightened Lady* (1940), scored By Jack Beaver. The most successful of these films was the Gainsborough film *Love Story* (1944) (also known as *A Lady Surrenders*), where Margaret Lockwood, who has one year to live, falls in love with Stewart Granger in Cornwall and writes a piano concerto. The film popularized Hubert Bath's *Cornish Rhapsody*, which is what Lockwood is writing in the film, and is included as a concert performance finale at the Albert Hall, at which she is the piano soloist. The concerto is a fantasia on the two themes that appear in the film and references the location through the musical imitation of seagull cries. Similarly, the portmanteau film *Train of Events* (1949) used Leslie Bridgewater's *Legend of Lancelot* while *The Woman's Angle* (1952) used Kenneth Leslie-Smith's *The Mansell Concerto*. Following the same format, *While I Live* (1947) conferred an instant popularity upon a piece of music written and performed within the film. The melodrama concerns a morbid spinster who does not accept that her concert pianist sister Olwen is dead, having walked off a nearby cliff. When a mysterious woman appears and plays Olwen's musical composition she appears initially to be a reincarnation of the dead woman. Upon the film's re-release in 1950, it was cut by 22 minutes and renamed *The Dream of Olwen*, recognizing that Charles Williams's music for the film, which was thus titled, had outstripped the film's renown and was the central audience attraction. Reviews noted the prominent piano music, *Kinematograph Weekly* commenting that the film was "... strenuously accompanied by the pianoforte ... "[31] Similarly, *The Glass Mountain* (1948) attained a great level of popularity for its film music while the film itself is now virtually invisible in any accounts of British cinema history. The film starred Michael Dennison as a married composer has an affair with a woman who inspires his new opera. While this was a routine romance film, and highly popular with audiences at the time, music was foregrounded as a feature in the film and prominent performers like Tito Gobbi appear, while Nino Rota's main theme became a bestselling piece both as sheet music and on record.[32] The use of Rota, an Italian-based composer who later firmly became associated with Federico Fellini, demonstrated the cosmopolitan activities of the film industry at the time.

Perhaps the most internationally renowned film music of the late 1940s was that for Carol Reed's *The Third Man* (1949). Anton Karas's ubiquitous zither music provided a memorable counterpoint to Joseph Cotten in Vienna, looking for his old friend Orson Welles, who is now a deleterious blackmarketeer. The main theme and the zither itself became world famous, while it provided the aural character of the whole film as well as denoting its setting. The score forged a continuity, both of timbre and of similar sounding themes, which unifies the film through its relative homogeneity. Karas's music involved strict rhythmic patterns and was highly obtrusive, dominating the film, and yet its prominence added immeasurably to the overall ambience and singular world of the film. The decision to use Karas's music was certainly bold, furnishing the film with a musical ambience that differentiated it radically from the dominant Hollywood fare with its fairly standardized orchestral "Classical film scores".[33]

The 1950s

British films regularly demonstrated a willingness to take risks with music, an example being the Two Cities film *Tawny Pipit* (1944) which allowed concert pianist Noel Mewton-Wood the opportunity to score his first and only film. Throughout the next two decades, the use of unusual timbres (instrumental colour and sonority) and other speculations were to become a definite current in British film music. Carol Reed's international achievement with *The Third Man* was followed by a less successful film, *The Man Between* (1953), which proceeded along similar lines to its predecessor. This tale of espionage was set in Berlin and was scored by John Addison. Rather than use a highly specific timbre, Addison's music involves some solemn and austere-sounding jazz-styles within the orchestral palette. The music connoted the specific location through referencing the modes of jazz prevalent in Berlin before the war as well as the music voicing the grimness of the shattered city.

Overall, the 1950s saw less of an international profile for British films. The contraction of British film production meant that there was less in the way of expensive and internationally oriented productions but this did not mean that the quality of film music was any less. Ealing Studios produced a series of notable comic films under the aegis of musical director Ernest Irving. It utilized the music of composers like French art film composer Georges Auric, who wrote some playful music for *The Lavender Hill Mob* (1951) and *The Titfield Thunderbolt* (1953)[34] and Benjamin Frankel, who scored *The Man in the White Suit* (1951).[35] Frankel's highly effective score for *The Man in the White Suit* built repeated music around a bizarre and idiosyncratic mechanical sound that signified the cloth-making experiments.[36] Another gentle comedy with a unique and exceptional musical score was *Genevieve* (1953). The film, which was produced by Sirius Productions and directed by Henry Cornelius, depicted a vintage car race between John Gregson and Kenneth More. The playful and lightly comic atmosphere of the film was fixed by Larry Adler's harmonica score and the central waltz theme. The highlighting of timbre playing an important part in the overall character of the film, much as did the music for *The Third Man*, and the highly specific sound of the solo harmonica throughout created a musical intimacy which doubled the film's empathy and mild manners.

Throughout the 1950s, film music composers like Stanley Black provided the music for a host of B pictures and second features. Black's other activities included conducting populist orchestral music, much like Mantovani, and he never had pretensions to the classical concert hall.[37] Nevertheless, his scores were often of a quality that was unmatched by the films themselves. Although the mode of production for these films involved a minimum of financial input, time and musical resources, it was still possible for a less prestigious or upmarket composer like Black to provide highly effective scores. An example of this is the Tempean production *Recoil* (1953), a film that owes a good deal to American *Film Noirs*, its music included. The score is for a small orchestra and uses a musical language that habitually involves the unresolved dissonance that had become a characteristic feature of twentieth century concert music, aiming for psychological impact through eschewing the use of memorable themes. Other more specialized film composers working at this time, like Philip Green, were also more interested in the possibilities of integrating popular music and jazz with the traditions of film music. Green and Stanley Black, along with Malcolm Arnold, were the most prolific composers for British films throughout the 1950s and most of the following decade.

Malcolm Arnold, despite having a significant concert hall reputation, became something of a film music specialist in the 1950s and 1960s, scoring a large number of feature films. His music for *The Sound Barrier* (US: *Breaking the Sound Barrier*) (1952) is of a high calibre, the heroic music sustaining the story of human achievement and electrifying the remarkable aerial sequences. This was one of the only times that Arnold fashioned a film's cues into a rhapsody for concert hall consumption.[38] He was perhaps more widely known for one of the most character-istic and identifiable comic themes in British film music, for *The Belles of St. Trinians* (1955). It served as a principal continuity between the series of subsequent films, the music not only functioning as narrative cement, but being equated definitively with the character of the series. This included a "school song" and a repeated theme on out-of-tune piano with ramshackle percussion accompaniment. Arnold's collabora-tions with David Lean, which had encompassed *Hobson's Choice* (1953) as well as *The Sound Barrier*, led to his biggest success, *The Bridge on the River Kwai* (1957), for which he was awarded an Oscar. While it had a bold main theme and the incidental music was of a high quality, the film also featured the *Colonel Bogey March*, a First World War march written by Kenneth Alford, which within the film is associated with the tragic absurdity of the men's endeavours. Arnold also includes another march which converges on *Colonel Bogey* and the two become super-imposed. Despite being prolific in all musical fields, Malcolm Arnold became possibly the most prolific composer in the British post-War cinema, scoring over 80 films between 1947 and 1970.[39]

Another most popular British war film of the 1950s was *The Dambusters* (1955). The music in the film revealed a noteworthy division between underscore and the featured march, with the musical labour divided between Eric Coates, whose *Dambusters March* became extremely popular in its own right, and Leighton Lucas, who provided the film's incidental music. During the Second World War, a solid tradition of popular British film marches had developed, and this was sustained by subsequent British war films. Conspicuous marches in films included William Alwyn's march in *Desert Victory* (1943), Leighton Lucas's march in *Target for Tonight* (1941), Coates's *Eighth Army March* in *Nine Men* (1942) which appeared within the film's overall score by John Green-wood, and F. Vivian Dunn's march in *Cockleshell Heroes* (1955).[40] *The Dambusters* was perhaps a highly successful continuation of this tend-ency, while also belonging to a collaborative mode of film music that had been operative both visibly and invisibly. *Way to the Stars* (1945) was nominally scored by Nicholas Brodszky, but with significant help from Charles Williams. Brodszky was really only a songwriter who needed crucial and extensive input from orchestrators and musical assistants, while other collaborations were due to the heavy workload with which composers were faced. An example of this is *The Cruel Sea* (1953) which is credited to Alan Rawsthorne and yet had a substantial input from

Gerard Schurmann.[41] The division of popular march and functional underscore in these films is highly reminiscent of the divide of pop songs and underscore that became prominent in some mainstream films of the 1980s and 1990s.

There was also a notable influx of musical style from twentieth-century orchestral music, particularly the "difficult" modernist music for the highbrow concert hall, and in the vast majority of cases in horror films.[42] The international success of Hammer horror films, with *The Curse of Frankenstein* (1957) and *Dracula* (1958), not only heralded a renaissance of the genre as a whole, but was also important for introducing highly dissonant music to the cinema. James Bernard scored both films and provided the best music for Hammer films from the 1950s onwards. His score for *The Curse of Frankenstein* evinced a gothic severity that went beyond previous genre conventions. Bernard's mature style introduced extended angular melodic lines often played in unison and with no stable centre of tonality. *Dracula* demonstrates these practices and exhibits Bernard's use of musical cells that are repeated and varied as well as the potential of strident brass. Bernard consistently built his title themes from the syllabic breakdown of the film's title, as a dislocated form of lyricism, and the three-note *Dracula* theme (or *leitmotiv*) occurred for each appearance of the Count and became associated at essence with the subsequent Hammer *Dracula* films.[43] In one of Bernard's later scores, for *Taste the Blood of Dracula* (1970), he establishes an opposition between the *Dracula leimotiv* and a lyrical theme for the young lovers who eventually defeat the Count, concluding in a triumphant quasi-religious chorale based on the love theme at the film's end. Bernard was notable for his very characteristic style. Indeed, his music is one of the most easily identifiable of any composer ever to write for films. His film music for Hammer is related to the trend of minimalism which only was emerging in the art music world at this time. Its techniques are systematic and highly transparent, which mean that they are very apparent to audiences and use a limited number of effects (often being based on repeated cells of music that rise in pitch).[44]

Other scores for horror films at this time also used a decidedly more modernist musical language, with Gerard Schurmann's music for *The Horrors of the Wax Museum* (1959), and Benjamin Frankel's score for *Curse of the Werewolf* (1960) which is reputed to be the first score in British films to utilize serial composition techniques.[45] Elisabeth Lutyens had been using serial techniques in her concert pieces, and although she was never as highly acclaimed for her film music as James Bernard, she produced some effective horror film scores throughout the 1960s, particularly *Paranoiac* (1962), *Dr. Terror's House of Horrors* (1964) and *The Skull* (1965). Modernist art music composers like Lutyens were particularly suited to scoring films using small-scale ensembles using chamber textures, rather than more traditional orchestral forces.[46] Other sinister music of note appeared in *Village of the Damned* (1960), where Ron Goodwin's forceful music included effective music for the children's telepathy that bore a resemblance to sound effects. However, Goodwin was from a popular music background, like Stanley Black and Philip Green. Some of his films clearly illustrate this, yet others emphasize how he continued the tradition of marches in British film music that had been prominent since the 1930s. Ironically, his best known marches came in *The Battle of Britain* (1969), where his music largely replaced that of original commission Walton, another composer who had regularly used marches in his film music as well as in his concert hall music.

The 1960s

In contrast, the novelty of "kitchen sink" dramas, what became known as the British new wave at the turn of the 1960s, was matched by their aim to have impact in terms of music that, in certain cases, was a featured part of the film. *Saturday Night and Sunday Morning* (1960), for example, had an exceptional musical score by jazz musician John Dankworth, his first of many film scores. It used a rough and ready jazz sound that equated with the film's downmarket but energetic depictions. The breezy and brash music was apt for this foundational film of the British new wave, the use of jazz further differentiating the film from British cinematic tradition. Similarly, *This Sporting Life* (1963) accompanied its bleak story with an austere score from modernist composer Roberto Gerhard.[47] Indeed, in the mid-1960s, British cinema showed itself to be highly adventurous with the commissioning of musical scores, in order to have singular music for films. Perhaps the best examples of bold film music experiments were two films that were scored by American jazz musicians who had never previously worked in the medium. *Alfie* (1966) had a score by saxophonist Sonny Rollins, while *Blow Up* (1966) was scored by Herbie Hancock, the pianist for Miles Davis's Quintet. Both scores worked well, the jazz manifesting the "Swinging London" soundtrack. Significantly, British film production was willing to assign film scoring to acclaimed jazz musicians rather than have established film composers use jazz as another component of their arsenal of film music techniques, as had largely been the case in the US (see Chapter 5).

The break up of the Hollywood studio system had far-ranging implications for the rest of the world, particularly Europe. It speeded the internationalization of the film industry, with American money and production companies increasingly looking to make films in Europe, an example being the series of international films produced in the early 1960s by Samuel Bronston. Although US had interests in the British film industry since the 1930s, investment increased throughout the late 1950s, with, for example, Hammer using Warner Brothers's co-production money, until the full internationalization of film making in Britain by the mid to late 1960s, where foreign (and almost entirely American) capital boosted film production in the UK. The early 1960s were a crucial time for film music in the UK. The years 1963 and 1964 saw a number of crucial scores produced that had ramifications for British film music to follow as well as being significant in their own right. The three films that are credited with inaugurating the boom in British cinema through attracting American finance, *Dr. No* (1962), *Tom Jones* (1963), and *A Hard Day's Night* (1964),[48] all contain music that was in some way significant.

Tom Jones won an Oscar for its bold music. John Addison's distinguished comic score consisted of a number of mischievous parodies of restoration music, which firmly refused a more conventional attempt at a solidly period style. The music plays a full and prominent part in the film's processes, nowhere more so than the opening where the film burlesques silent cinema and Addison's music spoofs the silent film pianist although using the period timbre of the harpsichord. *Dr. No* founded the James Bond series of films, one of the most significant British cinematic successes, while introducing to the world a pop music-inflected style of film score, and to John Barry who was to establish himself as the most significant British film music composer of the decade. Not only was the music in the Bond films brash and modern, as embodied by Vic Flick's trebly electric guitar in the Bond theme itself,[49] but the title songs also became media events, providing a succession of hit records for a roster of famous singers. The last of this triumvirate, *A Hard Day's Night*, heralded the pop culture explosion in the UK as well as introducing The Beatles to more of the world. Beyond that, its significance lies in the film's utilization of pop songs as non-diegetic (incidental) music. While this strategy became commonplace in the following decades as a part and parcel of the score compiled from pop songs, few films have been as creative in their use of pop songs as this stylish and innovative film (see Chapter 10).

In contrast, Maurice Jarre's music for two films directed by David Lean, *Lawrence of Arabia* (1962) and *Dr. Zhivago* (1965 UK/US), are commanding orchestral scores in their own right and suitably epic elements of the films. The main themes from the films, and particularly *Lara's Theme* from the latter, have become among the most popular and well known of any film music.[50] *Lawrence of Arabia* relies on large-scale orchestral forces for its impressive sound but attempts some Arabic-flavoured sections, while *Dr. Zhivago* utilizes the characteristically Russian timbre of the balalaika for some of its melodies as well as some Russian-style choral passages.

John Barry's 1960s scores for the James Bond series of films solidified a particular model for British film scores of the decade. Barry added pop music techniques to orchestral articulation and the film music vocabulary. Each title song was carefully co-ordinated to maximize commercial potential while the films' music is unified, both within each film and across the series, by the block reappearance of the characteristic Bond theme (often an existing recording simply cut into the film). Barry's other scores of the 1960s also have a propensity for playing with timbres. Indeed, this became something of a hallmark of film music of the decade, with the use of innovative instrumentation and non-orchestral ensembles becoming prevalent. In 1965, Barry received his first Academy Award for his score to *Born Free* (1965), the music being driven by the theme from the title song which became an international hit.

During the 1960s, Britain became associated with producing international spy films as a counterpoint to "Swinging London"-set films. Apart from the achievement of the James Bond films, there was a succession of films based on cold war spy novels by Len Deighton, starring Michael Caine as Harry Palmer. John Barry scored the first, *The Ipcress File* (1965), and rhymed Sidney Furie's baroque visual style with a suitably unique-sounding music encompassing the use of the cymbalom. The third of the series, *Billion Dollar Brain* (1967), was directed by Ken Russell and had music by Richard Rodney Bennett, which in its reiterated theme associated with Francoise Dorleac echoed Barry's play with timbres, although it frequently used electronics mixed with chamber music instrumentation that included a harpsichord – perhaps the most characteristic (and most faddish) musical colour of the period in British films and television.

Bennett already had some reputation as a concert hall composer, although he was better known in jazz circles, and provided an exceptional score for John Schlesinger's *Far From the Madding Crowd* (1967). His music adopted a concert music-style pastoral approach for the nineteenth-century costume drama, which stressed art film values, adapting Thomas Hardy's work of "high" literature. John Barry won his second

Oscar for *The Lion in Winter* (1968), a historical drama revolving around Henry II and his wife Eleanor. Yet another costume drama with a striking and strident musical score was the Joseph Losey and Harold Pinter production of *The Go Between* (1971). The music was written by established French film composer and hit writer Michel Legrand, and largely utilized parodic and very energetic baroque-style keyboards, the timbre being foregrounded. The score for the country house-based film concerned with the morality of the ruling classes is basically monothematic and incorporates a fugue on the main theme at a crucial point in the film's narrative.

The 1970s and 1980s

The 1970s saw an increased internationalization of the film industry. This meant that what once clearly had constituted "British" films was now less clear.[51] Directed by Donald Cammell and Nic Roeg, *Performance* (1970) had an outstanding score, consisting of diverse musical elements and genres, written by Jack Nitzsche, the Rolling Stones's string arranger. *Get Carter* (1971) had an engaging musical score by Roy Budd, which mixed rock, jazz and pop songs. Throughout the decade, Stanley Myers was one of the most prolific composers for the British cinema, although he also did scores for Hollywood films. From the 1970s onwards he became associated with Nic Roeg's films, and received an Oscar for *The Deer Hunter* (1978 US). Towards the end of the 1970s, Hollywood began returning to large, expensive and accessible orchestral music, particularly in the wake of the success and acclaim for John Williams's music for *Star Wars* (1977 US) and *ET* (1982 US).[52] The rejuvenation of the large-scale orchestral score coincided with the ascendancy of electronic film music, with *Midnight Express* (1978) being the first predominantly electronic score to be honoured with an Academy Award. It was written and performed by Giorgio Moroder who had previously been involved in the production of electronic disco music at the Munich Studios. Around this period there was an increase in the number of electronic scores that were being produced. The development of a new and cheaper generation of synthesizers heralded a new mode of musical production, one where a score could be produced at a very low cost in comparison with those that required a large number of hired musicians.

The 1970s film production had waned from previous decades, although to some degree this was reversed in the 1980s. In the early to mid-1980s there occurred what has been termed a "renaissance" of British cinema.[53] This was triggered by the international success of

Chariots of Fire (1981) and other films in its wake, the increased profile for the British film industry culminating in the proclamation of "British Film Year" in 1984.[54] *Chariots of Fire* had a highly distinguished score that not only won an Oscar but also made a hit single out of the main theme. The music was written and performed by Vangelis, a Greek electronic keyboard player whose success with this film led to a future of scoring Hollywood films. The score is electronic, utilizing both the characteristic timbres of synthesizers and more familiar quasi-orchestral tone colours. Some of the music, and in particular the main theme, pastiches the style of the romantic concert hall while affixing to it the trappings of modern pop music. The parodic "classicism" of the principal music has its antithesis in the dissonant synthesizer tones that are associated with the excessively "professional" American athletes before the race. Before this, Vangelis had been working on the margins of pop music, producing instrumental LPs as well as furnishing some films with music. The success for the main theme as a single was associated with the spectacle of athletes running in slow motion that was cut from the film to create a promo video. *Chariots of Fire* marked the first time for British scores when the sales of the LP had a significant effect, redoubling publicity for the film.[55] The soundtrack recording as an appendage to the film had replaced the concert suites made from film music that had been so prevalent in the 1940s, but had lessened considerably in volume during the 1960s.

Other films that followed in its stylistic wake were Nagisa Oshima's *Merry Christmas, Mr. Lawrence* (1983 UK/Japan), which similarly had a hit single. This record was an adaptation of the film's main theme, the score being provided by synthesizer player Ryuichi Sakamoto, one of the principal members of the Yellow Magic Orchestra pop group, who also appeared as a principal character in the film. *Local Hero* (1983) demonstrated a similar trend, where the reputation of a rock musician as film scorer provided an attraction for the film. Dire Straits guitar player Mark Knopfler's score is highly impressive and characteristic, using a rock ensemble but declining to use rock music throughout the film until the jubilant closing theme.

Certainly, the most unique and probably the most striking and energetic score from this period is without doubt Michael Nyman's music for *The Draughtsman's Contract* (1982). The film, a conundrum directed by Peter Greenaway,[56] was an art-house success across the world and although it never neared the level of popularity that *Chariots of Fire* achieved, it clearly indicated the creative potential of British films, and not least their music. Nyman's highly individual score for the film mixes restoration substance with modern style, utilizing fragments of Henry Purcell's music harnessed by a systemic structure that owes something to art music minimalism but perhaps as much to Western pop music. Each cue is particular, there is almost no repeated music, and it is autonomous, even within the confines of the film. Rather than being based on the momentary dynamics of the action, it tends to articulate the action itself, with the montage at times corresponding exactly to the pulse of Nyman's music. Nyman's music is like "autonomous" art music, pieces have their own integrity without the film rather than being a functional film score that only works in combination with the rest of the film.[57]

The 1980s saw very internationalized "British" films. This was especially true of big budget films, many of which were aimed as much as if not more than, at the American market as the British. Some film music received acclaim on the back of the film's success. Having an international aim, the music was sometimes of high profile. During the 1980s, George Fenton furnished two of Richard Attenborough's prestige productions with distinguished musical scores. The British and Indian co-production *Gandhi* (1982) was scored by Fenton in collaboration with Indian sitarist and film composer Ravi Shankar, while *Cry Freedom* (1987) was assembled in tandem with African musician Jonas Gwangwa. Both of these biographical films were international successes and the broad canvases used by director Richard Attenborough demanded music on a grand scale. Fenton declined to use a full romantic orchestra sound and opted instead for an appeal to an authenticity of location in his use of Indian and African music within the scores. These successes, much like those of John Barry and John Addison before him, led to his being exported to Hollywood where film composers can receive considerably increased remuneration for their work than that to which they are accustomed from the British film industry.

At the same time, British films increasingly were having music produced by foreign musicians as part of the international status of the film industry. An acclaimed film was *The Mission* (1986), which allied the high production values with music from Ennio Morricone, perhaps one of the most eminent film composers. He acquitted himself in an exemplary fashion, producing yet another remarkable score that characteristically displayed an overriding concern with instrumental sound. Novelist Clive Barker's film directing debut, *Hellraiser* (1987), was adorned with a subtle yet insistent orchestral score by the American composer Christopher Young. Émigré Hans Zimmer worked with synthesizers and collaborated with pop groups like the Buggles and the Damned before starting to write music for films. He collaborated with Stanley Myers on *Insignificance* (1985) and, like Miklos Rosza, used Britain as a stepping stone to Hollywood. *Waterland* (1992) had extraordinary music by American Carter Burwell, who had worked with half of British band New Order (in their incarnation as Thick Pigeon). His score integrated chamber orchestra and electronics, consisted largely of variations of a single theme's arrangement and was highly effective in its stateliness and affecting simplicity.

Nostalgic depictions of the days and splendour of the British Imperial past became something of a perennial theme during the 1980s for both films and television produced in Britain. David Lean directed another international success, *A Passage to India* (1984), and the music by Frenchman Maurice Jarre won another Academy Award 21 years after their last collaboration had done the same. Throughout the 1980s, films produced by the producer–director team of Ismail Merchant and James Ivory achieved a unrivalled international popularity among British films. The films' emphasis on quality and display of British heritage demanded music to reflect those values. *A Room with a View* (1986) was scored by the team's usual composer, American Richard Robbins, and yet a Puccini aria is featured prominently as a rather prosaic reference to high culture, and has become associated with the film in publicity.[58]

George Fenton produced a notable score for British–American co-production *Dangerous Liasons* (1988), which eschewed the use of a quasi-historical pastiche of music in favour of adding a modicum of period flavour to a contemporary orchestral score. This entails the inclusion of a harpsichord with the string-dominated ensemble and the inclusion of some pieces by Bach and Vivaldi, while for *The Madness of King George* (1994) Fenton adapted Handel.[59] The use of orchestral classical music furnishes a film with "distinction", providing a reference to high art and quality, very much like the impetus in the 1930s and 1940s to have music written by a "classical" composer.[60] However, the use of existing pieces edited into films was similar in process to the increasing use of pop songs as moments of music and tied-in products with films. The regular run of composers from pop music entering film scoring accelerated in the 1980s and was particularly encouraged by the proliferation of relatively cheap and substantial-sounding electronic keyboards that could provide the dynamics and density of sound previously only associated with large groupings of musicians.

At the end of the financial spectrum opposite to that of internationally oriented productions, films produced cheaply on occasions contained some exceptional music. A case in point is *Letter to Brezhnev* (1985), a low-budget independent film which contains a haunting repeated main theme by guitar player Alan Gill that mixes electronics with traditional instruments. Experimental pop group Coil provided the music to Derek Jarman's *The Angelic Conversation* (1985), where they furnished atmospheric backing to the spoken delivery of some of Shakespeare's sonnets. Films such as *In the Name of the Father* (1993 UK/Ireland) illustrates the increasingly common division of music within mainstream dramatic films. South African-born but British-based composer Trevor Jones wrote the underscore for the film, although pop songs appear more prominently. Apart from some pre-existing songs that appear, the film had title songs by Bono from U2 and Gavin Friday, with one song being sung by Sinead O'Connor. This example exhibits a common divide where pop songs are used for titles and montage sequences, while more traditional underscore enhances the drama at other moments in the film.

The 1990s and beyond

Michael Nyman managed to establish a career as a film music composer while retaining a highly distinctive musical sound. His minimalist-inspired music was derived from an art music career that proceeded in parallel.[61] His music has a scholarly flavour, often sounding like an oblique take on the traditions of film music, as illustrated by his music for Peter Greenaway in *The Draughtsman's Contract, A Zed and Two Noughts* (1985), *Drowning By Numbers* (1988), *The Cook, The Thief, His Wife and Her Lover* (1989), and *Prospero's Books* (1991) which included some startling operatic arias in the "masque" section. Nyman secured international fame with his music for the New Zealand–Australian co-production *The Piano* (1993), directed by Jane Campion. Other individual voices in British film music of the last couple of decades includes Simon Fisher Turner, who after beginning a career as a pop star went on to provide music for Derek Jarman's films *Caravaggio* (1986), *The Garden* (1990) and *Edward II* (1991), and Patrick Doyle, who has forged a solid alliance with director Kenneth Branagh. He has scored *Henry V* (1989), *Much Ado About Nothing* (1993), the UK–US co-production *Mary Shelley's Frankenstein* (1994) and *Hamlet* (1996), as well as many Hollywood films, and Ang Lee's British–American co-production *Sense and Sensibility* (1995). David Arnold started as pop musician but now overwhelmingly is interested in deploying the large orchestral forces that are *de rigueur* for expensive mainstream film productions. His first feature film was *The Young Americans* (1993), which also contained a hit record for Bjork that Arnold co-wrote. From there he progressed immediately to Hollywood films, including *Star Gate* (1994 US) and

Independence Day (1996 US). Arnold then went on to produce arguably the most outstanding music for the James Bond film series since
John Barry's heyday in the 1960s, including *Tomorrow Never Dies* (1997
UK/US) and *The World is not Enough* (1999 UK/US). Arnold had sent
producer Barbara Broccoli *Shaken and Stirred*, his record of Bond title
song reinterpretations. They called him in when a deal with John Barry
collapsed. He declared, "It was very exciting for five seconds, and then
you realise that you've got thirty five years of history to deal with, and
the whole world's asking 'what are you going to do?' "[62]

Like Arnold, Craig Armstrong came from a pop music background,
although he gained some prominence as a string arranger on pop
records. He provided an outstanding score for *Plunkett and Maclaine*
(1999), furnishing bold music for a very individual film,[63] and worked
on William Shakespeare's *Romeo and Juliet* (1996 US), directed by Baz
Luhrmann. Armstrong had already brought something of an orchestral
sensibility to some pop music, adding strings to artists such as Massive
Attack and producing a solo CD that consisted mostly of orchestral
pieces. Sometimes newcomers to film music can have an instant impact,
as was the case with Stephen Warbeck, whose bright and memorable
score for *Shakespeare in Love* (1998) won an Oscar for best comedy score.
Prior to this, Warbeck had only written music for television. In recent
years, British composers sometimes almost immediately are siphoned
off to Hollywood. In recent years, composers like David Arnold, Craig
Armstrong, Clint Mansell and David Holmes, as well as even younger
musicians like Harry Gregson Williams and Edward Shearmur, have
moved to greater financial success if not critical acclaim scoring Hollywood films.[64] This serves emblematically to (re)emphasize how significant Hollywood remains as a film industry that overshadows British
film production.

Conclusion

Apart from Hollywood's influence, British film music had a considerable influence from the languages of concert music and, from the
1960s, popular music. That British films spawned a remarkable series of
highly specific film scores is without question and the involvement of
"legit" composers in the 1930s and 1940s furnished a patina of "art" to
many films.[65] The fact that an industrial production line in the Hollywood mould was never fully established in Britain meant that British
composers and musicians had to be eclectic and flexible, able to write
music for a number of different contexts rather than simply specializing

in film music. Stylistically, in the 1930s and 1940s, British films had longer scenes and slower cutting. This allowed the opportunity for more autonomous music. In addition, Hollywood films instituted and relied upon the use of functional themes or leitmotivs while British films were less systematic and employed less in the way of themes.[66] The freedom that music had in relation to the image encouraged non-specialist musicians (from the concert hall in the 1930s and 1940s and from pop music in the 1960s) to write music for films in a way that Hollywood lacked. Vaughan Williams noted,

> you must not be horrified if you find that a passage which you intended to portray the villain's mad revenge has been used by the musical director to illustrate the cats being driven out of the dairy. The truth is, that within limits, any music can be made to fit any situation....I would...urge those distinguished musicians who have entered into the world of the cinema, Bax, Bliss, Walton, Benjamin and others, to realise their responsibility in helping to take the film out of the realm of hack-work and make it a subject worthy of a real composer.[67]

While British cinema certainly produced some film music of high quality, there was definitely something of a campaign to use art music in films to supply films legitimacy and cultural status, and to construe British cinema as an upmarket cinema of "quality".

At various times, Britain has been an important exporter of music, and films have taken advantage of this. The aura of art, of concert hall respectability, was readily exploited by British films in the 1930s and 1940s. This was signalled clearly by the highly prominent opening title cards assigned to Vaughan Williams, as if his music were one of the film's principal stars. In the mid-1960s, in the wake of The Beatles, British music again became very exportable and this led to a welter of films with pop music or being scored by pop or jazz musicians. A similar thing happened in the early 1980s, riding the wave of what some called the "Second British Invasion" of the US pop charts. In Britain, the divide of music between art music and popular music has been significant in the development of film music, although in recent years the division has been rather less pronounced.

In recent years, arguably some of the earlier impetus of British film music has moved into television. This is most notable in "prestige" television productions that aim at export and need to have the sheen of "quality" that an orchestral score provides. Examples include

Peter Salem's highly dynamic score for *Great Expectations* (1999 BBC), and Adrian Johnston's scores for *Shackleton* (2002 BBC) and *The Lost Prince* (2003 BBC). A good example of the intermittent continuation of the British film music tradition is evident in *Gormenghast* (2000 BBC), where Richard Rodney Bennett's impressive score sits alongside some "featured" ritual music by John Tavener, one of the most respected British art music composers. Television drama appears to have responded to aesthetic developments in feature films. Since the decline of the film musical, there is more music in "non-musical" films, and British films now contain more music than ever.

3
Wicked Sounds and Magic Melodies: Music in Gainsborough Melodramas

As I have noted in earlier chapters, history has taken little notice of British film music. In the case of music in Gainsborough films, it is an utterly neglected part of cinema history. While it has been easier for film music historians to weave a narrative around a personage, this approach is invalid in terms of Gainsborough's music as there were no "great composers" about which to wax lyrical. There was something else: a communal production of music, a production line of sorts, under the aegis of Gainsborough and Gaumont-British musical director Louis Levy.

The music in 1940s Gainsborough melodramas is distinct from the dominant styles and discourses that constituted British film music in the 1930s and 1940s. On the one hand, Gainsborough offered cheap and cheerful music that was seemingly in opposition to the large number of films that used prestige films scores at the time. While on the other, the melodramas offer music that is startling in its brashness and singular among music in contemporaneous British films for its lack of British restraint. This chapter will focus primarily on the melodrama cycle of the 1940s and the way that these films not only contain atypical and outlandish musical scores, but some incorporate song sequences to the point where they resemble musicals. While I realize that these films are perhaps too easily essentialized as the Gainsborough output, they are only one genre among many of the studio's output, but are, however, vessels for some extraordinary music that really deserves a degree of attention.

By the 1940s, British film music was regularly conceived as a prestige item in a quality British cinema,[1] and in particular as an opposition to Hollywood's industrial modes. This was reflected by the number of concert hall composers who wrote music for British films during the 1930s and 1940s. Before Second World War, Arthur Bliss, Benjamin

Britten, William Walton and Arthur Benjamin contributed regularly to screen music, while during the war many more British art music composers were inspired to write film music as their patriotic contribution to the war effort. The most famous of these was Ralph Vaughan Williams, who was something of a convert to the whole notion of film scoring, making his film debut at the tender age of 69,[2] while others who tried the waters at this time included Sir Arnold Bax, Lord Berners, Lennox Berkeley, Constant Lambert and William Alwyn.

In the mid-1930s, Muir Mathieson became the musical director for Alexander Korda's London Films. This meant he was in charge of music for all their productions, and he immediately invited respected concert hall composers to supply music for the company's films. Famous composers were a cinematic attraction,[3] and Vaughan Williams's name, for example, appeared boldly on the film's credits adding prestige to film production. By contrast, Gainsborough used composers who had little fame or eminence. Rather than cater to the lone artist–composer figure who moonlighted from the highbrow concert hall, Gainsborough had a musical production line that bore closer resemblance to the system of the Hollywood film studios.

Louis Levy

Gainsborough's music was masterminded by the music department of parent company Gaumont-British, based at the Lime Grove studios in Shepherd's Bush, and headed by Louis Levy from its inception in the late 1920s.[4] Levy's department had a number of staff composers and contracted composers and resembled, at least superficially, the large-scale music departments of the Hollywood studios. Among the major contributors to Gainsborough music were film music pioneers since silent days like Hans May, Hubert Bath and Levy himself, along with other department stalwarts such as Bretton Byrd, the senior musical arranger. According to John Huntley, Louis Levy ran " . . . a kind of music casting bureau whereby composers are brought in to score the type of pictures that suit their particular style".[5] Levy's department included arrangers and orchestrators,[6] reminiscent of Hollywood, where it was common practice for composers to have their music radically rearranged by orchestrators while other composers provided music for films without credit.

Apart from Bath, Byrd and May, Louis Levy used a large number of composers: Bob Busby (who did the music for *Waterloo Road* [1944]) joined the staff in 1942, had been another film music pioneer and worked for UFA in Germany; Henry Geehl (*The Magic Bow* [1946], *Jassy* [1947]); Cedric Mallabey (*The Man in Grey* [1943], *Fanny by Gaslight* [1944]); and Jack Beaver, another pioneer, who provided most of the music for the Tom Walls films as well as scoring *Dr. Syn* (1937). Levy also collaborated with several European emigrés, including Paul Abraham from Hungary, and Mischa Spoliansky, a one-time composer for innovative German theatre director Max Reinhardt, on *The Lucky Number* (1933), while German Jewish émigré conductor Walter Goehr provided some music for *The Ghost Train* (1941). John Greenwood, one of the first composers in Britain to become something of a film specialist, had also provided occasional scores, including one of the first British symphonic scores for Robert Flaherty's celebrated *Man of Aran* (1934), as well as reappearing at Gainsborough for the two Somerset Maugham portmanteau films, *Quartet* (1948) and *Trio* (1950). Bretton Byrd was musically self-taught and joined the Gaumont-British music department in 1930 after playing piano in cinemas from the age of 14 and managing to avoid any of the glamour that the music world had to offer until his film work in the 1930s.[7] He was chief music editor for Levy, and his modest background was a testament to Gainsborough's fundamentally different framework from that of the art music composers whom Mathieson procured for his prestige films.

As head of a music department servicing both Gaumont-British and Gainsborough films, Louis Levy was indisputably one of the most influential figures in British film music in the 1930s and 1940s. However, the lack of critical praise and respect that he received is striking. For example, by the time of Roger Manvell and John Huntley's book, *The Technique of Film Music* in 1957, Gainsborough and Gaumont-British film music is practically written out of British film music history.[8] This may be partially explained by the dominant paradigms for understanding musical production, especially that of the individual artist– composer figure. Levy does not conform to this – there were widespread (although unconvincing) rumours about his lack of musical ability. As the musical director for all the output of Gainsborough films until the late 1940s, his creative position remained unclear to people both inside and outside music.

The production of British film music was dominated by musical directors during the 1930s and 1940s. Mathieson was certainly the most famous, while Levy at Gaumont-British was certainly the more prolific, and Ernest Irving moved from conducting in London's West End theatres to Ealing Studios in 1937. Each of these had a high degree of influence over film music in Britain, choosing composers for films, overseeing the arrangement of their music and often conducting the orchestras, as well as writing and adapting music, directing the final form in which all the film's music would appear. Levy stated, "The musical director...is one of the first to start on a picture – and one of the last to finish. I come to things at the very first conferences on the new film. Sometimes a story is altered to suit my needs. Occasionally, even the title is changed."[9] He cites the example of Gaumont-British's Jessie Matthews film *It's Love Again* (1936), which was renamed from *Say When* to match the title of a prominent song in the film.

Levy's significance cannot be overestimated. Born in 1893, he attained an important position during the years of silent films, becoming the musical director for the Shepherd's Bush Pavilion cinema by 1921. This led directly to his securing the role as head of the Gaumont-British music department with the coming of sound. During silent days he apparently pioneered the use of the theme song before this became habitual in the US,[10] and by 1924 Levy was also a regular on the radio, leading his own orchestra in light music for the BBC. He wrote the *Music from the Movies March* which not only appeared at the start of his radio show of the same name which began in 1936, but also opened all of the Gaumont newsreels of the time. Levy was also responsible for narrative music such as the "coded" folk music central to the story of Hitchcock's 1938 film *The Lady Vanishes*.[11]

Levy's musical training, like that of many of his staff, had not been via the respectable and expensive London music colleges, but had rather come through earning a crust accompanying films in cinemas. Levy was also from a humble background, and it is tempting to see his class and Jewish background as having mitigated against his reputation. In addition to this, he had a realistic rather than romanticized vision of composition, that of perspiration outweighing inspiration,[12] which was at odds with dominant ideas of musical creativity. Another likely reason is that Gainsborough film music attempted to copy the modes of Hollywood film music rather than draft in respected concert hall composers as did Muir Mathieson, Levy's principal rival and musical Svengali at London Films. In contrast to Mathieson's project to procure film music from the cream of British concert hall composers and to establish British film music as a prestige item in British cinema, Levy's approach of using composers without art reputations, as well as foreign composers and Hollywood styles, was unlikely to win too many critical admirers in Britain.

While Muir Mathieson seemingly set standards across British cinema,[13] the idea of prestige film music by art music composers was not universally popular, however. As noted earlier in the book, film producer John Croydon complained about British art music composers, declaring that " ... they write their music with one eye on concert hall receipts."[14] Even Mathieson acknowledged that British composers cared less for the drama and tended to lack the technical dexterity of the Americans. He wrote,

> It would, I think, be fair to say that the standard of music in British films is at the present time as high, if not higher than any other country. This applies more especially to the serious type of film ... I would say that the technique of the Americans is more advanced, or at least infinitely "slicker" than ours ... [and] their composers seem to have trained themselves to write with precise care and appreciation of the dramatic significance of each turn of the story.[15]

This is stated in more direct terms by Gainsborough producer R.J. Minney:

> I do not say that psychology and the work of the great artists and composers should have no place at all in a film. They should. But they should supplement and emphasize the dramatic and the other qualities essential to a story's development and not eclipse or extinguish the story.[16]

Levy was interested directly in the craft of music in the cinema, in music enhancing the film through blending with it rather than being an almost separate attraction lumped together with the film. The 1930s Gainsborough comedies, vehicles starring either Tom Walls, Jack Hulbert or Will Hay, have unassuming film music that is largely of the quickly produced and highly functional variety. *Windbag the Sailor* (1936), for example, has a score assembled by Levy. It consists almost solely of instrumental arrangements of hornpipes and sea shanties that appear at regular intervals to connect scenes or accompany action. The cheap and cheerful character of this music is reflected in the rather utilitarian arrangement throughout, relying on low volume, similar orchestral textures and with the music taking no unexpected turns. Generally speaking, the music for relatively cheaply and quickly produced comedies might well be expected to have such a character, and Gainsborough's are certainly no different in this respect. It is precisely the melodramas of the 1940s where the music is not only most notable, but increasingly occupies the foreground of the film.

Levy's proclaimed desire to have well-crafted functional music in films should perhaps be explained in further detail. Claudia Gorbman has set out the pattern that classical Hollywood film music followed, involving "inaudibility", narrative cueing and structural functioning.[17] She notes that the film music of classical Hollywood tries to efface itself while emphasizing screen activity, and consistently uses repeated themes as a structuring device across the film. Gainsborough's attempts to integrate music with films correspond far more with Gorbman's schema than do the "prestige" British film scores of the same period. Film scores such as Ralph Vaughan Williams's *Scott of the Antarctic* (1948) in which the music was quite roughly cut to fit the film, or William Walton's *Henry V* (1944) where only the music for the battle directly homologizes screen action, tending predominantly to consist of autonomous musical pieces that were easily made into suites for the concert hall. Simply speaking, the Gainsborough films, like Hollywood, privilege the craft of the music fitting the film over the art of the concert hall. According to producer Harold Huth, Gainsborough composer Hubert Bath was " . . . a master in the art of writing 'unobtrusive film music.' Instead of hoping the music in *They Were Sisters* [released 1945] would add to his fame, Bath hoped that it would not be noticed. That, he considered, was the criterion of good background music."[18] Levy backs up this approach: "Musical accompaniment should never be consciously heard. . . . The music should play subtly on the emotions, and never intrude on the story . . . "[19] Yet heightened emotionality is regularly cued by highly prominent, even intrusive music, and this statement becomes increasingly difficult to substantiate when considering the melodrama cycle of the 1940s.

An example of Gainsborough's relatively unassuming music is *Dr. Syn* (1937), which was in some ways a precursor to the successful costume drama cycle. It has a musical score written largely by Jack Beaver and Hubert Bath,[20] although the sole screen credit is for Louis Levy as musical director. The score certainly aims to be unobtrusive, tending towards the unmemorable and having its volume electronically lowered to virtually disappear at times. The music does tend to match action in the manner of Hollywood film music and is also reminiscent of its American counterpart in that there is a large amount of it. Virtually, every scene in *Dr. Syn* is laden with some music although it still manages to hide in the background, if not through avoiding catching the memory (as one short theme comprises its repeated material), by using a volume control button.

Later, but along similar lines, *Fanny by Gaslight* (1944) has wall-to-wall music – in fact there is hardly a moment's silence in the film. The musical score, by Cedric Mallabey, is unobtrusive and profoundly functional, with one repeated theme associated with Fanny (Phyllis Calvert), while the rest of the underscore has no structural connection or associations. When Mallabey's underscore is silent, the film is bursting with pub songs, stage songs, one bawdy song plus waltzes, can cans and ballet. Despite its unobtrusive score, this melodrama certainly foregrounds music.

Gainsborough melodramas

The 1940s cycle of melodramas proved to be some of Gainsborough's most notable successes.[21] As Thomas Elsaesser points out, melodramas tend to foreground dynamic music that punctuate the emotional turns of the films. They share a "particular form of dramatic mise en scene characterised by a dynamic use of spatial and musical categories".[22] Levy seems to have had a melodramatic conception of film music: "Generally speaking, music is heard to the greatest advantage when the film is trying to create an atmosphere of (a) romance and (b) tension."[23] In the melodramas, music is geared precisely towards such ends. Sometimes the demands of the melodramatic material lead to a musical overload that breaks the rule of narrative integration. Indeed, the music in these films is extremely obtrusive, regularly encroaching on the action and fracturing the diegesis, as well as often appearing as diegetic songs that translate into non-diegetic character themes.

I shall now look at four films in some detail: *Caravan* (1946) and *Madonna of the Seven Moons* (1944) which have highly melodramatic musical scores to match their exotic and hyperbolic screen action; *Love Story* (1944) and *The Magic Bow* (1946), the first of which seems to have more "respectable" music in an essentially melodramatic context and the second which is an energetic and decidedly proletarian biopic of an art music hero, violinist and composer Niccolo Paganini.

Caravan concerns Richard (Stewart Granger) who is sent on a mission to Spain and is attacked and left for dead by cohorts of Sir Francis (Dennis Price) who wants Richard's fiancee Oriana for himself. She is informed that Richard is dead and marries Sir Francis. Meanwhile, Richard has amnesia and has been saved by gypsy and flamenco dancer Rosal (Jean Kent) with whom he lives happily in a cave. Oriana comes to Spain looking for Richard and the film climaxes with the deaths of Rosal and Sir Francis, allowing Richard and Oriana to reunite.

The film's exuberance and overstatement allows for music of a similar character, while the Spanish setting also motivates the appearance of some flamenco songs and dances. These last for a substantial amount of screen time, and underline composer Walford Hyden's reputation as "A specialist in Spanish music",[24] although Levy himself knew something about Flamenco music.[25] Levy called in Hyden precisely for this specialism as he had no reputation as a film music composer but had done more in the way of radio work.[26] His work was bolstered by music written by Bretton Byrd that has remained uncredited.[27] The flamenco sequences comprise both dances and instrumental performances; Jean Kent's dancing is outstanding (indeed, she had started as a dancer in the 1930s) and at certain points we are shown two flamenco guitar solos and also the songs sung by the flamenco guitar player. The narrative has virtually stopped for these interludes, which manifest a substantial block of screen time as a succession of direct musical performances. While Sue Harper dismisses the dance as pastiche,[28] the music sounds quite authentic (to my ears, at least), while Walford Hyden's reputation as an expert on Spanish music, added to Levy's previous endeavours with flamenco suggests that the flamenco music has some degree of authenticity or at least some truth to the original.

Caravan's title sequence consists of a Spanish song, which then dominates Hyden's underscore as a melodic theme associated with Rosal. Its manifestation as the title song is within a tight 12-bar structure and regular song form that plays upon a chord built on the flattened second of the scale, a defining characteristic of flamenco music. It is sung as a serenade, denoted by the image beneath the titles, that of a singing guitar player and woman at a balcony. It occurs later to underline Rosal's screen presence, and first occurs within the diegesis as a flamenco song as part of the succession of performances, and has its final appearance when she dies. The domination of this theme for Rosal concurs with Harper's suggestion that non-figurative elements in these films work to undermine the narrative. The narrative is ultimately concerned with the reunion of the central lovers, Richard and Oriana, but the music here privileges Rosal as the key figure in the action. Not only is Rosal assigned the film's principal theme, but her dances give her an extended time on the screen as direct spectacle for the audience, asserting her power and importance in the film.

At times, *Caravan* comes close to being a musical, with the narrative virtually stalling to allow the appearance of foregrounded music as an attraction in itself rather than integrated with the film. These songs and dances are motivated by the nominally Spanish setting, as Richard goes native while with Rosal, reverting to his mother's Spanish origins and invoking an extravaganza of non-British emotionality triggered largely by the rumbustious music. One of *Caravan*'s most striking moments involves Richard having to negotiate a patch of potentially lethal quicksand, following Rosal's orders and surviving to immediately realize his love for her. The underscore matches the action in the most unsubtle terms, with the use of cymbal crashes on each step across the quicksand that Richard takes, to be replaced by muted violins when he reaches his saviour Rosal. The music in this sequence is distinctly lacking in finesse, but direct in its energetic engagement with the screen action. Perhaps reflecting his inexperience as a film composer, Hyden's score is generally unsubtle. Yet his music, from the highly spirited and boisterous flamenco music to the brash and stormy underscore, remains distinctive.

Madonna of the Seven Moons (1944) has a striking underscore provided by Austrian émigré Hans May, who, like Levy, had been a silent film pioneer. He had worked on Giuseppe Becce's *Kinothek* of 1919, a groundbreaking library of printed music for silent films that gained widespread use. May had worked as a film composer in Germany until the Nazi accession to power in 1933. He arrived in Britain the following year and was involved in the music for films such as *Give Her a Ring* (1934) and *Radio Parade of 1935* (1934). After scoring Carol Reed's *The Stars Look Down* (1939), May went on to provide the music for Gainsborough's costume drama *The Wicked Lady* (1945), as well as the Boulting brothers's *Brighton Rock* (1947). *Madonna of the Seven Moons* is concerned with Maddalena (Phyllis Calvert), a respectable middle-class housewife in Rome. The reappearance of her maturing daughter (Patricia Roc) back from school in England precipitates a transformation that has already periodically taken place since her rape as a young girl. Maddalena becomes "Rosanna", a swaggering gypsy-type who lives at the Inn of the Seven Moons in Florence with her cutthroat lover Nino (Stewart Granger). Her "schizophrenia" is cured only by her death.

The musical underscore for *Madonna of the Seven Moons* is arresting in its dynamism. It mixes autonomous music, which was prominent in Britain and where the music is essentially a self-sufficient piece in itself (not subordinated to screen dynamics), with Hollywood-style direct matching of the action's nuances. The film's climax provides a case in point. As Rosanna (Maddalena) climbs the stairs to find that Nino's brother (who she believes to be Nino himself) is attacking her (Maddalena's) daughter, a dissonant but regular tension *ostinato* (a looped motif) sustains, interrupted only by brutal staccato stabs from the brass. The aggression of the musical stabbing effect (anticipating the imminent mutual death by knives) make the music decidedly intrusive, but effective as it becomes a key signal of the fever pitch of emotion to which the film builds. Immediately after Rosanna is hit by the knife, the film cuts to a deathbed scene and the music changes character and mode, into a regularly structured piece that does not rely on screen action for its logic, but on musical logic. The music thus moves from a direct emphasis of screen action to providing an overall mood that enhances but does not match the screen activity.

Thematically, the film is dominated by the theme for Rosanna. This appears as a plenitude as the song *Rosanna* with which Nino serenades her in the garden. The song follows the dominant formal schemes for popular songs, and is accompanied by guitar, although Granger was unhappy that his own voice was removed from the soundtrack to be replaced by one higher in pitch, and perhaps less masculine than his own.[29] The thematic importance of the *Rosanna* melody underlines the music's concentration upon her character, as well as emphasizing the importance of music in cueing the escape from middle-class banality. Its appearances as part of the fabric of the non-diegetic score are regularly as an arrangement premised upon lush strings, the common coding of emotion and love in both film music and light music. Although it tends to retain the same arrangement, it is slowed when compared with the song version. This marked slowing of the melody at certain points, almost like an improvisational *rubato*, tends to hang on the high notes, the music both coding and emphasizing desire. The *Rosanna* theme overwhelms the film – there is an organ playing on the soundtrack that is loosely associated with the Maddalena character, established at the convent near the opening of the film and reappearing at the film's conclusion when she is given the last rites by a priest. Thus, the underscore in *Madonna of the Seven Moons* is vaguely thematic, but not in the systematic way of most contemporaneous Hollywood scores, certainly those written by Hollywood's most prominent composers, such as Max Steiner or Erich Wolfgang Korngold. The *Rosanna* melody appears regularly, both as diegetic song, a musical box and whistling, and as non-diegetic underscore. It not only serves to trigger Maddalena's transformation, but the *Rosanna* song and theme, referring to the sensual and aggressive half of the character, underlines her power, in contrast to the weaker melody assigned to the demure Maddalena. In addition, the male lead (Stewart Granger as Nino) is assigned no music for himself, but becomes a vessel for Rosanna's song, thus further centring her character in the film. Overall, May's underscore is string-heavy and incorporates several "effects", where the music emphasizes action in a heavily intrusive, even crass manner. In this way, it is superficially reminiscent of Hollywood scores, in terms of the sheer amount of music and some crass matching of action (known as "mickeymousing"), although it lacks their systematic use of themes and includes a large amount of music that has no structural function within the film. But May's music always sounds purposeful and he varies the orchestral textures admirably throughout, to create probably the most impressive and distinctive score to a Gainsborough film.

Released in the same year, *Love Story* (1944) was a remarkable musical event. A piece of music which Hubert Bath had written for the film, the *Cornish Rhapsody*, became one of the most popular pieces of music of the decade. While this music had not quite crossed over with the highbrow concert hall like a few pieces of "quality" film music, the *Cornish Rhapsody* became one of the most famous light orchestral pieces of the time, and indeed remains the only piece of Gainsborough film music (underscore) ever, and still, available as a recording. As noted in the previous chapter, there was something of a fad in the 1940s for the featuring of concert pieces within films, inspired by the phenomenally successful *Warsaw Concerto* that appeared in the film *Dangerous Moonlight* (1941).

In the wake of the *Warsaw Concerto*, written by Richard Addinsell, many films surfaced that followed a similar format, including what were termed "tabloid concertos". The vast majority of these films focused on a central character who was a musician, allowing the motivation of foregrounded music within the films. In *Dangerous Moonlight*'s wake, *While I Live* (1947) used Charles Williams's highly popular *The Dream of Olwen*, while *Train of Events* (1949) and *The Woman's Angle* (1952) both had their own tabloid concertos. Levy maintained that with the *Warsaw Concerto* and the *Cornish Rhapsody*, "We had created an entirely new standard of screen music."[30] It was one that was not premised upon the highbrow reputation of the art music concert hall, but upon radio and popular light orchestral music. While both of these pieces bore no small resemblance to Rachmaninoff's orchestral style, neither of these pieces was the product of Britain's art music intelligentsia – both Addinsell and Bath were primarily film music specialists. In the aftermath of this success, Hubert Bath died in 1945 while sketching music for *The Wicked Lady*. Originally from Devon, he had studied at the Royal Academy of Music – in fact he was one of the few composers who worked for Gainsborough who had enjoyed such a privileged musical education. Bath had even written some music for the concert hall, but had joined the Lime Grove music department full-time in 1934 and spent most of his time arranging the work of other composers as well as providing music for many films. As stated earlier, Bath had been a film music pioneer, providing music for *Kitty* (1928), Britain's first partly sound film and Hitchcock's *Blackmail* (1929) the first all-sound film produced in Britain, although in both cases the score was pared down from the intended music for the silent version. He went on to provide most of the music for Hitchcock's Gaumont-British productions of the 1930s, wrote some concert hall music and once was music advisor to London County Council. Despite this seemingly full career, Hubert Bath's name is likely to be remembered solely for the *Cornish Rhapsody*.

Love Story concerns concert pianist Lissa (Margaret Lockwood) who, having only a year to live, goes to Cornwall. To her surprise, she falls in love with a man who seems to be dodging the war effort (Stewart Granger). He becomes the inspiration for her composition of the *Cornish Rhapsody* and finally redeems himself by saving people trapped in a tin mine. Lockwood leaves him for his own sake, however, and performs the *Cornish Rhapsody* at the Albert Hall, where Granger turns up to cement their love. The *Cornish Rhapsody* appears initially on the opening titles, and in its full form. For our next encounter with it is in fragments when Lissa is beginning to compose it in a summer house overlooking the cliffs of Cornwall. Finally, we have the full version, performed in a highly spectacular and climactic Albert Hall concert with Margaret Lockwood at the piano in front of a large orchestra. *Love Story* contains not only the highly evocative and emotive music, but this is matched by a suitably emotional performance from Lockwood as the doomed musician. The *Cornish Rhapsody* itself is based on two themes and includes "sea"-coded music and mimicking of seagull cries. While it is arguably clichéd, it is highly effective in its primal connotations. The music appears to be an emanation of both nature and Lissa's desire, the music thus functions to associate and unite elemental natural forces and female desire.

The Magic Bow

Gainsborough's historical biopic of violinist Paganini, *The Magic Bow* (1946), was one of the company's last films before the change in mode that resulted from Sydney Box taking up the studio's reins of production.[31] Stewart Granger portrays the violinist and composer who, as popular belief would have it, had sold his soul to the devil. Although the film's subject matter initially seems to smack of the high art that Gainsborough studios eschewed, their approach to the material falls distinctly within the house style perpetuated by their other melodramas.

Granger plays Paganini as an abrasive and unrefined character, in fact precisely as one lacking in middle-class decorum and restraint. While there seems historical veracity to this representation, Granger's performance arguably fits more closely with his persona in other Gainsborough melodramas, like *Caravan* and particularly *Madonna of the Seven Moons*.

The figure of Paganini as well as his musical performances act as a hypermasculine magnet for women. His performances are peppered with reverse shots of adoring women, especially Phyllis Calvert as Jeanne and, to a lesser degree, Jean Kent as his faithful but seemingly overlooked "companion" Bianchi. Granger emphasizes the spectacular nature of the performer, infusing the film with vigour and acting much like pop stars of recent times.[32] The film leaves us in no doubt as to the effects of both the music and Paganini on the female sector of the audience. During a montage sequence of his European tour, female members of the audience are shown mesmerized, in the thrall of this pied piper and his musical sorcery. The spectacularization of Granger's visual performance is matched by the quality of violin playing by Yehudi Menuhin to which he mimes most convincingly. The film's publicity was geared towards highlighting the authenticity of the acting performance and the music (the virtuosity of both Menuhin and Granger), certainly more than historical veracity of the film. Yet unlike the visual aspects of Gainsborough films as described by Harper,[33] the music did have considerable attention paid to its historical veracity.[34] Levy not only declares the authenticity of the music, but sees it as guaranteed through the "painstaking research" that has gone into its production.[35] For example, Yehudi Menuhin used not only a Stradivarius violin, but a Guarnieri, Paganini's personal favourite type of instrument. Such concentration upon the music was foregrounded in publicity. The press kit states, "Selling this film to the public is a pushover if you concentrate on the stars and the music", while it also suggests linking with local musical societies, collaborating with local music stores for window and counter displays, and competes with violinists "who can render pieces from the film" for prizes of cinema tickets.

Gainsborough's perennial concern with class surfaces again in this film. At a high society party at Jeanne's family home, Paganini finds out the hard way that music is not for those who appreciate it, but for the idle rich. His performance is initially hampered by broken violin strings, so he performs with the only one left on his instrument. The piece he then plays is interrupted by the partygoers' conversations and the snoring and hilariously loud awakening of an elderly man. Paganini is outraged by the lack of respect accorded to music by the rich and rather than persist with his piece he serenades them by making ass brays with his violin before storming out. What this incident underlines is that classical music is not for the sole use of the ignorant ruling class, but it is their dubious patronage upon which most well-known classical composers and musicians had exclusively to rely.

The Magic Bow has a large number of sequences of musical perform-ance, including *Campanella* (written by Paganini) outside the prison, *The Devil's Trill* (Tartini), *La Ronde des Lutins* (Brazzini), *Nel Cor Piu Nom Mi Sento* (Paganini), *Violin Concerto no.1* (Paganini) at the Parma concert hall,[36] *Caprice no.20* (Paganini), *Concerto Op. 1* (Paganini) and the final movement of Beethoven's *Violin Concerto Op. 61* at the climactic Vatican concert. The film's underscore uses a piece as the repeated main theme which is associated with the love between Paganini and Jeanne. It was written by Philip Green, marking his film debut before he went on to be one of the most prolific British film music composers of the 1950s, and is based on a theme from Paganini's *E minor Concerto*. Green's Love theme (*Romance*) is played over the opening titles and finally appears triumphantly within the diegesis, played by Paganini, to provide musical fulfilment to match the screen's union of Granger and Calvert. The piece became highly popular and even received a performance at the Albert Hall in 1946.[37] As *Love Story* had proved, musical tie-ins were relatively common during the 1940s, much like tied-in pop songs are with films today. The music in *The Magic Bow* demonstrates the Gainsborough production line approach, where Levy was in charge of the classical pieces that Paganini performs and indeed the whole musical side of the film, Bretton Byrd was the music editor, David McCullum was the music coach for Granger's miming, Phil Green provided a number of arrangements of the repeated theme of the underscore, while Henry Geehl provided the small amount of incidental cues that accompany action.[38]

The Magic Bow corresponded with some other films released in the immediate post-War period in that it prominently displayed classical music. Shortly before *The Magic Bow*'s release, *The Seventh Veil* (1945), with its numerous classical piano pieces, and *Brief Encounter* (1945), which popularized Rachmaninoff's *Piano Concerto no.2*, had both been successes. However, unlike these two films, *The Magic Bow* did not equate such music of culture with the ruling classes, rather it attempted to win such music for the masses. It is undoubtedly one of the most vigorous composer/musician biopics, with a remarkably charismatic performance by Stewart Granger in the central role. *The Magic Bow* demonstrates the interest in class that had been articulated by previous costume dramas,[39] but doubled this by proletarianizing art music, where it is for all rather than just a few rich highbrows.

Conclusion

Overall, Gainsborough's musical mode of production resembled Hollywood music departments far more than it did the single-composer system that was prevalent in Britain. This enabled Levy and his crew to produce cheap music quickly, using a number of composers and orchestrators in a production line for some of their scores. That Gainsborough's music differed radically from the prestige film music of the time is reflected by connections with radio light music (Levy and Hyden) outweighing those with the classical concert hall. The desire to have prestigious film music written by established art music composers had lost impetus by the early 1950s. Specialist film composers outnumbered the increasingly small band of essentially art music composers who were still slumming in the film industry. Louis Levy and his cohorts at Gainsborough were the forerunners of these specialists, caring for the overall effect of the music within the context of the film rather than its cultural status.

As pointed out earlier, once Sydney Box became chief producer at Gainsborough, the films changed character, as did the music department. Levy ceased to be used as musical director and musical production turned to the single-composer system that was and has remained dominant in Britain. Levy ceased to be musical director for Gainsborough films and Gaumont-British, being replaced by Felton Rapley in 1947.[40] He became musical director to ABPC in 1948 and worked for them at Elstree until his death in 1957.[41] After Levy's exit, some composers with certain reputations were imported by Gainsborough, most conspicuously Sir Arthur Bliss, who provided suitably prestigious music for the expensive-failure *Christopher Columbus* (1949). Other composers of perhaps more repute included Clifton Parker (*When the Bough Breaks* [1947]) and Doreen Carwithen (*The Boys in Brown* [1949]), who later married another film composer, William Alwyn. Also Benjamin Frankel, who having been a dance-music specialist and in more recent years rehabilitated as a respectable art music composer, scored *Dear Murderer* (1947) and *So Long at the Fair* (1949) on the way to a mixed career of film and art music.[42] It seemed that with the disintegration of Levy's music department, a whole mode of film music had disappeared from the British film industry, underlined by the appearance of

Muir Mathieson as musical director and conductor for some of the films produced under Sydney Box.

It seems strange that the music in Gainsborough films has been so completely neglected. Perhaps it is, as other writers have suggested, because of the studios output as a whole going against the grain of the dominant film culture. The music reflects the social class of the Gainsborough films, embodying the reality of their working-class popularity in opposition to middle-class morality and desire for art or quality. Gainsborough's costume dramas can be seen as contesting the consensual films of the time.[43] This attitude was also in operation when it came to film music: Levy led a functional music department that was unconcerned with concert hall kudos or critical backslapping. He was concerned with the craft of invisible, effective and cheap film music. That he managed to oversee the production of such a variety of remarkable film music is testament to his position as one of Britain's pioneer film musicians. Levy's humble origins and hustling attitude earned him little in the way of artistic recognition, indeed it earned him something of a negative reputation. His use of cheap and functional music and his encouragement of unrestrained music for the exaggerated posturing of Gainsborough's melodramas may not have helped his case. Such music could not usually be packaged as concert hall suites,[44] though it excelled within the overblown and emotionally charged contexts of the melodramatic films themselves.

4
Did You Hear the One about the Irishman? Sound and Music, Forging Ethnicity in *Odd Man Out* (1946)

Although set in Northern Ireland, *Odd Man Out* tried to avoid direct representations of the province's sectarian divide. The film attempts to promulgate a normative impression of Ulster – for an implied British/English audience – not only through the introduction into the narrative of characters who act as surrogates for this specific audience but also, perhaps more significantly, through the soundtrack.

Odd Man Out was released in 1946, directed by Carol Reed and set in Belfast, although it avoids stating this explicitly. While the film has pretensions towards the universal, in reality it merely projects a view of Northern Ireland from "Mainland Britain", namely England, and a highly specific point of view at that. In terms of its representations, the film tries to privilege the universal over the specific; yet, this is directly contradicted by the *highly* specific setting and milieu of the film. Film criticism and its concerns largely have duplicated the film's approach, attempting to repress the historical context and deny a voice to Northern Ireland. This is precisely underlined by the *Odd Man Out*'s articulation of sound. Against a backdrop of "Irish-style" music, the highly specific Ulster accent is repressed, to be replaced by southern Irish accents and English accents. While the spuriousness of the accents is doubtless (at least partly) due to the availability of actors, the effect is historically and ideologically specific, asserting a vocal and linguistic, as well as cultural hegemony.

Universality and specificity

Odd Man Out's story is as follows: During an Irish Republican Army (IRA) fundraising raid on a factory, unit leader Johnny McQueen (James

Mason) kills a man and shoots himself. He becomes separated from his unit and spends the rest of the film wandering through Belfast in rain and snow, gradually bleeding to death. This slow but inexorable demise gives the film similarities with *Reservoir Dogs* (1992 US) and makes it one of the most sustained spectacles of morbid fascination in the British cinema.

Odd Man Out was acclaimed at the time of its release as a film with a propensity towards the "universal" that pushes sociopolitical concerns to the background, and deals "sensitively" with the situation in Northern Ireland. *Kinematograph Weekly* called it a "British gangster melodrama set in Northern Ireland."[1] *What's on in London* declared: "a man, an idealist (if you like) hunted by the police for a hold-up carried out for money to help his cause...."[2], while Arthur Vesselo in *Sight and Sound* pronounced it "...the most genuine film of the quarter."[3] I will discuss the film's authenticity later, but *Odd Man Out* was perceived initially as being a boundless story of human suffering, a universal story of mankind. The urge to universalize is often achieved through the de-emphasis of specificity, or rather through its visual and aural distortion. Yet curiously, *Odd Man Out* does precisely the opposite, setting the film in a highly specific and highly charged *milieu*, demonstrating that manifestations of the universal usually turn out to be someone's, often someone else's, version of the "universal".

However, despite their appearance in the film, the IRA and the problems of Northern Ireland are never directly addressed, indeed they are repressed by the film history's attitude to *Odd Man Out*. Dai Vaughan's *BFI Classics* book about *Odd Man Out* makes hardly a mention of the IRA or the conflict in Northern Ireland.[4] This is hardly surprising. The film denies social and historical context to the IRA and the whole conflict. Indeed, as reviewers noted, the IRA are shown in a format that corresponds to the representation of organized crime, exactly the way that the British establishment has traditionally portrayed them. The film's opening rolling title card is a heavy-handed attempt at delimiting meaning. It says, "This story is told against a background of political unrest in a city of Northern Ireland. It is not concerned with the struggle between the law and an illegal organization, but only with the conflict in the heads of the people when they become unexpectedly involved." This caveat aims to excuse the film of precise representations, as well as attempting to remove the emphasis from the IRA. Thus, *Odd Man Out* tries to ignore the historical precedents and sedimentations of the film's location, characters and their motivations.

The aim at universalization was at least partially due to the adaptation (or bowdlerizing) of the film from the novel, by director Carol Reed and writer R.C. Sherriff.[5] The film's approach denies difference and specificity in Northern Ireland, by abstracting the humanist dimension of the story from a historically and culturally highly particular situation. Yet the seemingly universal aim of *Odd Man Out* is illusory, nothing more than a facade. While the film tries to remove specific material from the original narrative to create a patina of universality, the soundtrack, perhaps more than the other elements, betrays the fact that the film is not universal, but wholly British, or perhaps more pertinently English, in its construction, outlook and assumptions.[6]

Forging ethnicity

Odd Man Out has an exceptionally rich tapestry of a soundtrack, by any film's standards. Sound plays a fundamental part in the film's narration; yet it deals as much, if not more, so in paradigmatic aspects (cultural ideas and representations) than in the syntagmatic development of narrative. And these undermine the seeming universality of the narrative.

The film forges Northern Ireland, both in the sense of roughly fashioning it and in the sense of counterfeiting it in the most blatant of terms. The two principal zones in which the soundtrack functions are first that of speech, or rather accent, and secondly the virtually autonomous discourse of music within the film. While voices furnish the principal discursive matrix for the film's representations, the music provides a fabric through which the film's visual representations are filtered. Both voices and music enable the film to set up subject and object positions; Irish ethnicity as the film's object, and an English audience as the subject.

Northern Irish ethnicity is established principally through accent, specifically the marginalization of the Ulster accent and concomitant elevation of southern Irish and English accents. The implied English audience (as subject) seems to work as the "voice of reason". The English characters in *Odd Man Out* are surrogates in the film, who anchor and provide a normative point of view, offering a reference point for the film's other accents. The literal manifestation of the English voice of reason (in the face of the Irish irrationality) are the two sisters, Beryl and Maudie, and husband Tom, who are inclined not to give Johnny away, but also not to help him. As one recent commentator put it, "they epitomise the British temperament at its best...decent",[7] which

serves to emphasize their notable role in the proceedings. These characters represent the film's "moral centre". Other English characters have
similar positions: the publican trying to avoid involvement, which can
be read less as a professional response to the situation than a coding of
English neutrality in a conflict that regularly has been posed as a purely
Irish conflict. This is further underlined by the seemingly kindly English
soldiers, who help Johnny into a cab, thus disassociating themselves
from and contrasting with the film's ruthlessly efficient Royal Ulster
Constabulary. However, a more telling position is offered by Lukey the
artist (played by English character actor Robert Newton), who wants to
paint the ebbing away of life, and so openly vampirises Johnny's death,
a charge that could convincingly be levelled at the whole film. These
characterizations all imply an English audience. In addition to this, the
Northern Ireland *milieu* is constructed in terms that the English audience
of the time would understand. Apart from the numerous English people
who appear to live in Belfast, there is what has been constituted as a
"gangsters vs law" narrative, and the marginalization of Ulster accents,
replacing them with stock, stereotyped "Irish".

In terms of the spoken word, *Odd Man Out* seems to have an
unmatched polyphony. It renders a Belfast world through an amalgam
of accents that range from authentic Northern Irish, southern Irish and
English to fabricated Northern and southern Irish accents of varying
quality. I might add here as an aside that the scholarly investigation of
utterances is impeded because of the overwhelming academic concentration on linguistics (written language) to the detriment of phonetics
(the spoken sounds, the materiality of the word) – a situation which
strikingly matches the marginalization of sound in the study of film
and television. *Odd Man Out* notably lacks Ulster accents. The major
players all have southern Irish accents (including false ones) and English
accents. Cyril Cusack at least makes an attempt at an Ulster accent,
while the gang of children who appear in the film have *real* Ulster
accents. These children act as a direct signifier of the ethnic artificiality of the film, and are treated by the film as just another aspect of
the location shooting in Belfast, yet they provide a reference point,
an authentic centre, to contrast with the artificiality of the normative
English perspective. The treatment of voices is reflected by the stylization of sound in the sequence where Dennis asks a group of children
if they have seen Johnny. One boy repeats "Mister, give us a penny!"
at regular intervals seemingly irrespective of Dennis's actions. Another
boy answers the questions but, bizarrely, pinches his nose each time he
replies. This accentuates the sonic difference in voices. The boy's Ulster

accent is made more alien from the English (BBC/RP) norm in films of the time, and is counterposed with Canadian Robert Beatty's (Dennis) flagging attempt at a southern Irish accent. This stylized activity has the effect of undermining the narrative drive of this sequence, calling attention to the children and their disruptive positioning and attitude within the film.

This sequence evinces an astonishingly aestheticized use of sound.[8] It is orchestrated, structured like music, with the repeated "Mister, give us a penny" providing a rhythmic backbone for the action. This stylization of sound further enhances the dreamlike quality of the film, while distancing what the children say and what they are. Their voices provide the most solid co-ordinate points for the variations of accents on display. As real children – of Milltown Industrial School, Belfast[9] – they are a startling guarantee of the inauthenticity of the film's representations. They are props, but disruptive ones, which escape the limitation that the film tries to impose on them.

The absence of Ulster accents and their replacement with English and southern Irish is partially rooted in industrial expediency. The Abbey Theatre Company, Dublin, supplied many of the film's actors:[10] Cyril Cusack as Murphy, Kathleen Ryan as Kathleen, F.J. McCormick as Shell, Denis O'Dea as head constable (with an upper-class southern Irish accent that could easily pass for an English accent), W.G. Fay as Father Tom, Dan O'Herlihy as Nolan, Maureen Delaney as Teresa and Kitty Kirwan as Granny. All these have southern Irish accents, apart from the endeavours of Cusack, added to Ann Clery as Maureen and Joseph Tomelty as the cabby, who really were from Northern Ireland. Added to these are the English actors who retain their authentic accents: Robert Newton as Lukey, William Hartnell as the publican, Beryl Measor as Maudie, Fay Compton as Rosie and Arthur Hambling as husband, along with Welshman Elwyn Brook-Jones as Tober. Spurious accents appear from James Mason as Johnny, Canadian Robert Beatty as Dennis and Roy Irving as Murphy.[11] These accents are almost all southern Irish, and some of the false ones are highly unconvincing. Almost all of these are in stark opposition to the children. At one point in *Odd Man Out*, the children play excitedly, emulating their hero Johnny McQueen. They argue among one another, each shouting, "I am Johnny!" Yet the irony is that they are (or may have become) Johnny McQueen, a republican desperado, as opposed to James Mason, the upper-class British matinee cad who had so recently stalked through Gainsborough's melodramas. Robert Moss calls the children "an unconscious commentary on the... adults",[12] and De Felice refers to them as a "Greek chorus".[13]

While they hardly constitute the sort of commentary that these writers envisage, they certainly do provide a commentary of sorts: an index of the articulation of voice within *Odd Man Out.*

The dominant Northern Irish accent is known to specialists as "UAI" (Ulster Anglo Irish), which differs dramatically from the "brogue", as the southern Irish accent is commonly known.[14] While the Ulster accent is not confined by the political boundary of Northern Ireland, it is highly distinct from the "brogue", which is an accent far more in evidence in *Odd Man Out.* Inexplicably, one of the director's biographies states: "Reed wanted to ensure that every element of Belfast portrayed in the film was accurate, in particular the accents, which differed a great deal from those in the rest of Ireland."[15] While I have already pointed out that the spuriousness of the accents is doubtless (at least partly) due to industrial expediency, the effect is important; it is something historically and ideologically specific. The film constructs its character voices as simply either English or not English (i.e. "Irish"), using the English language and its articulation as accent, as a repressive and regulating device.

Killing the stage Irishman

Additionally, there is something *historically resonant* about the English replacement of the Irish/Ulster voice. This control of language regulates and allows the redefinition of people and their identity options. Renaming and linguistic redefinition recast the subaltern grouping's self-image – a contemporary response has been the defiant if occasional use of Gaelic in Northern Ireland within the republican community. The destruction of national languages in Ireland, Scotland and Wales fostered the wide belief in the English that these are lesser nations with little apart from English culture. That small repertoire of cliched national signifiers are displayed *ad nauseam* by the Scots, Welsh and Irish – for example, Scotland is equated with men in kilts eating haggis and playing bagpipes – serve to assert their difference from the dominant and dominating culture, that of England. English cultural hegemony persists in the using (and faking) of English spoken with an Irish accent, manifesting an appropriation of voice. This is matched more recently by Sinn Fein not being "allowed a voice", their outlawed word being subject to a broadcasting ban in the late 1980s and early 1990s, which bizarrely meant that the television image of politicians would have to be accompanied by a replacement voice – "that of an actor" as the titles on the screen declared. The irony of this matches *Odd*

Man Out's corruption of the Northern Irish voice and its replacement with surrogates.[16]

This array of voices in *Odd Man Out* engages with, and represents through, a number of half-concealed structural (and political) concepts that pattern the film. This matrix of discourses involves the whole "otherness" of the province to the English heartland; the domination of English voice, a voice of reason that marks the English as neutral; and that of Northern Ireland's problems being caused by Southern "outsiders". This configuration of ideas is still current in the British media and in perceptions of Northern Ireland from across the Irish Sea. Sound makes this more apparent than *Odd Man Out*'s other areas, especially the way that the accents abjectly fail to represent Ulster. As *The Belfast Telegraph* noted at the time of the film's release: "At times one feels the scene may have shifted to Dublin so rich are the brogues...".[17]

At the time of the film's release in the late 1940s, most of the population of the UK would have been relatively unaware of Northern Irish accents – certainly in comparison to now. Other accents had been canonized in films, giving a reductive scheme of ways of speaking in the British Isles. The BBC had a policy of accent standardization, which eroded any sense of a wide spectrum of different accents in the UK.[18] Films and professional "types" had done much to establish a minimal outline of UK accents: Cockney, West country (seemingly anywhere in the south outside London) and North (primarily an amalgam of Lancashire and Yorkshire, although Liverpool seems to have had a more individual sense), Scottish, Welsh, and a general Irish accent based on the brogue. There was little (wide) distribution of Northern Irish accent. A case in point is Sam Kydd, who was from Ulster and became one of the most recognizable bit-part actors in British cinema, yet only occasionally was he allowed to use his original accent, and indeed he is never thought of as Northern Irish.[19] Colin McArthur points out the charged aspects of the "tartan and kailyard" through which Scotland is represented (both by Scots and by foreigners),[20] yet Ulster has no signs that had currency in England, so those of southern Ireland were imported for the job.[21]

There is a tradition in British cinema of using English (more than other British) actors to play Irish people, adopting their ethnic voice. On many occasions this has involved the production of a degraded stereotype, often premised upon the figure of the "Stage Irishman", who graced English stage productions and was usually ignorant and spoiling for a fight.[22] While this tradition has receded to some degree, where films like *In the Name of the Father* (1993) took great care with accents, English actors still become conspicuously false and stereotypical Irish. A prime example is the recent film *A Man of No Importance* (1996), where an almost all-English cast of stars put on Irish accents of variable quality.[23] It is not simply a question of innocently "putting on an accent"; the situation has added significance in that it is replacing a subaltern voice that has been historically (and violently) repressed, and arguably still is.[24]

In films set in Britain, however, there is a tendency for accent to be used simply to *differentiate* from the English. So in *Odd Man Out*, the accents are English and "Irish". Northern Ireland is constructed through the familiar (English accent) and the semi-familiar (southern Irish accent), while the Ulster voice itself is marginalized – indeed consigned to children (which underlines its elision). In addition to this, the Irish accent perpetrated by star James Mason as Johnny McQueen is a variable attempt at a southern Irish accent. The effect of foregrounding southern Irish accents at the expense of Ulster accents is, first, to construct the IRA as southern Irish, which places the problems of Northern Ireland with the Republic of Ireland and, secondly, to imply that Ulster is the same as southern Ireland, which simply denies the existence of the loyalist community. The implication of the film is that the police are the film's only representatives of the loyalist community. Recent British films elide the loyalists, and tend to romanticize republicans.[25] *Odd Man Out* does precisely this, by removing their political and historical specificity. As John Hill comments, "British films about Ireland...have opted to focus on Irish violence while failing to place it in the social and political context which would permit its explanation. And, by doing so, they...have rendered the events with which they deal largely unintelligible."[26]

But an audience watching the film in Northern Ireland, or in the Republic of Ireland, could supply what was missing themselves, unlike a British audience. They could easily supplement what the film shows, as *Odd Man Out* certainly does not remove enough context to hide the IRA. *The Belfast Telegraph*'s review stated: "It is natural to question the suggestion of sympathy with a terrorist organization, but the direction of this film has been done so skilfully, and 'politics' avoided so meticulously, that good taste is rarely offended."[27] While this review desperately wanted to sidestep the very immediate question of glorification of the IRA, it seems that upon the film's release, this fear inspired action as well as words. *The Belfast Telegraph* reported criticism in the Ulster House of Commons of the cost of policing a Belfast cinema where *Odd Man Out* was being screened.[28] Although this was seemingly not reported elsewhere, it suggests that the film inspired fears in the authorities, either that it might become a focus for republicanism or that it might inspire a violent reaction from the loyalists.[29]

The Belfast Telegraph's film review was quick to try to deny the films political relevance: "The political angle you may completely ignore; as the director has wisely ignored it. In essence it is just another cops-and-robbers film. Why the 'hero' robbed the bank [*sic*] is his own business not ours. It may have been to get his 'doll' a mink coat or funds for his political party. All that concerns us are his reactions when, having killed a man, he, wounded and desperate, seeks to escape in a city which has been roused against him."[30] Belfast hardly seems roused in the film. The denial of the sociopolitical reality matches the fraudulent Ulster voices and Irish accents, which amount to a denial of voice commonly experienced by colonial/postcolonial peoples. A common strategy for subalterns is to channel the lost personal expression into music (or have that done for them). It could be argued that this process has taken effect in *Odd Man Out*, yet it too lacks "authenticity". The music is "Wardour Street Irish". However, it does occupy the foreground regularly and provide a "voice" for the figure of Johnny McQueen's dying trek across Belfast.

The Celtic musical soundscape

The film's music is outstanding and notably traverses the juncture of Hollywood-style film music and the indigenous British form of the 1930s and 1940s, which differed in many ways. It provides a mixture of Hollywood's highly developed action-matching underscoring with the predominantly British mode of autonomous pieces (with their own musical logic) counterpointed with screen action. As Michel Chion points out, "...music enjoys the status of being a little freer of barriers of time and space than other sound and visual elements."[31] So we might imagine that the music is not shackled by the film's processes, that it might not directly follow the film's ethnic construction. Yet in *Odd Man Out*, it decidedly does.

The film's musical score, written by William Alwyn, also engages with cultural discourses about Ireland, while its processes demonstrate perhaps even more nakedly the strategies of the film in its entirety. The musical score manipulates stereotypical signifiers for "Irishness" as part of *Odd Man Out*'s meditation upon the status of Northern Ireland. These stereotypical and reductive musical representations provide a frame for the reader that the text is positing: English cinemagoers. Music in the film is a primary signifier of location and ethnicity. It engages with stereotypical musical formations to represent "Irishness"; as Moss notes, "Occasionally the melodies suggest haunting old Irish airs..."[32] This "figurative" musical tradition used by the classical film score is responsible for musical shorthand for Native Americans and other nationalities and races. Music such as this trade upon the "already-known", in this case, English discourses about a general Ireland rather than the more specific Ulster. This is articulated through musical as well as iconographic and narrative stereotyping and clichés. Seen from this perspective, the music in *Odd Man Out* works as a frame for English audiences, a marker for point of view, allowing easy entry to a world of cliché and formula.

Broadly speaking, the music consists of an insistent "Irish"-style melody, plus art music harmony, structure and arrangement. This amalgam of the popular and melody-centred with the modes of the highbrow concert hall corresponds to the blueprint for orchestral film music that had been the norm since the mid-1930s, and had solidified into a strategy that manifested national identity as simply a number of musical tricks; for example, British soldiers regularly being accompanied by the appearance of the melody of a song such as *Rule Britannia* on the soundtrack, while native Americans usually cue the appearance of stereotypical rhythmic "Indian" music. In terms of matching the film's action, *Odd Man Out* has Hollywood-style action cues for the escape from the raid and the chase later in the film. In the first case, the music aggressively punctuates Johnny's fall from the car, while the vast majority of the film's underscore music does not follow the action. Arguably, the action follows the music. This is more than apparent in the scene at Teresa's, where the activities of Pat and Murphy take place accompanied by a record of Schubert's *Unfinished Symphony*.[33] The music and action match much like Hollywood film cues, in fact more so, as the two are absolutely integrated, adding to the overpowering fatalism of the film.

Odd Man Out has one repeated and overwhelming main musical theme, the Irish-style tune that is also pointedly the funeral tune for Johnny. Apart from this, only one other character has music consistently associated with them: Kathleen, who has a romantic string lullaby attached to her screen appearances; although Shell has a semi-comic clarinet tune that appears for him a couple of times. Kathleen's theme is precisely coded to indicate "emotionality", using gentle but chromatic strings. Apart from these repeated musical themes, there is only a repeated "Delerium" theme that cues Johnny's state of mind and hallucinations. This is musical paucity compared with the thematic wealth of

Hollywood film scores of the time. The point of the music is primarily to repeat the theme for Johnny, a funeral threnody, and thus to remain static, to freeze and fetishize the action of Johnny gradually dying.

The music provides a fabric through which the film's visual representations are filtered. It provides a grounding for the narrative action as well as fashioning a perspective upon the tale. As such, the music tells of inevitable death: the main theme is one long funeral march (the finale of the concert hall suite made from the film's music is called "Nemesis"). It starts with a rhythmic version of the "Fate" motto that inaugurates Beethoven's *5th Symphony* and is marked "Lento Funebre" (slow and funereal). It even goes so far as to include the tolling bell of the Albert clock, which marks out the 8 hours of the film's action, and is an obvious aural icon of the funereal.[34] Towards the conclusion of the film, this music comes into its own as an accompaniment for images of Johnny staggering about the streets of Belfast in rain and snow.

In *Odd Man Out*, the music works as a frame for English (perhaps British) audiences, allowing entry to a world of cliché, where the characters and situation is always ultimately distanced and fetishized by the foregrounded presence of the music itself. The music spectacularizes (monumentalizes) rather than elucidates, yet its processes reveal the film's processes – the "Irish" essence is manipulated for English ends, much in the same way that the Irish-styled melody is filtered through the art music conventions of orchestration and (art) musical development.

Alwyn's musical underscore is fully integral to the film, having been conceived and built up before the shooting started. The poetic quality of the film comes partially from the fact that it was shot as well as being cut to the music. Composer Alwyn stated, "Long before the shooting in the studios started. We worked on the pace of the music...Most of the scenes were shot to prerecordings and transformed and orchestrated afterwards. I worked in the closest collaboration with the editor, so that we knew what we were doing individually with sound effects and music, and the final result is a complete integration of sound and visuals – a sound-film in the real meaning of the word, where music had been allowed to speak in terms of film and fine art."[35]

The integral status of the music and its frequent appearance in the aural foreground amount to the music keying an immersion in *emotion*. The dreamlike quality of the film is partially caused by the music, creating a direct analogy with the attitudes of Britain to the "Irish problem", blurring the possibility of seeing reality clearly, and replacing it with simple oppositions and characterizations.

Conclusion: Who's listening?

Odd Man Out attempts to posture as universal, denying the historical context and the different voice of Northern Ireland and its people. However, the audience that is posed for the film is *not* universal, but is "mainland British", more clearly English, reflecting not only the origin of the film but also the target market. After all, Northern Ireland's population is insignificant when compared to other potential audiences for the film.

The film's repression of voice is sublimated into the film's foregrounded music, which is also a pastiche as the music is "paint-by-numbers" Irish. The music is rather a signifier of excessive (thus "not-British" or "not-English") emotion, invoking a fantasy scenario of the mystical Irish other, in this case a violent and morbid fantasy where British/English cultural hegemony manifests itself as unconscious aggression towards Ireland, inscribed upon the body of the dying Irishman.

The film manifests an uneasy sitting together, in fact a contradiction, between its use of the universal and the particular, the human-interest story and the charged local colour. Yet the film has attempted to subordinate the latter to the former, to create an imaginary Ulster at a cost to the realities of the situation: the sectarian divide, historical enmity and "mainland British" involvement and responsibility.

John Hill notes: "It is evident that the film tries to evacuate a number of concrete particulars...[but] there is still sufficient sense of particulars for the conflict of the film to have a specific, not merely general, context."[36] The film tries to deny specificity of location, yet uses location in a foregrounded way; and although it purports to concentrate on the personal aspects of Johnny, it denies that these are motivated by his IRA membership. *The Belfast Telegraph* registered the prominent locations.[37] Indeed, it would be difficult for anyone from Northern Ireland to miss the fact that film's opening shots embrace the Harland and Wolff shipyard and Cave Hill, both metonymic symbols of the two sides of the sectarian divide in Belfast.

The imaginary has displaced the historical. But it cannot be fully displaced, and the organization of the film's sound demonstrates nakedly the processes involved in the film's attempts at universality. Because of its extremity, local colour, in this case Northern Ireland, impinges heavily on the desire for universality. Film critics also have to work hard to establish the universal. Raymond Durgnat chose to contextualize the film within a British tradition of film narratives rather than site it in its historical and political context of Northern Ireland. He named a number of films where "A sensitive man commits a crime of violence, and is hunted down for it" and suggested that this is a quite common pattern in British films,[38] while Robert Moss linked the film to the "moods" of French cinema.[39] Ernest Lindgren even stated that *Odd Man Out* "...is concerned with something deeper and more fundamental in human experience than anything which happened in Ireland at a particular moment in history."[40]

Related to the ultimate in universal narratives, *Odd Man Out* exhibits a self-consciously Christ-like, mystical portrayal of a dying man. From the absolute inauguration of the film the music proclaims death, cueing the British cinema's projection of a violent and mystical fantasy onto an ethnic other. The use of Christian imagery, set in land riven by sectarian divisions, is ironic in that the film has been at pains not to show those divisions. But its pretensions to universality are never fully successful. The last word should remain with the English trade press at the time of the film's release. *Kinematograph Weekly*'s considered opinion on *Odd Man Out* was "...not only the last word in gangster fare, but an astonishingly accurate study of Irish life and psychology."[41]

5
Experimenting with Film Scores, 1967–1970

In a handful of British films of the late 1960s, pop musicians attempted to forge anew the film's soundtrack. In 1968, the protean energy of pop music and "Swinging London" films came into intimate contact in films that boldly decided that their musical scores should be constructed and performed completely by popular musicians, marking radical experiments within mainstream cinema and following radically different procedures from the dominant film music patterns evident in mainstream Hollywood films. The following were the films in question:

1 *Here We Go Round the Mulberry Bush* (1967), music by Traffic and the Spencer Davis Group
2 *Wonderwall* (1968), music by Beatle George Harrison
3 *Up the Junction* (1968), music by Manfred Mann and Mike Hugg
4 *The Committee* (1968), music by Pink Floyd
5 *Performance* (shot in 1968 but released in 1970), music primarily by Jack Nitzsche.

During the 1960s, there was pressure for "up-to-date" soundtracks. Probably the most famous instance of this was Hitchcock's *Torn Curtain* (1966), where he fell out with his musical collaborator Bernard Herrmann over the desire for an "up-to-date" score for the film. While such pressures may have had a negative effect, they also led to a degree of experimentation. This involved the introduction of some pop musicians to the medium of film. In the case of these five British films, all of them are "scored" by pop musicians in manners that do not follow dominant traditions of musical accompaniment to film. While some of those involved had a small amount of previous involvement with films, in some of these cases such activities were a stepping stone to further involvement with audiovisual culture.

Analysis sometimes divides the "film" from the "soundtrack" in an untenable manner, making each an independent and coherent concern. In the case of this group of films, however, it is unavoidable to address the music as a separate item from the rest of the film in that they were constructed in such an atomized manner and have music that is semi-autonomous, in some cases perhaps even fully autonomous from the film.

Historical moment

The year 1968 was a watershed year for British pop/rock music, including a mad rush of counterculture and psychedelia. It was the middle period (perhaps the high point) of what most commentators characterize as an outstanding period of creativity. The Beatles made their own film, *Magical Mystery Tour*, which depicted the effects of drugs in close-up for a bemused mass audience across Britain when it was broadcast on Boxing Day in 1967.[1] They had already made *Sergeant Pepper's Lonely Hearts Club Band* in 1967 and were on the way to making *The Beatles* (known as "The White Album") which was released later in 1968. Historian Arthur Marwick has developed the notion of "the long sixties" running from 1958 to 1974. He places 1968 at the apex of the sub-period, which he calls "the high sixties", which confirms its importance as a cultural moment in Britain.[2] This was an extraordinary moment for British cinema. The cycle of "Swinging London" films emerged from a short-lived window of time roughly between 1965 and 1970. Although the films themselves are fairly diverse, they are unified by a common temperament and the premise that London was the centre of the world for modernity, fashion, music and the emergent ideas of the burgeoning youth culture, not least open sexuality. In 1966, American *Time* magazine coined the term "Swinging London",[3] and there is an undoubted travelogue dimension to these films, which is little surprise seeing as these films were driven by the influx of Hollywood production interests and investment to British film production at the time.

These films certainly comprise one of the boldest periods in British film production and, although they may appear mannered to more recent tastes, are astounding in their wide range of both visual and musical techniques, amounting to a technical bravura arguably unmatched in British cinema history. They showcase the new industries that were elevating Britain at the time: fashion and pop music. Many of these films show red London buses and at the least allude to Carnaby Street fashion in a travelogue manner for implied overseas audiences. Indeed, according to George Melly in *Revolt into Style*, "Swinging London" had already dissipated before most of these films were in production.[4]

The key to the developments in the British film industry was the copious amount of American money that had entered the country and buoyed production. In 1969, (British) Film Production Association President Clifford Barclay stated that the United States was "...the world's richest film market...[and] the main source of finance for British films...".[5] Not long afterwards, American finance went home, leaving British film production an impoverished ruin. "Swinging London" films still are celebrated, probably the most iconic of them being Richard Lester's *The Knack...and How to Get It* (1965), Michelangelo Antonioni's *Blow Up* (1966), *Alfie* (1966) and *Georgie Girl* (1966). Music was fundamental for these films and an essential part of Britain's exports at this time, as testified to by *The Beatles* being awarded MBEs, medals for service to Britain. *Blow Up* had the Yardbirds perform on stage, *Alfie* had Cher singing a Burt Bacharach song on the titles and *Georgie Girl* had a Seekers title song. However, the former had a score by an American jazz musician (Sonny Rollins), as did *Blow Up* (Herbie Hancock).[6]

It is worth noting that the excitement of the time and place attracted Michelangelo Antonioni and Jean-Luc Godard to London to make films. However, the exuberance of the time allied to the buoyancy of the film industry entailed by US money decamping to the UK led to an excess as well as leading to projects whose failure ended Hollywood investment. Bizarre individual projects, such as Anthony Newley's *Can Hieronymous Forget Mercy Humppe and Find True Happiness* (1969), demonstrated how far almost any project was able to get substantial funding, in that particular case leading to a surreal but virtually unreleaseable project that starred his family and seemed to figure its imminent disintegration. For British cinema, the release of *Performance* (1970) and *Let It Be* (1970) ought to be seen as a symbolic end for the "Swinging Sixties". These films mark a dark end to Sixties optimism as well as the decade's prosperity and large-scale American funding in British cinema.

A moment of experiment

The late 1960s marks a moment of experiment in the use of pop songs in films that were not musicals in the traditional sense of the term but in most cases mainstream narrative films. In the United States, *The Graduate* (1967 US) had songs by Simon and Garfunkel used as non-diegetic music, along with a small amount of score by Dave Grusin, while *Easy Rider*

(1969 US) was fitted up with a succession of rock songs. This is not to say that these were the first to use such techniques, as Kenneth Anger had "fitted" pop songs to film a few years earlier.[7] In Britain, however, films were arguably bolder, leading to some remarkable experiments with pop music in film. This was precipitated by the buoyant film industry and the international success of British pop and rock music. Additionally, it was aided by London's retention of a "village" mentality, where different arts and artists were in close proximity and, crucially, art and the avant-garde were not remote from other culture industries, most notably the film and pop music industries.

British psychedelia was also qualitatively different from its American counterpart. In some ways, it was perhaps less overtly drug-inspired, less "multi-coloured" and more multi-media, more of an arts collaboration. A good example is the emblematic The Beatles's *Sergeant Pepper's Lonely Hearts Club Band* album cover designed by pop artist Peter Blake. Items like this suggest that British psychedelia was more design oriented and interested in stylistic juxtaposition more than its American relation,[8] some poster art notwithstanding. As part of the differences between British and American, it is clear that the American version had a stronger political agenda.[9] It is tempting to suggest that, in significant ways, the American was a *counter*-culture while the British was a counter-*culture*.

Each of the films under scrutiny in this chapter might be seen as having at least some psychedelic aspects. Testaments to the convergence of the popular arts in Britain at this juncture were the artists working on the films I am discussing. Art directors for these films included pop artist Richard Williams (*Here We Go Round the Mulberry Bush*), The Fool (*Wonderwall*) and Christopher Gibbs (who was "consultant" on *Performance*). In 1966, Paul McCartney had written music for *The Family Way* (1966), orchestrated by Beatles producer George Martin. It sounds like traditional, conventional film music. A year later, his colleague in The Beatles George Harrison was told when he sent to score *Wonderwall* (1967) that whatever he recorded would be used in the film. This amounts to a profoundly different conception of incidental music in film and an unparalleled scope for a popular musician not simply at the time, but at any time before or since.

Aesthetics

The conventions of incidental music for mainstream films were originated in the production line of Classical Hollywood's studio system. This created what Kathryn Kalinak has called the "Classical film score".[10]

This denotes a particular craft that followed a number of fairly strict conventions, and ending with a final product that deviated little from a standard industry blueprint. Over the years, there were a number of innovations and amendments, where new techniques were assimilated into the dominant practice.[11] The common procedure for constructing a musical score still follows the same pattern: from a near final cut of film, a "cue sheet" of precise timings and detailed notes about screen activity is made and composed by skilled film composer, who is very much a "professional" craftsperson. As something of a caveat, it is worth noting that incidental music in British films often involved less precise action matching, and thus more in the way of autonomous pieces. Such music therefore was more amenable to being reused elsewhere as concert hall suites. This was at least partially due to the historical existence of less technical ability to match action, emanating from the lack of large-scale music department like in Hollywood, which led to the use of smaller ensembles, more individual and less standardized music. As I have discussed in earlier chapters, it would not be unfair to say that British films had a cheaper mode of production than Hollywood, as evinced most clearly perhaps by the regular use of less music in films than their American counterparts.

The films under discussion here in each case contravene the dominant conventions for incidental music in film. Generally speaking, the music in these films only rarely matches action closely and often totally ignores screen dynamics. Songs are used regularly as underscore, along with pre-written mood pieces, in both cases mostly not conceived as "accompaniment" in the traditional sense. Additionally, these pop musicians brought new timbres with them to films instead of writing music for the traditional orchestral ensemble, introducing the sounds of 1960s rock and pop music into the underscore as well as in the form of songs. The music for this series of films was trusted to musicians with no experience of creating film music in the traditional sense, and thus they produced music that bore more resemblance to the sort of music they had been producing already than it did to traditional film scores. They did not simply produce song compilations but wrote scores for these films, even if they were a succession of songs. This manifested a new conception of the musical score – as a decidedly "modern" part of film (self-consciously so), less as simple support to action and more as a featured aspect. This entails the conception of music and film as the partnership of two arts rather than one yoked in support of the other. This also, of course, illustrates a further development in the financial relationship of film and music as industries, despite their close relations since the coming of sound.

Musical logic has to be taken into account when discussing the use of music in films. The easiest way to integrate music with film is to follow, one way or another, the existing conventions for importing music to film, the traditions of the film musical. These strategies include the use of song sequences, on-stage performances and audio dissolves that allow the movement of music into the sonic foreground. To a lesser degree, there was also an embryonic tradition of the pop promo, which arguably had been derived primarily from film anyway. In 1965, The Beatles made 10 song promos with Joe McGrath and in 1967 made some with Peter Goldmann.[12] Here, music was prime and the images were conceived as accompaniment, a logic that is evident in certain sequences in films in the late 1960s. Pop groups were accustomed to making pop records, which usually were written and recorded as three-minute songs for release as singles. When they were faced with scoring films, unsurprisingly, they tended to produce music that still followed the patterns they knew rather than producing conventional "film music". Indeed, "classically trained" musicians were more used to writing with precision and dealing with formal and temporal variation, whereas pop musicians tended to use the standard format of verse–chorus structures in the 32-bar song.

The films in question

Here We Go Round the Mulberry Bush (1967) concerns a teenager's frantic quest for sex and love. Directed by Clive Donner, it is set in the new town of Stevenage rather than London, which not only foregrounds the location's modernity but also suggests a reaction against London as the sole locus of the "Swinging Sixties". The film's music is by the Spencer Davis Group, who had fragmented into two parts at the time; the other was Traffic, a vehicle for the 19-year old prodigy Steve Winwood. Traffic was formed in April 1967 and already had hits with *Hole in My Shoe* and *Paper Sun* before the release of the film's title track in December. The Spencer Davis Group has formed as an r'n'b group in 1963, but had successfully developed into a pop group with massive hit records, including back to back number ones with *Keep on Running* and *Somebody Help Me* in 1965, *Gimme Some Lovin'* in 1966 and *I'm a Man* in 1967. They had already appeared in their own film vehicle *The Ghost Goes Gear* (1966), a cheap and unsophisticated comedy following in the wake of The Beatles's *A Hard Day's Night* (1964) and *Help!* (1965). The Spencer

Davis Group provided the lion's share of the music for *Here We Go Round the Mulberry Bush*, with eight songs, although one (*Waltz for Caroline*) had been recorded some time beforehand (before the group's halving), while Traffic contributed three songs. A crucial role was the film's music editor and arranger Simon Napier-Bell, a pop impresario and manager, whose responsibility was to edit, place and remix the songs to fit the film's requirements.[13]

Director Clive Donner has stated that the process of getting a pop group to supply the music for the film was "brand new", furnishing the "first score of pop songs" for a film. Crucially, he also states that music clinched the film deal, after he suggested to United Artists that the film could have a soundtrack by a group from their roster of artists.[14] Film and music are not fully integrated in the traditional sense. Music is cut to fit the film, making it fragmented, while on occasions it looks likely that the film was cut to fit the temporal requirements of the music. A principal musical strategy in the film includes songs regularly appearing diegetically on a radio, in the family kitchen or in the amusement arcade. Basic descriptions of the film's requirements were shown to the groups and then they wrote music that they thought "fitted" the situations. The repetition of some song material provides certain cohesion for the film in musical terms. The film's title song, which has accompanied the opening sequence shot in Stevenage town centre with Jamie cycling reappears later as Jamie runs around the town centre, while it also appears in an instrumental version (without vocals) as Jamie walks to his house shortly afterwards. A few songs repeat in fragmented form. One, the song *Long Time*, is crudely cut in as excerpts that function like a traditional film score's repeated main theme. It appears five times, and although different sections of the song appear, these retain a coherence that provides something of a unity to this "thematic" usage.

The Spencer Davis Group appear on screen at a fete/dance. They perform two songs but are relegated to the background by the activities and dialogue of the diegetic characters. Unconventionally, they are never shown in tableau shot (the conventional establishing shot that establishes the whole group). Instead, they remain in a handful of close-ups, some of which merely show the disembodied heads of the musicians. This is another unconventional aspect, in that visually the film failed to establish their musical activity through a long shot followed by close-ups of the individual musicians, and betrays a lack of interest in their on-screen appearance.

Overall, the way that *Here We Go Round the Mulberry Bush* cuts songs up leads to a sense of musical fragmentation but critically this removed any pressure from the film makers to include sustained song sequences. In addition, the songs as fragments provide bursts of the energy of contemporary youth culture, but without overwhelming the on-screen activity.[15] The music by the Spencer Davis Group and Traffic is in many ways a "parallel product", which does not impinge on the film, and has something of a semi-detached character. Songs appearing on the radio in the film highlight their status as independent pop songs rather than as music made to fit the requirements of the film's action. Furthermore, the music as tied-in product included an LP and two singles (*Here We Go Round the Mulberry Bush*, *It's Been a Long Time* [sung by Andy Ellison, once of John's Children]). The singles were released before the film, the latter in August of 1967 to the film (and LPs) release in February of 1968. This suggests that the music was not conceived as a mere appendage to the film, but the products were seen as intersections that would not be compromised from their regular modes by their interaction. The sense of parallel commodities developed to this degree was a new development, prefiguring the saturation tie-ins a decade later.[16]

Up the Junction (1968), directed by Peter Collinson, should not be confused with the earlier television version directed by Ken Loach and produced by Tony Garnett as *The Wednesday Play* in 1965. Both adapted Nell Dunn's 1963 novel about a young woman from rich Chelsea who goes looking for love and adventure in working-class Clapham. The film version ameliorated the insalubrious elements of the earlier versions in favour of glamour and youthful vigour, and a notable part of this process was the commissioning of a score from the Manfred Mann group. Manfred Mann had achieved massive hits with *5-4-3-2-1* (1964), which was then used as the theme tune for pop television programme *Ready Steady Go!* (1963–1966), *Do Wah Diddy Diddy* (1964, number one) and *Pretty Flamingo* (1966, number one) amongst others. However, not only were they a group that mixed rhythm'n'blues with pop but they also played jazz, as can be ascertained from their LPs. This flexibility was absolutely crucial in allowing them the scope to produce underscore as well as songs for *Up the Junction*.[17]

The group was in a state of flux at this time, with the departure of singer Paul Jones. *Up the Junction*'s music was recorded primarily by organist Manfred Mann and drummer Mike Hugg, and only the title song involved the group's full new line up, with singer Mike D'Abo and bass guitarist Klaus Voorman joining Mann, Hugg and Tom McGuinness. *Sing Songs of Love* was performed by Hugg's brother's band Cherry Smash. The Manfred Mann group had previous film involvement, including recording a song, *My Little Red Book* (written by famous American song-writing team Burt Bacharach and Hal David), for the film *What's New Pussycat* (1965). In the wake of *Up the Junction*, Mann and Hugg recorded some music tied to *The Charge of The Light Brigade* (1968) and the song *My Name is Jack* for *You Are What You Eat* (1968 US), which was a large hit for them in 1968. (This was a light-hearted song about someone who lived in "The Greta Garbo Home for Wayward Boys and Girls".) Hugg and Mann went on to write the music for a BBC *Wednesday Play* (*The Gorge* [1968], about a day trip to Cheddar) and the Jess Franco film *Venus in Furs* (1969), where Mann also appears on screen as a jazz musician.[18] They both went on to produce music for television adverts,[19] while Hugg did music for television comedy *Whatever Happened to the Likely Lads?* (1973 and a film spin-off in 1976).[20]

The group saw rushes and rough cuts of the film, and then composed and recorded blind, to their impressions.[21] The music mixes jazz tracks and pop songs that are vaguely reminiscent of the Beach Boys's *Pet Sounds* era, along with more "contemporary" sounds like electric guitar with "wah wah" effects pedal. The songs are used predominantly non-diegetically and tend to work for the film as a Greek chorus, providing a commentary on the action in terms of their song lyrics, which thus become similar to a voice-over. This was hardly a novel process, a clear earlier example would be Fritz Lang's *Rancho Notorious* (1952 US), although as this example suggests, such a procedure was a marginal tradition in mainstream film. Songs appear in *Up the Junction* as kernels of narrative and/or emotion, which has the effect of almost rendering the rest of the film an accompaniment to them.

Songs are used both as diegetic ambient music, played on juke boxes (*Sing Songs of Love*), and as non-diegetic music (*Walking Around*). In the latter case, diegetic sound recedes in an audio dissolve that foregrounds the song with visual accompaniment and, which, despite no synchronized connection between sound and image, is reminiscent of situations in the classical musical film. This is a substantial sequence, of over two minutes with no diegetic sound. The visuals are divided between shots of Polly (Suzy Kendall) looking and reverse shots of the people she sees in the street. The song has a strong demarcation between verse and chorus, yet these two structures are in no way homologized in a clear fashion. This sequence adds little to the film's narrative but is of high symbolic significance in that it spatializes the film's premise: of the middle classes "cruising" the working classes. The use of music at this juncture monumentalizes this moment and offers repose from narrative development for two minutes of reflection.

Manfred Mann's jazz background was useful for the rendering of the film's title song as temporally more flexible underscore, first appearing in the sequence that establishes Clapham Junction railway station. In this sequence, initially there is no diegetic sound, like the *Walking Around* sequence earlier. Jazz is used more easily under dialogue when it merely supplies a sheen, a musical "groove" of similar and unchanging dynamics. In these cases, there is less of a requirement for the crass use of the volume control as is evident at other moments in the film. Indeed, this is most notable at *Up the Junction*'s inauguration, where the music is "sneaked" with a volume control, but kept at low volume for portions of the opening and closing of the song. This simply underlines how the music was not written to fit the film and, indeed, follows the fairly standardized requirements of song form rather than anything else. This is borne out by the way that the group's songs tend to dominate sequences in which they appear, while their more jazzy instrumental music appears to adopt the foreground less.

The film is fairly fragmented rather than making a coherent unity, with music as one side of a multi-faceted object. Thus, *Up the Junction* resembles more recent multi-attraction films, which hedge their bets through the inclusion of something for everyone. Music has a crucially important role in the film, providing a "positive" and happy character that helps convert the potentially downbeat story to a happy "Swinging London" film.[22] Like *Here We Go Round the Mulberry Bush*, there were tied-in discs. The film's title single was released in February 1968, like what became known as a "scout single", before the release of the film and LP in March.[23]

Wonderwall (1968), directed by Joe Massot, is without doubt Ur-text psychedelia, which at the start ostentatiously announces its musical score is by "George Harrison MBE". It got a patchy release and was not picked up by a major distributor. The film's story concerns a scientist who spies voyeuristically through a hole in his apartment wall at the events in a young woman's life. Despite the problematic focus of the film, it is a comedy of sorts, from a story by Gérard Brach. The film's startling art direction was by Dutch art collective "The Fool", who had also painted the mural on the Apple building. It furnishes striking psychedelic design for the neighbouring flat. On the scientist's side, the wall has two quotations on it: from Alfred Tennyson's *The Daydream* (about sleeping beauty) and from Christina Rosetti's *An End*. There is also a picture on his side of the wall that was an illustration for Tennyson's "Guinevere and Other Poems" (by Florence Harrison), an accompaniment to the death of King Arthur.

George Harrison's songs often were marginalized in The Beatles's output by Lennon and McCartney. This music was the first Beatles solo recording, as well as being the first album on their Apple record label, The Beatles's own record label. It was being recorded at the same time as *Magical Mystery Tour* was on release.[24] Harrison's music includes some wild stereo movement and some electronics. His second solo album was *Electronic Sounds* (1969), which was an experiment using Moog synthesizers with the help of Bernie Krause. Interestingly, Harrison's experimental work has been shunted aside by concerns with the experimental and avant-garde status of work by Lennon and McCartney – to the point where there is a whole book about McCartney's dealings with the avant-garde.[25]

George Harrison remembered Massot saying "Anything you do, I will have in the film". Harrison agreed, despite worry about not knowing "how to do music for films".[26] He saw a rough cut and then composed music – clearly not to precise timings as it was "uncut" – yet George Harrison claimed that he used a stopwatch to spot-in music, then composed and recorded it. Some of the music was recorded in London, some in Bombay. In London, Harrison used musicians including the Remo Four (including pianist Tony Ashton), Tommy Reilly on harmonica, Eric Clapton and Ringo Starr. So this marks a project where Harrison oversaw a number of musicians and produced the recordings on both continents.[27]

Wonderwall contains little dialogue and includes a few sequences of speeded-up action, both aspects of which suggest a notable similarity to silent cinema. Consequently, most of the film's music is unsynched. This uncoupling of sound and image track leads to an experience of aesthetic and sensory counterpoint. Thus, the music becomes a notably powerful element in the film, empowered well beyond its traditionally assigned role as a support to the image in the cinema. The assumption in mainstream films is that sound and music are synched. Eisenstein discussed parallel and counterpoint in film and music.[28] The latter is where music can work irrespective of on-screen dynamics and action, thus creating something of a dialectical relationship – a counterpoint – between image and music. In *Wonderwall*, the degree of separation between image and music is at times large and dramatic. This suggests how far music is important to the film. It contains a large amount, far more than was released on the soundtrack LP. The importance of the music as accompaniment downgrades the traditional significance of the divide between diegetic and non-diegetic sound. Furthermore, *Wonderwall*'s paucity of dialogue and diegeses of ambiguous status have the effect of making the music track all the more important, more prominent, in what constitutes an uncoupling of image and sound tracks. It would not be hard to argue that Harrison's status sells the film itself, the music being the primary object. Of course, one does not need to know that Harrison provided the music for the film to "work" as an experience, but his cultural prominence at the time (and after) suggests that the music should be seen as the primary object and the film only secondary. During the 1990s, it was certainly easier to access Harrison's music as a recording than it was the film as video or DVD.[29] The fact that Harrison's album contains a number of stereo experiments which would not have been apparent for almost all British cinemas, where monophonic sound overwhelmingly dominated, merely underlines that this was not simply "accompanying" music, and that the experience of it in tandem with the film was perhaps only a secondary experience.

The Committee (1968) was a bizarre, highly stylized film.[30] It was an hour long and based on illustrating abstract and philosophical ideas. It starred Paul Jones, who once had been singer for Manfred Mann, and had starred in Peter Watkins's *Privilege* (1967). It was directed by the young Australian Peter Sykes, who went on later to direct the Hammer horror film *To the Devil...a Daughter* (1976). It also included a startling cameo by The Crazy World of Arthur Brown, who appears without warning to perform *Nightmare*, which includes Brown wearing his renowned hat of flames. It was a small-scale and low-budget production, which engendered Pink Floyd writing and recording the incidental music very quickly. They approached the film's music with a "make do" attitude, retaining an improvisational quality across all the music, which clearly was recorded very rapidly by the group's standards. It evinces a concern with textures, timbres and sonority, and is most unlike their other scores – *More* (1969) or *Zabriskie Point* (1970). These tended to consist of songs and mood pieces. The music for *The Committee* was mostly either variations on their song *Careful with that Axe, Eugene*, or sparse instrumental textures for momentary atmosphere. It was recorded during May of 1968 and they supplied just over 17 minutes for the film.[31] Due to the brevity of material and its uncommercial character, the group elected not to release on disc the music they had provided for the film.[32] For *The Committee*, Pink Floyd looked towards spare textures and sustained atmospheres that bore more resemblance to their earlier improvised stage pieces such as *Interstellar Overdrive* rather than their more conventional songs. Their score, for this highly singular film, marks an isolated experiment, by a group who wanted increasingly to foster an image of being experimentalists. The film, along with their other film work, doubtless expanded their boundaries as an aesthetic unit.

Co-directed by Donald Cammell and Nic Roeg, *Performance* was shot in 1968 but released in 1970. Production was troubled, with Warner Brothers holding up the film's release for two years and forcing re-edits on the film's co-directors.[33] Rarely is music as central to a dramatic film as it is to *Performance*. It is the key film concerned with late 1960s British pop music culture and its embracing of counterculture and the "underground" (as well as the gangster "underworld"). *Performance* is aptly named because its narrative foregrounds "performances", first to those of gangster Chas (James Fox) and later to those of reclusive rock star Turner (Mick Jagger). On the run, Chas hides out in the house of Turner, a rock musician who has lost his demon, where the two of them investigate and seemingly converge identities.

In the run up to the shooting of the film, there were reports that the film's star Mick Jagger was writing the score for the film.[34] Ultimately, this was not to be the case; instead, the Rolling Stones studio arranger Jack Nitzsche provided the music and was on the project fairly early. However, it clearly was not totally unbelievable to suggest that a pop singer was going to provide a musical score. Indeed, Jagger went on to provide the music for Kenneth Anger's *Invocation of My Demon Brother* (1969), producing some very austere and repetitive synthesizer music. Jagger ended up only contributing a single pre-recorded song for the film, which he performed in a set-piece song sequence (*Memo from Turner*).[35] Jack Nitzsche assembled an impressive cast of rock and other musicians for the production of the film's highly adventurous music, most of them Los Angeles-based session musicians and friends. Prominent among them was slide-guitarist Ry Cooder who, during the sequence of Chas going to Turner's house at Powis Square, plays a piece of music that was later to reappear intact in Cooder's acclaimed score for the film *Paris, Texas* (1984). Cooder later claimed that Nitzsche did not write a score for much of the film, but asked musicians to improvise and develop their own material.[36] This underlines that Nitzsche's music for *Performance* is a diverse "composite score" or assemblage,[37] not constructed in any way that resembles the through-composed especially written scores traditional to dramatic films.[38]

While British pop music culture was showcased, much of the music was not British at all. It starts with American singer and composer Randy Newman singing a blues rock song *Gone Dead Train*. This is quickly superceded by dissonant and futuristic electronic music, still within the title sequence. The body of the film includes more blues and rock,

Indian sitar music, middle-eastern santur music, echoed piano non-diegetic "score", what seems to be commercial "muzak" or easy-listening music, and "improvised" music (consisting of guitar, jew's harp and wailing). Eschewing an especially written orchestral underscore, the film pulls together a wealth of heterogeneous musical genres. *Performance's* composite score comprises an aggregate of disparate musics, culled from the library of world culture. There is less focus on melody and harmony, and more on timbre and rhythm. Allied to this is a tendency to articulate music as large pre-existing blocks rather than weave a coherent unity across the film. If it is easy to see the film's music in the light of the 1960s' tendency to "plundering" other cultures, also evident in the film's design and Asian/middle-eastern references.[39] The range of musical genres within *Performance* is a palpable symptom of the film's emanation from late 1960s pop music culture, underlining it as a site where these disparate musics converged. Perhaps the best example is the popularity of Indian music for Western audiences in the late 1960s, personified by sitar player Ravi Shankar who appeared at the Woodstock festival. While the film's foregrounding of pop music culture motivates the variety of musics in circulation within the film, pop music culture conceives of other musics as a zone for "miscegenation", where pop music plunders ethnic and other musics to create hybrids and pastiches, or simply relocates them within the pop music context of usage. Music is a major material element in the film, however, with action often cut to music and diegetic sound being marginalized for it on many occasions. This extraordinary strategy of eclectically bringing together bits and pieces of music into a composite score for the film, rather than merely functioning as support to the action, allows music opens up massive possibilities of texture, reference and invocation. The fact that *Performance* was shelved for two years suggested that its degree of experimentation was too much for the film industry.

Conclusion

The division of "film" and "music" can be a problematic conceit of some analysis, yet in the case of this group of films the two were most decidedly separated in terms of conception and production. Michel Chion may suggest that there is in fact no soundtrack as a coherent unity in itself,[40] yet in the case of these films the music must be seen as an organic unity – indeed, it might be argued that it works better on disc than in tandem with the films. Furthermore, in some cases the soundtrack recording has sustained better than the film, having remained available for periods when the "accompanying" film was only a distant memory.

In the 1960s, there certainly was a trajectory towards modernizing the music on the film soundtrack. In *The Sounds of Commerce*, Jeff Smith discusses the "pop score" in relation to American mainstream film, where he identifies a number of pop techniques brought to the traditions of film scoring by composers such as Henry Mancini and John Barry.[41] In Britain, later in the 1960s, rather than simply introduce a selection of pop techniques to the arsenal of film music techniques, pop musicians were given free rein to produce film soundtracks as they saw fit. The films under discussion display musical characteristics derived from pop/rock music rather than the tradition of film scoring. These include the retention of continuous beats and the alternating verse/chorus-type structures evident in song form, at the expense of flexible film time and the music precisely following the dynamics of action or mood. When songs are used, they are usually non-diegetic and obtrusive, often appearing for montage sequences that lack or marginalize diegetic sound, which allows the song to occupy the foreground. In many cases, music is faded in and out, or cut (sometimes quite crudely), which clearly demonstrates that music was not written to the precise requirements of film development; indeed, in the majority of cases one can easily see that images are more or less obviously cut to the requirements of the music. These aspects of musical relationship with image not only add up to a less clear "innovation" than the "pop score" as discussed by Jeff Smith, but also mark a fundamental rethink of the relationship between music and film, a situation that has come back at various times rather than simply becoming assimilated into the mainstream modes.[42]

George Harrison's score for *Wonderwall* ("do anything you want") was clearly a unique situation for a feature film. There were almost no films that followed suit. The aftermath of this short but creative period saw pop musicians occasionally score films, although more often they would simply provide songs for a film (like Traffic and Spencer Davis had for *Here We Go Round the Mulberry Bush*).[43] The pop musicians involved in the films under scrutiny were not film scorers: they had no experience of the craft of writing music to accompany film. Consequently, they used different techniques, and the music in these films is not really conceived and constructed as an accompaniment to the image, but is conceived as having a more loose relationship than most film scores. The groups and musicians in question did not simply produce song compilations but wrote scores for these films, even if they resembled a succession of songs. If these were not "ruptures" in the dominant traditions of film music, they certainly were utilizing marginal practices in film scoring. This manifested a new conception of the musical score, or at least an alternative dominant conception of "incidental music". Music in these films was conceived less as a simple support to action and more as a featured aspect, resembling to some degree the way that songs worked in film musicals. Like musicals, these films aimed at some degree of egalitarian partnership of music and film world, two arts rather than one simply yoked in support of the other. Indeed, to varying degrees, these films were reconceived as a *whole process*, where image, sound and music are a productive unity, rather than being conceived as one where the visual and dialogue is finished and then the music is added as a dressing.[44] This short period and the films under discussion should be seen as a historical staging post on the way to more recent "synergy", where the music and film industries have collaborated in order to sell each other's products. It should also be noted for the utilization of a number of techniques that later reductively were seen "MTV aesthetics" when they began to creep back into the arsenal of film techniques in the 1980s and 1990s.

6
Pop Music Culture, Synergy and Songs in Films: *Hardware* (1990) and *Trainspotting* (1996)

The low-budget science fiction film *Hardware* (1990) is seen by some as one of the British film successes of the last 20 years. Reputedly, it was made for less money than a Michael Jackson video, and was well aware of musical pedigree and how much a judicious choice of existing songs on the soundtrack could add to a low-budget production. Similarly, *Trainspotting* (1996) was in some ways premised upon the logic of licensed pop songs and pop music culture. It arguably was one of the most successful examples of pop songs being used in films in recent years. This chapter will investigate the two influential films and their use of pop songs. Both *Hardware* (1990) and *Trainspotting* (1996) demonstrate a form of cinema where music functions as a central aspect, in a similar manner to film musicals.[1] In films that are not musicals, music usually is conceived and theorized as an afterthought to what are usually seen as the "primary" aspects (the film's images, dialogue and narrative development or the diegetic world on screen). Yet plenty of films seem to contradict this notion to a greater or lesser extent. These two films, released six years apart, are good illustrations of developments in British films, if not elsewhere. One has a musical score allied with a few significant songs, while the other uses a selection of songs as a replacement for the unity of a film score. It is not difficult to see the musical logic of these films as having been inherited from the film musical, and it is notable that the songs tend to appear for set-piece spectacles where dialogue is forced into the background to allow music to take at least something of the foreground. Furthermore, the songs are embedded and sold, much as they were in the Classical Hollywood film musical and its British counterpart. Indeed, at times, these films seem less interested in devising a scenario than they are in other things, such as articulating pop music as an internal momentary logic of the film.

The development of MTV and the frantic exploitation of record label–back catalogues in the late 1980s and 1990s are both vividly inscribed across *Hardware* and *Trainspotting*. MTV started broadcasting in the United States in August 1981, Euro-MTV started 6 years later, although European terrestrial television shows were already showing pop videos and exhibiting the "MTV style". What was identified as style, derived from MTV, loud pop songs, glossy images and rapid editing, was decried by film critics as an embodiment of style over substance. Pop promo videos became increasingly important throughout the 1980s, both as marketing tools and as cultural objects in their own right. Many commentators have proclaimed their influence on film negative, yet they have been part of the influence of the film musical format in mainstream dramatic films, where the urge to music can erupt in films without their being musicals in the traditional sense.[2] If dramatic film structures traditionally are built around a strong narrative drive, then films that have a weakened narrative allow other elements of the film to adopt the foreground, as was the case in the classical film musical. In *Hardware* and *Trainspotting*, aspects such as spectacle and music as semi-independent attractions have partially replaced the idea of developmental narrative.[3] Kathryn Kalinak notes the way that the enduring principle of the film score has been in some films thrust aside by the use of songs:

> the pop score represents the most serious challenge to the classical score among the various attempts to update it in the fifties and sixties. Specifically, the pop score's insistence on the integrity and marketability of the nondiegetic song frequently brought it into conflict with some of the basic principles of the classical model. Unlike earlier innovations which added new idiomatic possibilities, like jazz, or demonstrated the adaptability of the leitmotif, like the theme score, the pop score often ignored structural principles at the center of the classical score: musical illustration of narrative content, especially the direct synchronization between music and narrative action; music as a form of structural unity; and music as an inaudible component of the drama.[4]

These two films demonstrate the ways that pop songs not only can replace a coherent, purpose-built score but also how a "song score" can be used as a featured element that has a notable importance for the film in aesthetic terms. Arguably, certain films have retained the impulse of the film musical although they refuse to follow its traditional generic format. Instead, they retain its concern to publicize and sell songs as well as having music as an elevated, even crucial, component in the film's mixture of elements.

Hardware

Hardware was a British-made science fiction film set in a post-catastrophic future, where there is a desert "zone", a continuous war and constant radio broadcasts about dangerous radiation levels. It was an international success that was made cheaply, costing only $1 million to produce.[5] The film is set in the future and is about a prototype military robot that rebuilds itself and goes on a killing rampage among civilians. The music in the film consists primarily of songs from the 1980s, some of which are then articulated as if they were songs from the film's diegetic world's past. *Hardware* figures the present (including the recent past) in "the future" of the film's diegesis through its articulation of music.[6] Not only through the songs themselves and references in the background score, but also through the figuration of an MTV-like channel on the television as well as the film's structuring of two sequences using a pop video aesthetic, all of which firmly places a contemporary understanding of pop music within the futuristic world portrayed in the film.

Pop/rock music has an evident and important position in *Hardware*. Its position may to only a small degree be accounted for by commerce, as more significantly it provides cultural co-ordinate points for the film. While *Hardware* embodies the increased integration between the music and film industries, it is also a product of the interaction in aesthetic terms, between the cinematic medium and the pop music discourse. It features, or rather showcases, two pop songs, *The Order of Death* by Public Image Limited and *Stigmata* by Ministry, both of which appear for significant durations. In addition to this, the songs are foregrounded in the film in a manner directly reminiscent of pop videos. *Hardware* also features a largely electronic musical underscore (incidental music) composed and performed by Simon Boswell, who was associated with the independent fringes of pop music as well as film scoring. Boswell described his score for *Hardware* being "...as if a Celtic Ry Cooder on acid had discovered God and decided to write an opera...[climaxing in] a scene in heaven – with Jimi Hendrix, Stravinsky and the Moscow State Choir all jamming in a very small room."[7] As in the case of many musical scores in recent years, *Hardware*'s incidental music as distinct from the pop music may be characterized as eclectic, an amalgam of technological innovations, pop music techniques and the historically accrued musical style and functions of film music.[8] The film contains cameo appearances by three pop performers and *Hardware* articulates a discourse concerning pop music that, while not being of any real importance for the film's narrative development, seems to have a high degree of prominence. *Monthly Film Bulletin's* review of *Hardware* noted the characteristics associated with music and music video:

> ...Richard Stanley's feature debut is an impressively glossy high-tech thriller which eschews narrative intricacy in favour of pop-promo production values....contributing greatly to the movie's impact is the droning, mechanical soundtrack which underscores much of the action...*Hardware* is a palatable exercise in trash aesthetics whose flashy visuals and seamless soundtrack belie the relatively low budget.[9]

The film clearly exhibits the pace of action that had become commonplace for pop music and its associated images since the proliferation of pop promos on music television. However, the film is certainly not simply an excuse to sell songs. Instead of symbiotically marketing a number of licensed songs through (alongside) the film, *Hardware's* sound-track album is very much conceived as an experience that is very directly an adjunct of the film. One review of the soundtrack album noted, "You can almost smell the burning shrapnel as you load the tape..."[10] The music certainly is distinctive, and the pop songs match the overall mood of the rest of the underscore.

The film moves between musical spectacles to narrative development in a manner reminiscent of traditional film musicals. *Hardware* contains two pop video-like sequences, for *The Order of Death* by Public Image Limited (PiL) and for *Stigmata* by Ministry. The former is a voyeuristic display of sex, with the PiL song cueing the limits of the sequence and the act of sex itself, while the latter is a distinct montage sequence of a sculpture being made. In their integrity, these sequences both bear striking resemblance to pop videos.[11] PiL singer John Lydon was originally to provide the voice of the disc jockey "Angry Bob" in *Hardware* but withdrew to be replaced by Iggy Pop.[12] It is possible that PiL produced the song as a part of the soundtrack for the film *Order of Death* (1983) (alternatively called *Cop Killer*) in which Lydon starred but the song failed to be included, although the piece's availability under another name suggests otherwise. Indeed, the song in *Hardware, The Order of Death*, not only lends itself to use within a film but also in many ways resembles film music more than it does the traditional pop song.

The discretion of the *Order of Death* sequence is principally achieved by the music that destroys almost all diegetic sound to become the foregrounded motor of the action. The edits take place around important moments in the music's development (the entry and exit of the guitar tune, for example), giving the firm impression that the images were cut to fit the music. Upon the first guitar entry, the prototype robot Mark 13's eye lights up and upon the inauguration of its second block of four bars the film cuts to a *Psycho*-referencing shower shot (from underneath the shower head). The cut to images of sex on the bed arrives at the point of a dramatic chord change (from I minor to IV major). It is not common in film and pop videos to cut the action on the first beat of a bar, but this takes place on one occasion during the sequence. The effect is to dramatize the action at that point, where the sequence replaces the micronarrative of Mark 13's vision with the spectacle of sex. The cut coincides with the main variation in the music, where the guitar tune enters, so achieving maximum effect for the conduit into the spectacle. The piece is based on the alternation of four bar blocks. The regularity and easily recognizable (even subconsciously) format sets up certain expectations in the audience. The principal effect of utilizing the music to drive the action of the sequence is that film time (editing rhythm, narrative time) is replaced by musical time (metronomic rhythm, musical beat).[13] The temporal organization of the sequence is thus built around a repetitive beat, a forward movement that is perceived as inevitable, and the image track is subordinated to musical organization as the central carrier of filmic development.

The second pop video-like sequence in *Hardware* (using Ministry's *Stigmata*) involves another discrete action set-piece in the image track, that of creating a sculpture with the head of Mark 13 as the crown of the finished item. In this sequence the music is diegetically motivated, by Jill turning the television to an MTV-like channel that is broadcasting what appears to be a pop video. Jill leaves the music channel on as a soundtrack to her sculpting and while the earlier parts of the sequence intercut TV images (of the group and other things), as the sequence progresses there are increasingly only shots of the act of sculpting. The foregrounded song, *Stigmata*, has a duration of 1 minute and 56 seconds on the soundtrack and fades to the sound of Jill's drill as she finishes the assemblage. The sequence is certainly kinetic; the act of sculpting involves welding, drilling and spraying and is intercut with dramatic TV images that appear to be part of the pop video. On the TV is the group who appear to be the source (the diegetic motivation) of the song that encapsulates the sequence, and yet it is not the images of

Ministry that are shown but of Gwar, a notoriously theatrical heavy metal band sporting outrageous costumes. This sleight of hand certainly adds to the esoteric level of the film and the observation of this would have given pleasure to members of the audience. This in-joke is a clear example of how the film made an effort to establish "cult" appeal, as well as illustrating the film's intermittent music discourse that is almost totally uncoupled from the film's story. The television appears to show a montage of images as effects, with the flow of footage including the group Psychic TV's video that was banned, as well as images from Psychic TV collaborator Monte Cazzaza and experimentalists Survival Research. Some of the images look like a snuff torture movie, although it also includes what appears to be some footage from a slaughterhouse.[14] The TV pop video includes images that then appear intermittently with the sculpting activity, these are images of torture, war, explosions and violence. They are implicit and explicit, doubling the words of the song and creating an overall effect of kinesis and aggression, the TV images and the song denoting an extremity of word, sound and image.[15] The television's music track ceases to accompany its images and assumes a role as accompaniment to the sculpting. Musical structure, in the case of both songs, has a much higher degree of significance, setting up particular time schemes for the film to access momentarily before its successive movement to another attraction, be it another piece of music, visual spectacle or violent set-piece.[16]

In addition to its songs, *Hardware* includes a number of important cameo appearances, further establishing a significant esoteric level in the film. It showcases a couple of brief song excerpts, and as a counterpart to these contains brief appearances by three musical performers: Carl McCoy, Lemmy and Iggy Pop. McCoy, the singer from The Fields of the Nephilim, is the first person to be seen in the film, a mysterious figure (a "zonetripper").[17] Lemmy, the singer from Motorhead, appears briefly as a taxi driver concurrent with his radiocassette playing the Motorhead song *The Ace of Spades*, a brief and highly self-conscious interlude, where, referring to his group's song, he asks "Do you guys like music? Check out these boys!" The excerpt is largely the song's kinetic introduction, a full four bars, after which dialogue forces the verse into a lower volume. The third cameo is in voice only, where a disc jockey is featured on the soundtrack although no radio source is seen on the image track. The voice belongs to Iggy Pop and the first of his two voice-over appearances concludes with one of his own songs, *Cold Metal*, which he introduces as "…a golden oldie." The film emphasizes music as a discourse in itself, through having both Iggy Pop and Lemmy introduce their own songs.

The effect of this is firstly on an esoteric level, as a kind of "wink" at the audience, while secondly it establishes a familiar type of music (if not the song itself) in a less familiar setting, manifesting a reassurance for the audience. Cameos, like the songs in the film, provide crucial cultural co-ordinate points for the film's consumption. These are not mainstream pop stars, like Cliff Richard or Phil Collins, but artists with more extreme reputations, which lend a strong sense of the esoteric to the film. Indeed, McCoy, Iggy Pop and Lemmy arguably are not full recuperable to (dominant) mainstream pop culture.

Trainspotting

Trainspotting (1996) was made with a £1.5 million budget and within 6 months had a British gross of £12 million.[18] Robert Murphy has noted that the film was perhaps "a harbinger of a real renaissance in British film production".[19] Its success and influence have been considerable, and its use of pop music was one aspects of the film that added considerably to the final product. In a similar manner to *Hardware*, *Trainspotting* used a whole wealth of pop music on its soundtrack, although it also eschewed the common Hollywood strategy of tying-in some new songs as potential hit singles. Instead, it mixed a liberal number of "classic" songs, all of which were less "populist" album tracks rather than singles, with a number of contemporary pieces of music, the vast majority of which were not written or recorded with the film in mind.[20] *Trainspotting* contains many more songs than *Hardware*, obviating the need for a musical score to furnish mood and dramatize events, which in many cases is managed by the pre-existing songs and musical pieces used in the film.

The film is an adaptation of Irvine Welsh's very singular novel, made into a screenplay by John Hodge. The latter has pared the book down into a more straightforward dramatic story, retaining the character of the source novel as a succession of episodes rather than a developing storyline. It was made by the same team that had produced *Shallow Grave* (1994): director Danny Boyle, screenwriter Hodge and producer Andrew MacDonald. It also featured Ewen MacGregor as the leading character, Renton. The energy of *Shallow Grave* is also evident in *Trainspotting*, with the former's opening sequence being a voice-over with sped-up images shot from the lower bumper of a car travelling around Edinburgh. Similarly, *Trainspotting* starts with a kinetic sequence of the main characters running down an Edinburgh street after stealing drugs from a chemist's shop, also accompanied by a voice-over. In both cases, music is prominent and important. In the first, there is some energetic and repetitive dance music by Leftfield, while in the second there is the introductory section from Iggy Pop's *Lust for Life*. Each opening sequence leaves us in little doubt as to the importance music will play in the coming film.

Trainspotting bears a certain comparison with Quentin Tarantino's highly successful films *Reservoir Dogs* (1992 US), *Pulp Fiction* (1995 US) and *Jackie Brown* (1998 US). Each of these films cedes a notable importance to music, which often involves old songs being wielded in a creative manner in the film. One might argue that these films are "music-based" and consequently have a best-selling tied-in album, while using specific music for a "hip" effect (signification) as well as for its kinetic qualities. Indeed, like Tarantino's films, *Trainspotting*'s succession of songs is reminiscent of a selection from someone's record collection, something that Tarantino noted himself as has been discussed by Ken Garner.[21]

It is noteworthy that *Trainspotting* attempted to ride the wave of "Britpop" of the mid-1990s. Director Danny Boyle pointed out that the film connected with the Britpop explosion,[22] featuring Blur (and their singer Damon Albarn alone), Pulp and Sleeper. "Britpop" was a loose grouping of guitar-based bands that made bestselling albums and were to some degree successful in the United States as well as in Britain. The white heat of Britpop was in the early and mid-1990s, and centred upon the successes of Oasis and Blur. Other groups who headed the movement included Pulp, Cast, Ash and Primal Scream. Some of these were evident on the soundtracks of British films of the time.[23]

Trainspotting uses a constant run of pop songs, and its episodic character lends itself to the use of songs. The songs become an essential part of the film's system of narration, along with dialogue and action, as ways to move the film forward. A clear strategy is to match a montage of compressed time and space with the prominent appearance of a song on the soundtrack, allied with a voice-over from the film's protagonist (the element that clearly holds the film's narrative together as a progressive enterprise). In *Trainspotting*, the songs regularly function in material terms to hold together diverse montage sequences, and as cohesion in the face of a simultaneity of fragmented action and voice-over. They also provide punctuation, while emphasizing kinesis. In cultural terms they provide a vague periodization, the film plots a history of sorts, which acknowledges that both music and drugs have changed. The novel appeared to be set during the 1980s, but the film's music seems to be primarily from the mid-1970s and the mid-1990s, with a few 1980s moments in between.

As I have already noted, Iggy Pop's *Lust for Life* (originally released in 1977) appears over the opening sequence of running protagonists, one that echoes the start of The Beatles's *A Hard Days' Night* (1964).[24] The beat provides a spine for the succession of highly kinetic images and the voice-over breathlessly listing the prosaic aspects of stereotypical modern life ("Choose life, choose a job, choose a career, choose a family..."). The dynamic structure of the song largely dictates the layout of the sequence. The song is built around temporal structures of four bars, at the end of the first four bars the bass guitar enters to join the drums and Renton's voice over enters at the same moment. At the 16-bar point, there is a chord change from what we have previously heard and at this significant moment there is a freeze frame of Renton on screen, leaning on the front of a car and with his name emblazoned across the screen. The climactic point of this opening montage sequence has, in quick succession, Renton finish his voice-over monologue, a football being kicked, in reverse shot hitting Renton on the head, which then cuts to him slowly falling down from a standing position as a result of a heroin "hit". This is intercut with him falling from the impact of the ball at the soccer game. The key point, where the football hits, is succeeded immediately by Iggy Pop's singing entering after the extensive introduction to the song. After the lengthy build-up, the singing enters and Renton dramatically falls backwards. The temporal format of the images is dictated by the musical structure, the regulated musical time of the song, which has provided a temporal and dynamic frame to which they have been edited.[25]

The next piece of music to appear in the film is the opening section of the *Habanera* from Bizet's *Carmen*, which accompanies Renton's preparation for coming off heroin. The simultaneous voice-over lists things required. The music fades out when Renton goes for a last hit and shortly afterwards fades back in as he dives into a toilet to retrieve his suppositories. As soon as he is swimming under water, the music changes instantaneously to Brian Eno's *Deep Blue Day*, a piece of music from the *Apollo and Soundtracks* album (released 1983) and inspired by (and suitable for) footage concerning space and human endeavours in that direction. Renton and Sick Boy in the park with an airgun is accompanied by Primal Scream's *Trainspotting*, a piece written especially for the film, which functions as a "groove" behind the dialogue and action. This means it never matches dynamic development in image and dialogue but merely fleshes out sound space and provides a background atmosphere. At the club, Heaven 17's *Temptation* is played diegetically as Renton looks for a willing woman in the club, accompanied by his voice-over. The following song in the club is *Atomic*, a massive hit for Blondie in 1979, but here covered by Sleeper – especially for the film. This begins as we are shown Diane at the bar and carries on outside the club as Renton follows her. In the morning at Diane's house, she sings briefly and then shortly afterwards we hear *Temptation* by New Order (released 1982), appearing diegetically, as Renton talks to Diane's parents at the breakfast table. The montage when they decide to go back onto heroin, including breaking into a car, in the flat, Sick Boy talking about women in Bond films, voice-over about activities on screen is accompanied by Iggy Pop's *Nightclubbing* (released 1977) and Renton's voice-over. The slow electro beat with sparse piano, wah wah guitar and baritone voice fades out to Alison's screams as she discovers her baby dead. Shortly afterwards, Blur's *Sing* (released 1991) provides a very emotional sound as well as functionally holding together a montage along with Renton's voice-over. It fades in as Sick Boy cries at the death of the baby, continues for shots of the group of friends running in the Edinburgh streets from the start of the film and concludes with the sequence in court where Spud is sent to prison and Renton is released. After fading out, the song returns (fades back in) as Renton leaves the pub via the back door and climbs the wall. As Renton jumps from the wall and with a match on action appears to land at Mother Superior's flat for a hit, the music finishes with a final chord upon his landing, another example of musical structure providing punctuation for the film's action.

The sequence that uses Lou Reed's *Perfect Day* (originally released in 1972) is the highly memorable overdose sequence, which is accompanied ironically by a song that has been seen as a love song to heroin. *Perfect Day* runs to its full length, without fades or cuts, meaning that the action is cut to fit its requirements. The sequence proceeds from Renton injecting, through his overdose (which is rendered visually through a "distancing" effect of what appears to be carpet obscuring Renton's point of view shots that are interspersed with his illness), until he is put into bed at home by his parents.[26] Almost immediately, the very repetitive and beat-based Underworld piece *Dark Train* (a remix of *Dark & Long*) begins to accompany Renton's hallucinations in his bedroom during his "cold turkey", including the memorable appearance of the crawling baby on the ceiling.[27] This highly kinetic sequence lasts for nearly seven minutes and includes hallucinated television footage of a game show featuring television personality Dale Wynton and questions about HIV, Renton's HIV test, in a pub and visiting Tommy, at which point the music's relentless beat fades out.[28]

Upon Renton's announcement (in voice-over) that he was moving to London, there is a montage sequence accompanied by Ice MC's *Think About the Way*. This is euphoric dance music that certainly lends much of its character to the seemingly ironic but impressively glossy succession of tourist guide images of London. This is what is known as "uplifting dance music", aimed at a positive reaction from dancers and comes as a massive contrast to the music and images of the previous part of the film set in Scotland. This track returns underneath the sound of Diane's letter being read by her in voice-over as Renton eats a Pot Noodle and reads. Pulp's track *Mile End*, a song about living in squalor, about "how low a human being can go", fades in under dialogue between Renton and Begbie, the latter of whom asks for a Pot Noodle and throws an empty cigarette packet on the floor. The club sequence uses *For What You Dream Of (full on Renaissance Mix)*, performed by Bedrock featuring KYO. When Sick Boy arrives in London and they eat chips, Elastica's *2.1* plays underneath a voice-over, a succession of street scenes and in the new flat. On the bus from Edinburgh to London, Renton tests the heroin and his voice-over notes that it was a "final hit", while the accompanying music is Leftfield's *A Final Hit*, which builds slowly with a very deep bass sound and dance beat.

In the joy among the group of friends in the wake of the drug deal, the rock sound of the Sleeper song *Statuesque* fades in as non-diegetic music, but then as the image cuts to a pub the music takes on the acoustic quality of diegetic music, a good example of music's capacity to provide continuity film's across time and space compression. The climax of the film, as might be expected, is partially achieved through the prominent and sustained use of a single piece of music. Underworld's *Born Slippy (NUXX)* starts with Begbie blowing smoke in Renton's face, continues as he lies awake while the others sleep and then accompanies him when he leaves and the film seems to conclude. The duration of the music is over four and a half minutes, accompanied by Renton's voice-over, which carries on as vertical lines and the title *Trainspotting* cross the screen as an apparent closure, although briefly afterwards there is an interior shot from a left luggage compartment of Spud collecting his money. The following titles are accompanied by Damon Albarn's *Closet Romantic*, where the voice lists James Bond films, aspects of which have been under discussion among the group of friends earlier in the film.

More unmistakeably than *Hardware*, *Trainspotting* demonstrates the path that music and film industry "synergy" was attempting to follow in the 1990s. This development was part of the re-organization of the music industry, which included a re-branding of what had been "independent" music as a more mainstream "alternative" music, and the rush into repackaging old albums for sale on CD. This latter process, of re-selling old music, is highly evident in *Trainspotting*'s soundtrack albums. The film had two tied-in soundtrack albums made available, both of which sold well. These albums clearly aimed to be coherent in themselves as well as being the record of music in the film. Thus, they had a hybrid character in that they were not specifically a subset of the film but more an intersection with the film. Songs that had appeared all too briefly could be heard in their full plenitude and some music that had appeared in the film was not represented on the first album. The second album mostly consisted of music that had not appeared in the film. Indeed, the film's relationship to these two albums sums up the contemporaneous attitude to what the converged film and music industries had been calling "synergy", where one product sold the other and the effect of publicity was more than the sum of the parts. Denisoff and Plasketes discussed the notion of synergy in relation to American films of the early and mid-1980s, a time when films were used by record companies to sell songs by their current roster of artists. With the advent of CD in the early 1990s, this strategy was amended by record companies's desire to sell back catalogues, and films became full of older records with newer pop music being pushed to the margins. *Trainspotting* evidently is an important part of the reselling of old material, as the film includes much from the 1970s. However, it also has a notable current musical input, embracing both the current trend of "Britpop" and the 1990s development of electronic dance music.

The second soundtrack album (known as *Trainspotting #2*) contained a number of songs that appeared in the film but had not featured on the first album.[29] The other music on the disc has no direct connection with the film, and thus marked an extension of the film.[30] However, the album's sleeve notes inform us that these pieces of music were under consideration for inclusion in the film. For example, David Bowie's *Golden Years* was going to be sung by Diane to Renton, although in the final film she sings New Order's *Temptation*. This song is one of the many mentioned in Irvine Welsh's original novel. Other songs on the second soundtrack album include the Fun Boy Three's *Our Lips are Sealed* and Primal Scream's *Come Together*, for which placements in the film could not be found despite the intention to include them at some point. Also on the album are Goldie's *Inner City Life*, Joy Division's *Atmosphere* and the hit single by PF Project *Choose Life*, which is premised upon a sample of Renton's opening speech from the film accompanied by dance music. The second soundtrack album, while supplying the missing songs from the film that were not included on the first, also adds a number of seemingly unconnected pieces to make for a coherent listening experience and thus make it into a fairly solid compilation album rather than a record of the music from the film. In Welsh's book, a whole section concerns an Iggy Pop song, *Neon Forest*. It is worth noting that this was not used in the film, in favour of Pop's better-known material, his songs that the audience are more likely to recognize. Indeed, there is a certain homogeneity about some of the film's music, Iggy Pop's two songs and Lou Reed's *Perfect Day* all being produced in collaboration with David Bowie. While they wanted a Bowie song for the film, his absence as an artist in his own right is striking.[31] Producer Andrew Macdonald said that Bowie, Reed and Pop provided a foundation for the film in the 1970s, but then the music branches out from there.[32] The book was published in 1993 and its setting is the 1980s, roughly 1982–1988. This accounts for the handful of early to mid-1980s songs that appear in the film, although it updates dramatically to include 1990s dance music.

Films are uniformly slow to translate cultural explosions in pop music to celluloid. The summer of 1989 was a boom period for house music, especially "acid house", which was a new form of dance music premised upon new digital synthesizers and sampling technology. In many ways, it revolutionized the pop music industry, allowing records to be made at home computer keyboards rather than by working bands of musicians, while as a movement it permeated fashion, club culture and design. Yet there were no immediate attempts to represent this exciting new pop music culture on film. The first mainstream British film to use a certain amount of the new dance music was *Shopping* (1993), a film about fast cars and drugs that had Sabres of Paradise and Orbital on its soundtrack. This was followed by the opening titles of *Shallow Grave* (1994). Later in the decade, *Trainspotting* underlined its significance through using the new dance music to signify the change in culture, particularly drug culture, which had been brought about at the turn of the 1990s.[33] The use of dance music in the film was symbolic of the new youth culture developments, which are represented in the film (club and electronic dance music culture – "music is changing and drugs are changing"). Indeed, *Trainspotting* was one of the first films to use such music notably on the soundtrack. Apart from music by Bedrock featuring KYO and Ice MC, the pieces by Underworld and Leftfield appear at significant moments in the film, the conclusion and the hallucinations caused by Renton's withdrawal from heroin respectively.

Conclusion

Cultural recycling was endemic in the mid-1980s, with record companies keen to exploit other markets. Denisoff and Plasketes detail the industrial strategy called synergy, involving the coordination of record releases from a film soundtrack as mutual publicity.[34] Since the 1990s, song collections often predate film being produced, with film makers often looking into what pop songs they can afford to license very early in the project. While *Hardware* uses a couple of songs in a foregrounded manner and makes a number of knowing pop culture references, *Trainspotting* is premised upon a regular succession of pop songs, fragmenting the film into successive incident accompanied by music and voice-over, a reflection of the tessellated pattern of Irvine Welsh's original novel.

Tom Gunning notes the similarity between some contemporary cinema and the "attractionism" of early cinema.[35] His approach sees film as a grab bag of effects and fragments of (often discrete) interest, rather than a fully integrated work. Overarching narrative is therefore of less importance and micro-narratives and incident tend to be of more interest. Other elements of the film can also take on more significance, and in the case of *Hardware* and *Trainspotting* most clearly, music seems to have a degree of importance in the film that has almost no direct bearing upon the film's narrative or diegetic world. Within the body of *Hardware* the pop/rock songs presented like pop videos and the pop references function as discrete attractions and micro-narratives which break up the narrative elision.[36] The music remains another (almost independent) dimension in the film, setting up its own time schemes (of regulated musical time) and not bowing to those of dominant cinematic convention. The dual context of the pop/rock music (within and without the film) means that it signifies intertextually, relating to the specifics of the music itself and the pop music discourse outside of the film's bounds. *Hardware* and *Trainspotting* are both very conscious of their musical pedigrees. *Trainspotting* mixes some established "classics" with some obscure pieces (along with a few "respected" hit records).[37] Since the advent of CD, the music industry's selling of old back catalogues has been a big business. The relationship of the nostalgia industry and the record industry's repackaging of old songs has been mutually reinforcing. The retreading of the musical past has speeded up, allowing a nostalgia for the 1980s despite its relative historical proximity. Films such as *Peter's Friends* (1992), *Boston Kickout* (1995) and Mike Leigh's *Career Girls* (1997) were set in the 1980s and used songs of the period that were yet to achieve quite the "classic" status accorded to older songs.

By the early 1990s, it certainly was not uncommon for British films to have a number of pop songs incorporated with a view to soundtrack LP publicity. Sarah Street notes that Polygram's publicity campaign for *Trainspotting* did not limit the film's image to any single generic category but instead simply targeted a youth audience.[38] In both *Hardware* and *Trainspotting*, the pop and pop music culture references were exploited as a means to court a specific audience: in other words, the films specifically were targeting a youth market, but perhaps more precisely, through their musical soundtracks, the films aimed at an audience particularly interested in music, one that might well know the songs being used and one that might be persuaded to buy the songs being used. Yet this is not to deny the aesthetic efficacy of the songs in the film; at times, they make the film.

7
History of British Film Musicals

Some are surprised to discover that British film musicals were at one time a thriving concern, seeing as in recent years the musical film, let alone the British musical film, has become something of an occasional treat rather than a consistently productive film genre. The 1930s were a particularly rich decade for the British film musical. In fact, British cinema was buoyant on and off throughout this decade and held its own in the home market against Hollywood imports.[1] Musicals, like most other British films, had many similarities to Hollywood films and followed similar genres, although with a varying degree of local difference from the internationally dominant American cinema. Generally speaking, the British film musical has followed a similar trajectory to the Hollywood film musical, in that it was a successful genre that has been in a consistent decline. In both cases, they developed from being a staple of the film industry in the 1930s to being sporadic productions from the 1970s onwards.

Since the advent of synchronized sound films, there has been a reciprocal relationship between music and films, with the mutual promotion of films and sheet music, and later films and recordings. As a result, the appropriation of cinema as a medium for popular musicians and singers had been a common practice since the late 1920s, American examples including Kay Kyser in the 1930s and Frank Sinatra in the 1940s. By the late 1950s, the principal inspiration behind putting British rock'n'roll singers in the cinema certainly came from the success of Elvis Presley's early films. His films had not only supplied a showcase for his songs but allowed a broadening of his appeal, with the possibilities of increased record sales and the films proving attractive beyond an audience whose immediate interest was Presley's singing. Tied-in products had been involved with films since the 1910s, while songs had been involved with films since before the widespread use of sound in the cinema. Yet musical product placement certainly accelerated with the introduction of pop music to the cinema. Denisoff and Plasketes assert that "Since the start of the rock era and *The Blackboard Jungle* (1954) music placement has been an essential ingredient in promoting the film and its music."[2] Yet film musicals were already premised upon selling music to audiences, either as sheet music or as recordings later. In most cases, appearances in musical films were little more than adjuncts to successful careers as singers on stage, radio and recording. A good example is the first British film musical, *Auld Lang Syne* (1929), which starred Scots music hall star Sir Harry Lauder. It had been filmed as a silent but had six song sequences hurriedly synchronized for release.[3] Film musicals were in many cases a series of songs or turns, and sometimes a more "organic" form of drama with songs interspersed with the action.

The 1930s

The film musical was one of the most popular British film genres in the 1930s. Stephen Guy points out that "Out of just over 1500 full-length feature films made in that decade, at least 220 can be described as musical films."[4] This compares with the popularity of the musical in American cinema of the time, and demonstrates the British film musical's popularity in itself.[5] The Cinematographic Films Act of 1927 vastly expanded British film production to fill the quotas it established of British-made films to be shown in British cinemas.[6] This led to the production of many films that were cheap and of modest pretension, known as "quota quickies", a proportion of which were musicals, although many musicals were of higher budget and some were made at great expense in the hope of success in the lucrative American market.

This was a period when popular films were often star vehicles and this logic tended to dominate British cinema as much as Hollywood cinema. British film musical stars almost always came directly from the stage – the exception was Jessie Matthews, who was created as a film star rather than progressing from top billing at live shows to screen stardom. Probably, the most significant British film musical stars of the decade were Jack Buchanan, Jack Hulbert, George Formby, Gracie Fields and Jessie Matthews, all of whom inspired notable peripheral fan culture and tied-in products appended to their film appearances, ranging from recorded discs to photographic cards in cigarette packets.

Jack Buchanan had a reputation for sophistication, having attained fame from the upmarket end of the London stage, from whence he took his talent into films. He was famed for his immaculate dress-sense, and was Glaswegian despite his polite BBC/received pronunciation accent.[7] Buchanan was signed to work with film director Herbert Wilcox in 1931, in the wake of massive stage success on Broadway as well as in London.[8] Buchanan's success in *Brewster's Millions* (1935) as well as his stage reputation ultimately led him to Hollywood and a role in Vincente Minnelli's *The Band Wagon* (1953 US) nearly two decades later.[9] A more comic star was Jack Hulbert, who was married to another star, Cicely Courtneidge. His films were primarily comedies with a musical garnish. His film debut was in *Elstree Calling* (1930) while his most successful film was probably *Jack's the Boy* (1932), directed by Walter Forde. He made a series of successful films in the mid-1930s, which emphasized comedy rather than music. In parallel, Hulbert made a number of successful discs. Hulbert regularly appeared alongside his wife Cicely Courtneidge (as well as his brother Claude). She made films that included *Falling for You* (1933) and *Soldiers of the King* (1934), which featured the song *All for a Shilling a Day*.

Jessie Matthews was an accomplished singer and outstanding dancer with no little charm, and affected the sort of BBC, middle/upper-class accent that was *de rigueur* for many in the fields of entertainment, and was perhaps most internationally evident in Charlie Chaplin's accent. However, Matthews had a rather baroque, camp intonation.[10] So, while Matthews may have had a sheen of upper-class sophistication, her on-screen persona was configured in a manner that was aimed more at working-class audiences. Matthews had been a success on stage in a Noel Coward revue and in 1930 in Rodgers and Hart's *Evergreen*, a role that she repeated on film a few years later. Her films included *There Goes the Bride* (1932) and Hitchcock's musical *Waltzes from Vienna* (1933). She then forged an alliance with film director Victor Saville that lasted much of the 1930s, and led to her being known as "the Dancing Divinity". He directed her in a highly successful adaptation of J.B. Priestley's *The Good Companions* (1933), about a group of travelling performers (and also featuring a young John Gielgud) and *Evergreen* (1934), a stage adaptation about a woman who pretends to be her mother making a stage comeback (and included the songs *Daddy wouldn't Buy Me a Bow Wow* and *Dancing on the Ceiling*). Both were backstage musicals. The latter film was a notable success, with songs by American songwriters Rodgers and Hart, although a song by the British songwriter Harry Woods, *Over My Shoulder*, became a theme song for later use by Matthews. Her follow-up was *First A Girl* (1935), where she masqueraded as a female impersonator in a film based on the German film *Viktor und Viktoria* (1933). Matthews next starred in *It's Love Again* (1936), about a dancer who adopts a new fabricated persona.[11] She was not limited to appearing in musicals and became Gaumont-British's biggest star of the 1930s. Her films not only managed significant success in the British market, but also achieved some success in America too. Her next two films *Head Over Heels* (1937) and *Gangway* (1938) were directed by her husband Sonny Hale and were conceived as decided and quite successful tilts at breaking into the lucrative US film market.[12] *Gangway* is replete with Americanisms, and is a slick production, including some singing along the lines of operatic recitative and some memorable duets using the lip-synch mode (such as *That's Life*). With the outbreak of Second World War, she went to the United States and her film career stuttered to a halt, although she later made a notable comeback to appear in *tom thumb* (1958) and as a long-running character in BBC radio's *Mrs. Dale's Diary*.[13]

George Formby provided a distinct contrast with Jessie Matthews. His persona and films appeared aimed at a solidly working-class audience and drew upon the traditions of the northern working men's club circuits and seaside seasons,[14] both of which exhibited coarse risqué humour and eschewed the sophistication evident elsewhere on the British stage.[15] Formby, who had renamed himself after a British seaside town, always appeared as an innocent abroad and played with blatant double entendre and seaside postcard cheekiness. However, he also had a good degree of charm and peppered his films with individual musical performances. Almost all of these were solo performances using the performance mode,[16] where Formby sang a fast, witty song in his Lancashire brogue while accompanying himself on what he called his "ukelele" (which actually was a banjolele, more banjo than ukelele). Formby's film successes started playing a character called "John Willie" in *Boots! Boots!* (1934) and *Off the Dole* (1935). He made 11 features for Associated Talking Pictures, including *It's in the Air* (1938), *Let George Do It* (1940), *Spare a Copper* (1940), *Turned Out Nice Again* (1941) and *Bell-Bottom George* (1943). In these films, Formby essentially played the same character but in a different context, as the film titles suggest, as a sailor or as an airman. He was a good example of the mutual relationship between the music, stage and film industries. Starting on the stage, he had his first disc releases in 1932, two years before making a career in films.[17]

Gracie Fields was another star whose immediate constituency was the same Lancastrian, northern English background that was paraded in her films. She had a very robust and highly individualistic singing voice, and in a number of her films she appeared as light of happiness in a miserable and down-beaten working-class community.[18] Fields became a mainstay at Basil Dean's Associated Talking Pictures (ATP), "the studio with team spirit" as they liked to be known. ATP had been set up with the backing of Hollywood studio RKO, who in reality were only interested in making cheap films aimed purely at the British market.[19] Later in the decade, Fields was joined at ATP by Formby.[20] The studio made many musicals, led by Basil Dean's vision of the British stage as the principal source for their films.[21] She made her film debut with *Sally in Our Alley* (1931), directed by Maurice Elvey, and then made a succession of films under the direction of Basil Dean, including *Looking on the Bright Side* (1932), where she has a songwriter lover, *Sing as We Go!* (1934), with its celebrated chase sequence shot in Blackpool, *Look Up and Laugh* (1935), *Queen of Hearts* (1936) and *The Show Goes On* (1937). Her last British film was *Shipyard Sally* (1939), directed by Monty Banks and set in the shipyards of Glasgow. Jeffrey Richards calls Gracie Fields "consensus personified"[22] and, indeed, her debut film, *Sally in Our Alley*, ends with the superimposition of her face on a Union Jack flag. However, James Park notes that *Sing as We Go!* is "…one of the few [British] films of the 1930s to make any reference to unemployment",[23] anchoring her work further in a sense of working-class community. Her films of the 1930s finished abruptly with the coming of the war. She was married to Italian-born director Monty Banks and fled to Hollywood with him at the start of the war to avoid his being interred as an alien.

Herbert Wilcox was a pioneering figure in British cinema, having worked as a film distributor and producer immediately after First World War and helping to found Elstree Studios. Wilcox directed a number of successful musicals during the 1930s, starting with *The Blue Danube* (1931), and then *Goodnight Vienna* (1932). He then went on to direct *Bitter Sweet* (1933), an adaptation of the very prominent Noel Coward play. While it may have been a stage success, it was not turned into a success on film. Like Hollywood, British film musicals also exploited the tradition of stage operetta, derived usually from imports from mainland Europe. For example, Wilcox's *Goodnight Vienna* was a great success, and had been based on an existing radio drama with music by George Posford and Eric Maschwitz. It starred Anna Neagle and Jack Buchanan, both of whom continued to develop notably under Wilcox's aegis. Other operettas included *Princess Charming* (1943), directed by Maurice Elvey, *Two Hearts in Waltztime* (1934) and *Blossom Time* (1934), a notable success that helped establish Austrian Richard Tauber as a singing romantic lead. Other operettas included *Pagliacci* (1936), directed by Karl Grune, and *The Lilac Domino* (1937), directed by Fred Zelnick.

Some British film musicals were simply derived directly from the stage. *Chu Chin Chow* (1934) was one, attempting to emulate its original success.[24] Similarly, Victor Schertzinger's *The Mikado* (1938) was a direct transfer of the Gilbert and Sullivan play as performed by the D'Oyly Carte company. *The Lambeth Walk* (1939) was an adaptation of *Me and My Girl*, which had been tremendously popular as a stage musical. The story concerned a cockney who (played both on stage and in film by Lupino Lane), after learning that he is heir to a lordship, goes to live at a large aristocratic hall.[25] (There is further discussion of the relationship between stage and screen in Chapter 8.)

There were also a number of films whose stars were bandleaders rather than acting singers. *Say it with Music* (1932) starred bandleader Jack Payne and his band, *She Shall Have Music* (1935) starred Jack Hylton and his orchestra and *Music Hath Charms* (1935) starred Henry Hall and his orchestra. The films very much reflected the British music industry of the time, where bandleaders were feted on radio and in disc sales, despite an often high degree of personal anonymity. During the 1930s, musical films were made by musicians and performers who had achieved fame elsewhere, much as in Hollywood. Variety stars from the stage, singers from BBC radio and dance bands that had nationwide fame were the chief components of the British musical.[26] The films featuring dance bands were invariably second features, produced on low budgets (often as "quota quickies") and were rarely rerun or reissued. These films include *She Shall Have Music*, featuring Jack Hylton's band, *Everything is Rhythm* (1936) starring Harry Ray and his Band and *Radio Parade of 1935* (1934), a revue starring Will Hay. The revue form, as was Hollywood's version, was merely a succession of diegetic performances by acts from the theatre, or in the cited case radio, with a minimal narrative or a master of ceremonies – the latter format mirroring the theatre variety show. As a format, it already existed on the radio with films like *On the Air* (1934) simply adding visuals to the sort of show that was popular on the BBC,[27] and musical performances were usually central.

The 1940s and 1950s

While Britain changed radically at the end of the 1930s, due to the onset of the Second World War, George Formby continued to make musicals, including *Much Too Shy* (1942), *Get Cracking* (1943), *Gaiety George* (1946) and *George in Civvy Street* (1946). Vera Lynn cemented her role as singer to stir the nation's wartime aspirations with the films *We'll*

Meet Again (1942), *Rhythm Serenade* (1943) and *One Exciting Night* (1944). While musical feature films were few, they had a wide range of subject matter and style. American singer Paul Robeson appeared as a singing Welsh miner in *The Proud Valley* (1940), Wilfrid Lawson appeared as the eponymous composer in the Technicolour biographical film *The Great Mr. Handel* (1942), and music hall star George Robey appeared in *Variety Jubilee* (1943), which showcased a number of stage acts. Other music hall-based films included Ealing Studios's *Champagne Charlie* (1944), starring Tommy Trinder and Stanley Holloway and directed by Alberto Cavalcanti, and *I'll Be Your Sweetheart* (1945), a backstage musical about a music hall star (played by Margaret Lockwood) and her rise to fame. Her singing was lip-synched to the voice of Maudie Edwards.[28] Cheaper productions, such as those by John E. Blakeley and the Mancunian Film Studios, included *Demobbed* (1944) and *Holidays with Pay* (1948) that mixed regular star Frank Randle with club comedienne Tessie O'Shea and Irish tenor Josef Locke.

The post-War era in Britain saw musicals appear as scarce as many of the consumer goods were still officially rationed until the early 1950s. Not only were British musical films a rarity but when they appeared they were often highly distinctive rather than being simple genre pieces or star vehicles. A notable example was Powell and Pressburger's *The Red Shoes* (1948), which was an attempt to make a ballet musical with high art overtones, derived from an E.T.A. Hoffmann tale. It starred Moira Shearer as the dancer who ends up possessed by the pair of dancing shoes, with Marius Goring as the composer and Anton Wallbrook as the director. It is an impressive film that lacks any songs, the characteristic of the musical comedy as a form. Instead it has some extensive musical passages, including the extended *Red Shoes* ballet sequence. While there may be debate about whether this film should qualify as a constituent of the film musical genre, it should be noted that there was an impetus to produce a "high art musical" in the immediate post-War years, as evidenced by Vincente Minnelli's *The Band Wagon's* (1953 US) narrative, which featured Jack Buchanan, and *An American in Paris* (1951 US), with its extensive reference to figurative art and to ballet and modern dance. Powell and Pressburger followed *The Red Shoes* with another musical film, also based on the stories of the same writer, in *Tales of Hoffmann* (1951). Director Michael Powell had a declared interest in the notion of what he called "the composed film",[29] which was not conceived as a film musical in the traditional generic sense but as a new Wagnerian *gesamtkunstwerk* art form where music would interact with other filmic elements in an integrated and highly aestheticized manner. Similar attempts at musicals using more "legit" sources and performers included Austrian singer Richard Tauber's films *Waltz Time* (1945) along with Kay Kendall, and the stage adaptation *Lisbon Story* (1946).

There were still occasional films such as *London Town* (1946), which graphically depicted music hall culture and featured Claude Hulbert, Jack Parnell, Kay Kendall, Tessie O'Shea, and a succession of stage acts, while being directed by American Wesley Ruggles. After the 1930s, the 1940s look poor for British musicals. According to Andrew Spicer, the reason was due to industry instability,[30] while according to Stephen Guy the reason was changing audience taste.[31] The austerity inaugurated by Britain's involvement in the Second World War doubtless discouraged the production of expensive film musicals.

Anna Neagle used the same director, Herbert Wilcox, for the vast majority of her films and married him over a decade after their first collaboration, on *Goodnight Vienna*. She was originally a dancer more than a singer, but became world famous for her dramatic role as Queen Victoria in *Victoria the Great* (1937) and its sequel *Sixty Glorious Years* (1937). She collaborated with director Wilcox and actor Michael Wilding on a series of very successful London-set musicals in the late 1940s: *Piccadilly Incident* (1946), *The Courtneys of Curzon Street* (1947), *Spring in Park Lane* (1948) and *Maytime in Mayfair* (1949). In the 1950s, Neagle starred in two Ivor Novello stage adaptations along with Errol Flynn, *Lilacs in the Spring* (1954) and *King's Rhapsody* (1955), and then made a few films with singer Frankie Vaughan. Indeed, her career spans a wide range of genres and even a range within film musicals, going from operetta through to attempts to negotiate emergent rock'n'roll in her later musicals.

The 1950s were a decade when Hollywood musicals reached what some see as a peak of sophistication in the MGM musicals produced by the Freed Unit. British musicals failed to compete on a level of production values, and were shunted aside in the home market by their glamorous American counterparts. There were far fewer British film musicals produced in the 1950s than in the previous two decades. The 1950s were also a decade when momentous changes took place in popular music. The advent of rock'n'roll in the middle of the decade sent shockwaves across the popular music industry, making overnight stars and consigning many singers and songwriters to the dustbin of history. British musicals reflected these developments, with the appearance of rock'n'roll musicals later in the decade, although many more traditional films were still being produced.

Launder and Gilliat made *The Story of Gilbert and Sullivan* (1953), which starred Robert Morley and Maurice Evans as the lyricist and composer respectively. The song sequences were adapted from current D'Oyly Carte productions and the film was one of the first released with the capabilities of stereo sound reproduction. Moving from success on the stage, Max Bygraves made a few films, including *Charley Moon* (1956) and *Bobbikins* (1959), on the way to a long-term career on television. In the former, Bygraves as the eponymous character sings *Out of Town* (twice, once using the lip-synch mode and once using the performance mode), in what is primarily a traditional backstage musical. There was a remake of J.B. Priestley's *The Good Companions* (1957) that mixed young performers (Janette Scott and John Fraser) with the more established (Celia Johnson and Joyce Grenfell).[32] While the production updated the setting from the earlier version, it had an added edge in that the sort of variety the company are involved in was on the decline at this point. ABPC's expensive production failed to recoup costs against a backdrop of dwindling cinema audiences and the ousting of traditional backstage musicals such as this by rock'n'roll films. Film musicals with similar problems were *It's a Wonderful World* (1956), *Stars in Your Eyes* (1956) and two adaptations of Ivor Novello stage plays with songs, both starring Errol Flynn, who was at the twilight of his acting career: *Wonderful Things* (1957) and *Let's be Happy* (1957).

Hungarian director George Pal, who had produced *When Worlds Collide* (1951 US) and *War of the Worlds* (1953 US), came across from Hollywood to make *tom thumb* (1958), another film premised upon special visual effects to create a world of giants surrounding the minuscule lead character. The lead part was played by American actor Russ Tamblyn, who had come to some prominence as the vigorous and athletic youngest brother in *Seven Brides for Seven Brothers* (1954 US). It also featured Jessie Matthews, making a comeback as his mother, and Alan Young who later was best known for sharing a television show with a horse, the famous *Mister Ed* (1961–1966). *Hello London* (1958) was a vehicle for Norwegian ice skater Sonja Henie, although well after her Hollywood successes. She is meant to be on tour and the film includes large number of acts and actors playing themselves (such as Stanley Holloway, Dora Bryan and Eunice Gayson).

There were continued attempts to make high-art musical films. Hungarian-born Paul Czinner continued making films in Britain, concentrating on adapting and filming stage and ballet productions. He directed *Don Giovanni* (1955), *The Bolshoi Ballet* (1957), *The Royal Ballet*

(1960), *Der Rosenkavalier* (1962) and *Romeo and Juliet* (1966), the last with Margot Fonteyn and Rudolf Nureyev.[33] Similarly, Michael Birkett directed Robert Helpmann in *The Soldier's Tale* (1963), a ballet written by Igor Stravinsky.

The coming of rock'n'roll was incontrovertibly a dramatic point in the history of international popular music. The established hit factory was turned on its head and had to react one way or another to the new type of music that was becoming so popular. While some upcoming rock'n'roll singers were signed up by the major record companies, others were manufactured by them and others still who were already contracted were reborn from previous careers as crooners. The rapid change in musical taste gave dramatic opportunities to smaller record companies as much as it did to unknown singers. Similarly, the production of rock'n'roll films gave scope to small independent film production companies. *Rock You Sinners* (1957) was distributed by The Small Film Distribution Company, *The Golden Disc* (1958) was made by Butchers, *Sweet Beat* (1962) was made by Flamingo Films and *Expresso Bongo* (1959) was made by Conquest Films.

The first British films with rock'n'roll were *Kill Me Tomorrow* (1957), *Rock You Sinners* and *The Tommy Steele Story* (1957), the latter two of which were musicals of sorts. Subsequent notable films included *The Golden Disc*, starring Terry Dene, *The Duke Wore Jeans* (1958), starring Tommy Steele, and the television spin-off revue film *Six-Five Special* (1958). Backstage musical (and stage adaptation) *Expresso Bongo* satirized the exploitation of young rock'n'roll singers in the entertainment industry, and allowed Cliff Richard a few songs. *Monthly Film Bulletin*'s review of *Rock You Sinners* stated: "The plot of this film is negligible, most of the footage being occupied with rock'n'roll numbers."[34] In most cases, these films were aimed at a quick financial return and sacrificed much sense of quality. A concerted attempt to merge the old and the new took place, where "adaptations" or "compromises" between the traditional film musical genre and the new musical style were attempted. A significant part of the compromise was the inclusion of older, established actors and artists. For example, throughout a distinguished career, Herbert Wilcox had become something of a specialist in making film musicals. In the late 1950s, he made *The Lady is a Square* (1958) and *The Heart of a Man* (1959), which paired his wife, Anna Neagle with Frankie Vaughan, a crooner being recast as a rock'n'roll singer.

Concurrently, in the late 1950s and early 1960s, Dixieland jazz became popular in Britain, but renamed as "trad jazz". This popularity and some of the bands involved led to films like *Jazz Boat* (1959) with singer and actor Anthony Newley, the vehicle for Acker Bilk and his band called *Band of Thieves* (1962), *Take Me Over* (1962) with the Temperance Seven and Richard Lester's *It's Trad, Dad!* (1962), a backstage musical that mixed trad jazz and pop groups.

The 1960s

The late 1950s and early 1960s were a period of highly dramatic flux for popular music, where careers were made or broken overnight. Films played an important part in these cultural developments, not least in that they served to establish the status of rock'n'roll singers. By the early 1960s, films also served as an important means to attempt to extend what was conceived as a short commercial lifetime. Despite the emergent rock'n'roll's relatively rapid absorption into the established (and conservative) modes of musical entertainment, it effected drastic changes in the music industry, and its induction into films stimulated the relationship between cinema and the music industry. Rock'n'roll recast the music and film industry partnership, paving the way for the saturation of tied-in musical commodities which had become so prevalent in the years since.

Cliff Richard starred in a succession of traditional musicals that tried to merge youth concerns and music with the existing film musical format, the most successful of which were *The Young Ones* (1961), *Summer Holiday* (1963) and *Wonderful Life* (1964) (see subsequent chapter). Many, if not most, of the pop musicals of the early 1960s were vehicles for singers, with Billy Fury in *Play It Cool* (1962), Tommy Steele in *It's All Happening* (1963) and Mark Wynter in *Just for Fun* (1963).[35]

A good example of the endeavours to assimilate pop music and youth culture to existing formats was *The Cool Mikado* (1962), which used W.S. Gilbert's lyrics and Arthur Sullivan's music from *The Mikado*, but had the musical style updated by Martin Slavin. There had already been a number of updates of *The Mikado* on stage, but this version was more self-consciously current, featuring the John Barry Seven. It was directed by Michael Winner and starred Stubby Kaye and Frankie Howerd. At the same time, traditional film musicals were still being made, if only occasionally. Ronald Neame directed Judy Garland in *I Could Go On Singing* (1963), a fairly straightforward backstage musical about a singer's career. Rock'n'roll singer-turned mainstream entertainer Tommy Steele starred in the Anglo-American co-production of *Half a Sixpence* (1967), which was derived originally from an H.G. Wells story, and Carol Reed directed a massively successful film in the Dickens adaptation *Oliver!*

(1968). Both of these were traditional integrated musicals that used the lip-synch mode for all their songs. In the same year as *Oliver!*, *Chitty Chitty Bang Bang* (1968) was a highly successful children's film very much in the vein of Disney's *Mary Poppins* (1964 US).

The early 1960s saw a boom in cheaply made revue films, which showcased a succession of acts, much as did stage shows and television pop shows at the time. These revue films often placed pop music alongside trad jazz. The films' close relationship to television pop shows was underlined by *The Six-Five Special* (1958) emerging directly from the television pop show of the same name. Another revue film, this time set at a television studio, was *It's Trad, Dad!* (1962), which also used the "putting on a show" format familiar from Hollywood musicals, while *Live It Up* (1963) also involved "putting on a show" with a climactic concert. *Kinematograph Weekly* noted the salient points about *Live It Up*: "Pop-music parade tagged on to a local-boy-makes-good story.... The story, acting and direction are incidental to the pop music, of which there is plenty.... It should send the kids home twanging."[36] In such films, pop music acts began to dominate what had originally been a development from cabaret shows, mixing in a few elements of narrative cinema. *It's All Over Town* (1963) saw Willie Rushton and Lance Percival in bed dreaming of seeing variety acts around town. *Kinematograph Weekly*'s review of *Just for You* (1964): "There is no story, but...the popular artist in nearly every case presents numbers that have already appeared successfully in the pop-parade..."[37] *Just for You* was unified merely by Sam Costa in bed pushing buttons to summon each successive act, with the cabaret turns being overwhelmed by pop groups, from Peter and Gordon and Millie, to the Merseybeats and the Band of Angels. The disappearance of the revue form can be largely attributed to the institution of *Top of the Pops* on television in 1964. This new pop show offered a different selection of acts each week, thus dooming musical revue films to look like a cheap weekly television show. At the same time, the pop musical was revolutionized by The Beatles's film debut in *A Hard Day's Night* (1964), which used a massive range of film techniques to double the energy of the group's music with on-screen kinesis. (There is more detailed discussion about this elsewhere in the book.)

In 1966, *Time* published an article that crystallized and coined the term "Swinging London",[38] which probably manifested itself most tangibly in a cycle of British films that used Hollywood finance. While music was a key aspect of many of these films, there was only really one musical. *Smashing Time* (1968) was a film musical in the classical sense, but articulated the locations and character types that epitomized

"Swinging London". Two provincial women (Lynne Redgrave and Rita Tushingham) run away to the metropolis and become successful in the two areas of cultural activity that define the period and location: pop music and photographic modelling. As an integrated musical, almost all the songs are premised upon the lip-synch mode's "spontaneous" outbursts. Looking back to earlier pop musicals, *Smashing Time* attempted to update the traditional formula of the integrated film musical through a youth-oriented and contrived "Swinging London" setting.

After the successes of *A Hard Days Night* and *Help!*, The Beatles made the psychedelic home movie *Magical Mystery Tour*, which was broadcast on BBC television at the end of 1967. This included song sequences and was arguably a musical. Perhaps most notably, *Your Mother Should Know* parodied classical musicals, particularly American ones from the 1930s or 1940s. The Beatles's next film was *Yellow Submarine* (1968), although its production concerned the group minimally. The voices of the animated Beatles characters are even spoken by doubles[39] and the group were unhappy about their contractual stipulation to supply new songs and ended up contributing some unreleased outtakes,[40] which then nestled among the film's roll call of the group's hits and famous songs. *Yellow Submarine* cobbled together a story from the nonsense-words of the song *Yellow Submarine*, which had appeared on *Revolver* in 1965. While the film demonstrates a high degree of visual imagination, its articulation of music is quite traditional and, in cultural terms, *Yellow Submarine* shifts the new psychedelic culture into the relatively safe compartment of the children's film.[41]

The 1970s and 1980s

British film production changed both qualitatively and quantitatively at the turn of the 1970s. Alexander Walker wrote of the development in film production that "London slid from its 'swinging' euphoria into its 'hangover' period."[42] The American finance that had buoyed film production in Britain since the mid-1960s was quite suddenly absent, setting up a crisis of investment for British film production.[43] While there was an unequivocal renewal of confidence in American-made films, other financial determinants did come into play. The US tax authorities continually challenged Hollywood studios's investments abroad throughout the 1960s, so the corollary by the early 1970s was that American production money remained in the United States. Consequently, the studios's overseas production arms began to wither.[44] This, along with the spectacularly expensive failures at the close of the previous decade, dealt a decisive blow to film production in Britain.[45] Top British producer John Boulting succinctly summed up the predicament facing British film production: "...for about seven years...the British production industry has been something like 80 per cent financed by the American companies, and if the American companies are not making films [here] immediately or not in the foreseeable future, then I think you have a crisis."[46] The collapse of Britain as a major film producer and thus exporter of films led to a surge of cheaply made films aimed at the home and commonwealth markets.[47] The expense of musicals meant that they appeared even more infrequently than previously.

Cliff Richard returned to the cinema screen in 1973 with a very traditional musical. *Take Me High* was set in Birmingham and concerned the development of a fast food called "the Brumburger". It was something of an anomaly in that it was the first traditional pop star vehicle since the middle of the previous decade. However, its modern concerns are demonstrated by the use of songs as non-diegetic music as well as using the performance and lip-synch modes. *Take Me High* is thus a remarkable attempt to update the by-now virtually extinct traditional pop musical format. Pop groups were promising material for the backstage musical format. Slade made *Flame* (1973), a gritty story of the rise then demise of a pop group.[48]

The hyperbolic tendencies of progressive rock culminated in what became known as "rock operas". They involved copious use of the lip-synch mode with their song sequences resembling the strategies evident in classical musicals as well as the highbrow form from which they derived their name. As films, these constituted a subgenre of the film musical, yet they went beyond the traditions and conventions of that genre. In essence, they were the cinema's equivalent of the concept albums that had become endemic since the end of the 1960s. Rock operas were uniformly of a grand scale, regularly had outlandish sets and costumes, and usually displayed the artistic pretensions characteristic of progressive rock. Rather than follow the tradition of musicals, with numbers as set-pieces that are interposed with the narrative, rock operas functioned more like operas. The music had a primary role, driving the progression of the films and treating dialogue-led sections as something less than the principal aspect of each film. America produced two Christian-inspired rock operas, *Jesus Christ Superstar* (1973 US) and *Godspell* (1973 US).

The year 1975 seems to have been the key year for the appearance of British rock opera films, with the release of *Tommy*, the rock opera *par excellence*, *Lisztomania* and *The Rocky Horror Picture Show*, which could be read as a parody not only of the Classical musical and its offspring the pop musical, but also of the excesses of the rock opera itself. Ken Russell became one of the British directors to specialize in musical films, making a number of highly acclaimed dramatized documentaries for the BBC, about the lives of composers such as Edward Elgar and Claude Debussy. Russell's *The Music Lovers* (1970) was made for the cinema and portrayed the life of Pyotr Illyich Tchaikovsky (played by Richard Chamberlain) in spectacular terms, illustrating events in his life through his pieces of music. Russell went on to produce something similar in *Mahler* (1974), but then turned to the rock music world for his highly singular biographical film of Franz Liszt, *Lisztomania*. *Tommy* had already been staged as a successful rock concert and stage show developed by The Who around their concept album of the same title.[49] The film's song sequences regularly provide more narrative than the non-musical interludes that appear between them, so that the film is driven by the songs and their words rather than by action and dialogue. Notable song sequences include *Fiddle About* (with Uncle Ernie played by The Who drummer Keith Moon), *Acid Queen* sung by Tina Turner, *Eyesight to the Blind* by Eric Clapton (as a preacher) and *Pinball Wizard* sung by Elton John, who plays a piano that is simultaneously a large pinball machine. At times, in the manner of operative recitative, characters simply convert dialogue to singing.[50]

Following in a similar stylistic vein, Russell's *Lisztomania* attempted to imbue art music with the excitement of rock music, through a biography of composer and pianist Franz Liszt. Songs were forged from Liszt's instrumental pieces, and again The Who's singer Roger Daltrey took the lead role. There were more traditional transmissions of high culture; some were plain and reverend, like Southern Television's filming in 1977 of Peter Hall's staging of Mozart's *Don Giovanni* at Glyndebourne (with Bernard Haitink with London Philharmonic Orchestra). It includes some superimpositions of close-ups of faces over the domination of long shots of the whole stage. Others aimed to make high culture more accessible, such as the film *The Tales of Beatrix Potter* (1971), which used sumptuous costume (and occasional close-ups) and sets (by Christine Edzard) to make the performance by the Royal Ballet more than a simple recording of an event on stage.

The Rocky Horror Picture Show, while not often being called a rock opera, certainly shares some of their stylistic aspects and, indeed, parodies them. Its overblown song sequences and outrageous *mise en scene* is, however, consistently played for irony and comedy. The *Time Warp* song sequence, for example, parodies traditional dance sequences in film musicals by inserting shots of narrator Charles Gray, whose flat speaking of the song words and dancing instructions break the continuity of the musical sequence. All the songs appear using the lip-synch mode, relating the film strongly to the traditions of the film musical, which it is burlesquing. It includes a reference to Busby Berkeley's sets in film musical films of the early 1930s in the *Don't Dream It, Be It* sequence, which is staged in a swimming pool and begins with an overhead shot. The film was developed from Richard O'Brien's stage show and made quickly with almost the same cast.[51] It features the rock singer Meat Loaf, before his international success, who appears and sings a self-consciously clichéd rock'n'roll song *Hot Patootie – Bless My Soul* after arriving on a motorcycle. While initially not a notable success, *The Rocky Horror Picture Show* has become a significant cult film, perennially able to fill cinemas since its release. Andy Medhurst contends that since the mid-1960s, "... pop and cinema ceased to interrelate in any meaningful way [and that]... since the mid-60s the pop film was at best marginal to what remained of British cinema".[52] While the type of film that was based on pop music had changed, it was still a notable aspect of British films, many of which were not musicals in the traditional sense. For example, Lindsay Anderson made a sequel to his highly acclaimed *If...* (1969) in *O Lucky Man!* (1973), where lead character Mick Travis (Malcolm MacDowell) had gone from public school to working as a travelling salesman. The film had a highly singular musical commentary, at times performed on screen by Alan Price, one of the successful 1960s group The Animals. While the use of such a Greek Chorus, musically commenting on the action, was hardly new, the use of Alan Price within the film's diegetic world added an extra dimension to a highly imaginative film. In a different vein, Alan Parker made *Bugsy Malone* (1976) with a cast that consisted wholly of children, including American child actors Scott Baio and Jody Foster. It was a gangster drama set in prohibition-era US and included much in the way of stereotypical paraphernalia parodied through the use of children in adult roles. For example, gunfights involved guns that shot messy cream rather than bullets. Attractive to adults as well as children, Bugsy Malone managed a rare energy, with strong acting and some vigorous song sequences. In fact, in some ways it proved to be one of the most traditional film musicals of the decade.

According to Andrew Higson, "The late 1970s... was the end of the low budget British genre film, one of those cinematic forms that proved to be no longer commercially viable. In effect, this whole category of film-making has moved into television."[53] However, there was a regular supply of concert films throughout the decade, even if film musicals, particularly of the traditional sort, had become something of a rarity. Even so, the new form of musicals involving pop groups had become one of the low budget films par excellence of the 1960s and 1970s. At the end of the 1970s, the advent of punk rock primarily centred on music and fashion, proclaiming a new aesthetic or anti-aesthetic. The Sex Pistols made *The Great Rock'n'Roll Swindle* (1980), which was a spoof rockumentary that also included some more traditional film musical elements.[54] *Breaking Glass* (1980) mixed the traditional with a sheen of punk style. It has a highly conventional storyline about a music star and her relationship with an exploitative manager. This was also in effect a backstage musical, so it consistently used the performance mode for stage appearances. *Breaking Glass* contains two hit singles, *Eighth Day* and *Will You*, and the film made singer and actress Hazel O'Connor a short-lived star.[55]

The 1980s

The 1980s saw something of a revival in British film production, although this was not focused notably on musical films. *Pink Floyd: The Wall* (1982), directed by Alan Parker, was constructed around the group's very successful concept album released three years earlier. Formally, it follows the rock operas that had appeared in the middle of the previous decade. There is virtually no dialogue in the film. The songs provide the progression which, in the case of the climactic *The Trial*, embody a parody of operatic recitative's interaction between characters, rendered in a ponderous approximation of the style of Gilbert and Sullivan. Most of the songs provided a degree of narrative, which adds to the somewhat elliptical visual narrative development to form a relatively coherent whole. Almost all of the songs appear as non-diegetic music, aiding the visual unfolding of the story.[56] In fact, the film's images provide little more than an extended visual accompaniment to the soundtrack which had already been a best-selling LP,[57] as had the single *Another Brick in the Wall* (Part Two).

An older established artist, Paul McCartney returned to films with an extraordinarily unadventurous musical, *Give My Regards to Broad Street* (1984). The traditional attractions of The Beatles's songs meant that the film was imbricated with nostalgia, and yet oddly proved less effective for nostalgia marketing than other areas of pop music culture. McCartney wrote and starred in *Give My Regards to Broad Street* which was an unmitigated financial and aesthetic disaster: "... one of the most embarrassing experiences for everyone involved, including CBS Records and 20th Century Fox, who just couldn't bring themselves to tell the emperor he had no clothes on."[58] What on-paper must have seemed a surefire success ended up as a lifeless failure.

There were some more singular musical films during the decade, such as *Shock Treatment* (1981), made by the team behind *The Rocky Horror Picture Show* and *Billy the Kid and the Green Baize Vampire* (1985), which was a traditional film musical directed by Alan Clarke, who had made his name with hard-hitting social realist television dramas. The story was about snooker competitions, leading to a climactic contest between Billy the Kid (Phil Daniels) and the Green Baize Vampire (Alun Armstrong). This was something of an anomaly in British film production of the time, where film musicals of a traditional sort – an integrated musical with songs sung using the lip-synch mode – were extremely rare, and was co-produced by Lord Grade's ITC television production company. In the same year, however, Britain produced its most expensive film musical for decades, *Absolute Beginners* (1985). This was a highly bold musical, featuring lavish sets, detailed choreography and stars such as David Bowie (and is the subject of a detailed analysis in a later chapter in this book). However, it was at least partially responsible for the collapse of the British film "renaissance" through the financial ruin of Goldcrest.[59] Subsequently, Bowie traded in his reputation for being at the cutting edge of pop music in the 1970s for an appearance as the king of the fairies in *Labyrinth* (1986). He sings a few songs in this children's film directed by Jim Henson of *The Muppet Show*, which was hardly befitting his earlier more controversial musical image. Henson had already made two spin-offs from the successful television puppet series: *The Muppet Movie* (1979) and *The Great Muppet Caper* (1981).

Aria (1987) was an interesting attempt to reinvigorate the film musical form, through mixing the format of pop video with operatic arias. It had sections directed by Nic Roeg, Robert Altman, Bruce Beresford, Jean-Luc Godard and Ken Russell, and in some ways it looked back to Russell's musical work of the previous two decades.

The 1990s and beyond

In the 1990s, while London's West End stages have been dominated by musicals played to packed houses, the British film musical has been only an occasional occurrence. A notable strand followed a trend in the 1980s and has attempted to take advantage of Britain's significant heritage in terms of pop music. *Velvet Goldmine* (1998 UK/US) looked back to the glam rock era of the 1970s and included characters who were thinly disguised representations of real pop stars (Jonathan Rhys Meyers as the David Bowie character and Ewan McGregor as the Iggy Pop character).[60] American director Todd Haynes was sensitive to the period, utilizing many songs of the period on the soundtrack, reworked by contemporary musicians.

There was something of a revival of the British pop musical, which had remained relatively dormant since the rock operas of the 1970s. Backstage rock musical *The Commitments* (1991 US–UK–Ireland) was a British–American co-production shot in Ireland. It was a great success, and directed by Alan Parker, who had made something of a habit of directing film musicals, having directed *Bugsy Malone* and *Pink Floyd: The Wall*, and going on to direct Madonna in *Evita* (1997 US–UK), adapted from a British stage play about the wife of a fascist dictator. *The Commitments's* use of American soul and blues songs mixed with the Dublin setting gave a vigour that marked it out as a highly distinct film. Less financially successful and less critically acclaimed was *Buddy's Song* (1990), which built the short-lived musical career of its star, Chesney Hawkes.[61] It revived in a remarkably precise manner the "rise to the top" format of the earliest British films to utilize pop music, pop musicals of the late 1950s like *The Tommy Steele Story* (1957) and *The Golden Disc* (1958). Similarly related to pop music film tradition, *Spice World* (1997) followed remarkably closely some of the strategies of The Beatles's vehicle *A Hard Day's Night* (1964). The whole proceedings were imbued with an irony that, by the late 1990s, was probably the only way to deal with an unsophisticated narrative about a group on tour.

An inventive take on the musical was *Hear My Song* (1991), directed by Peter Chelsom and starring Adrian Dunbar as a club owner who has to find the real Josef Locke (Ned Beatty) after presenting a fraud in concert. Another innovative musical was *Wild West* (1992), an engaging film about the endeavours of a British–Asian country and Western band. *Back Beat* (1993) was a biography of The Beatles before fame, focusing on Stuart Sutcliffe (played by Stephen Dorff). This backstage musical paved the way for *The Beatles Anthology*, the first part of which was released in 1996, including three double-albums and a television series.[62] Indeed, the 1990s saw a number of backstage musicals, such as rock musicals *Velvet Goldmine* and *Still Crazy* (1998), while *Little Voice* (1998) used many old show songs and was perhaps the nearest thing to a traditional musical that Britain had produced for some years. A rather less glamorous film was *Still Crazy* (1998), written by successful team Dick Clement and Ian La Frenais (who had written television series including *The Likely Lads, Porridge* and *Auf Wiedersehen Pet*). This charted the reunion of an aging group of rockers, a subject that was increasingly relevant in the face of the welter of group reunions that began taking place in the late 1990s (such as the Sex Pistols in 1996).

One new pop music phenomenon that merited a film vehicle was the all-female group the Spice Girls, who promoted what they called "Girl Power" and were very popular among young, often pre-teenage, girls. After bursting into the British charts in 1995, within a couple of years they were big enough to have their own film vehicle. This was a rarity since the pop group vehicle's heyday in the 1960s with The Beatles, Gerry and the Pacemakers and the Dave Clark Five. *Spice World* (1997) was premised upon a series of songs by the Spice Girls, which appeared as non-diegetic music, diegetic ambient music and as fully blown performances. The film was a backstage musical, and showed the four Spice Girls doing promotional and musical activities. They occupy a tour bus with a union jack flag painted on the roof, which also has a space for each group member reminiscent of The Beatles's communal house in *Help!* (1965). *Spice World* had more similarities with The Beatles's debut film, *A Hard Day's Night* (1964), and makes very literate references to both pop music culture and pop culture more generally. A review at the time noted: "Mums and dads unmoved by the less subtle of their offspring's noisy pleasures (Michael Barrymore's jerky dancing, Spice music itself) can pass the time unravelling dozens of affectionate references to 1970s pop culture, or revelling in the script's self-awareness. . . . With fantasy sequences, parodies and much offstage inter-Spice interplay, it sends up the amiable idiocy of pop packaging – and also the slow-witted mass-media response to it."[63] *Spice World* has its tongue firmly in its cheek. Perhaps by the late 1990s, irony was the only way that pop group vehicles could be credible. Such sophistication was not evident in some of the pop musicals of the 1990s.

The Full Monty (1997) was a notable international success, and a rare British attempt to produce a dancing musical, being set among unemployed steelworkers in Sheffield who start up a male striptease troupe. Another success, also based in a post-industrial landscape in the north of England, was *Billy Elliott* (2000), a dance musical about a young boy's dreams of success as a dancer against unsympathetic surroundings. Both of these films had an international impact and neither were musicals in the traditional sense. Similarly, *Babymother* (1998) was an energetic film that depicted the reggae "dancehall" culture of north London. Directed by Julian Henriques, the film included some songs where characters interacted using the lip-synch mode, and thus followed the traditions of the film musical, which was something of a rarity in such films. *Julie and the Cadillacs* (1999) followed the progress of a Liverpool-based pop band in the wake of The Beatles, which was publicized as the first "genuine" British musical of the 1990s. Made for £2 million, and modelled to some degree after *The Commitments*,[64] it sank without trace, while *I'll Be There* (2003) was perhaps more of an unexpected failure. It stars the matured child prodigy singer Charlotte Church as the long-lost daughter of an ageing pop star (played by the film's director, Craig Ferguson). Church had gained fame at an early age with traditional songs aimed at a mature market. This film was part of a seemingly successful attempt to re-brand her, allied with newspaper stories of drunken escapades and the recording of some pop singles.

More upmarket attempts at musicals included Nic Roeg's *Othello* (1995 UK-US), an opera adaptation, and *Lucia* (1998), where a brother and a sister decide to stage a Donizetti opera (*Lucia di Lammermoor*) in their stately home. This individual film was directed by veteran producer Don Boyd. Mike Leigh's *Topsy-Turvy* (1999) was an extraordinary attempt to make a backstage musical about Gilbert and Sullivan. Set around the performance of *The Mikado*, the film appears to leave behind many of the usual concerns of Leigh's work. Andrew Lloyd Webber's massive stage success has been translated to only a couple of musicals: *Evita* (1996 UK-US) and *Phantom of the Opera* (2004 UK-US). The former was directed by Alan Parker, something of a musicals specialist, and starred Madonna. Eschewing the use of dialogue, it reinvented the operetta form, where every word of dialogue is sung, although most are songs in themselves (arias, one might say). *Phantom of the Opera* was a major international success, starring Gerard Butler and directed by American director Joel Schumacher, it was a stylish and sumptuous production with extended song sequences to match those of the stage version.

Conclusion

This chapter provided a panoramic overview of British film musicals, running from the beginning of sound cinema to the present day. From the successes of British musicals in the 1930s with stars such as Gracie Fields, Jessie Matthews and George Formby, the British film musical declined dramatically, although it still made occasional appearances in later years. To some degree, it was enlivened by pop and rock music, most notably from the mid-1960s to the mid-1970s. The late 1950s and early 1960s are characterized by attempts to include pop music within the existing modes of musical film, as the pop musical and the revue. The pop musicals of this period were the dominant form for films featuring pop stars. They used the style of traditional film musicals but changed the content, mixing in pop music and youth concerns with the recipe of the classical musical. By the 1970s, the tendencies of progressive rock allied to the large-scale business operation that rock music had become, resulted in the crassly extrovert and pretentious rock operas. Although these were quite quickly forgotten by film criticism and film historians, their opulence and bravado mark them out as among the most distinguished British films produced since the Second World War. In the mid-1980s, musicals such as *Pink Floyd: The Wall* and *Give My Regards to Broad Street* looked back very directly to the rock operas of the 1970s. Since that time, it is tempting to reason that pop and rock music that could have fed into rock musicals is now feeding into musical stage shows in London's West End and on Broadway. Good examples are *Mamma Mia!* which uses the music of Abba and *We Will Rock You* using the music of Queen.

Despite its success in the 1930s, the film musical did not manage to establish itself as a perennial of British cinema in the same way that the forma managed in Hollywood. John Huntley declared in 1947:

> Britain has not had very much to do with the evolution of the big scale musical...For a time, we went on steadily turning out modest but quite good pictures, occasionally incorporating musical numbers, rarely designed on the Hollywood pattern.[65]

It is John Huntley's view that due to an inability to compete with the Hollywood film musical, British film production tended to neglect that form in favour of cinematic forms in which it had had more international success. While there may be some truth in his argument, the plethora of British music hall stars and stage or radio singers who made a successful transition to the cinema screen suggests otherwise. Similarly, the way that British pop singers in the late 1950s and 1960s managed to adapt the traditional film musical format and the way that rock operas took off in Britain in the 1970s suggest that Huntley was wrong to see Britain as marginal to the film musical.[66]

8
Stage to Screen: Whatever Happened to the British Musical Adaptation?

There has been a familiar relationship between the British stage and the British cinema, which has been manifest most clearly in the relationship between stage musicals and film musicals. This is what might be expected, in that the overwhelming majority of stars, musicians, songs and shows in musical films have originated on the stage. However, there have been some distinct surprises in what has failed to be translated from stage to screen. Some very successful British stage musicals have not managed to make the transition to the screen, while others, conversely, have been made into film musicals in Hollywood rather than at home. London's West End theatres consistently have been full of highly successful musicals, many of them home-grown. The abiding question is to wonder why these have only rarely translated to musical films. Over the past few decades, there have been massive stage successes for Andrew Lloyd Webber's stage musicals, not only in London's West End but also on Broadway and elsewhere abroad, and yet these have not yet been exploited by British cinema to the degree that might have been expected, although Hollywood has cashed in on a few of them.

A number of notable individuals have had a great impact on the British musical stage, with varying degrees of success in films too. It is something of an enigma as to why Noel Coward never made a British film musical. Even his successful stage musicals were only rarely made into films. It is interesting how maverick talent on the British musical stage (and in the popular music industry as well) has failed to be exploited by the British film industry to the degree that it might have been. Apart from Coward, this chapter will look at the career of another renaissance man, Anthony Newley, who made a British film musical but found more success in Hollywood, and other figures such as Andrew Lloyd Webber, whose films have been adapted after some time by Hollywood rather than by Britain. This has been against a backdrop of very successful runs in London's West End, where the musical has been a perennial while on screen it gradually has become marginalized in film production, evolving into a more occasional production rather than a staple of cinema.

In terms of scholarly attention, there has been a surprisingly lack of interest in the transposition of musical successes from the stage to the screen. Geoff Brown's article on the relationship of British film to theatre concentrates overwhelmingly on non-musical stage productions and their adaptation, making hardly a mention of musicals.[1] This chapter will chart a perspective on the relationship between the British musical stage and the screen, concluding with a more detailed consideration of three notable figures of the British musical stage and their relationship to the screen.

Traditions

What became known as the "English musical comedy tradition" can be traced largely to plays with music in the eighteenth century, most notably John Gay's *The Beggar's Opera*, which debuted in 1728 and used familiar song tunes. This tradition was crystallized by the later series of successful musical comedies of Gilbert and Sullivan. This pairing produced 14 comic operas between 1871 and 1896, including *Ruddigore, H.M.S. Pinafore, Iolanthe, The Mikado* and *The Gondoliers*. These were massively popular and have remained something of a perennial ever since. They certainly cast a shadow over stage musicals in the early part of the twentieth century. In his review of the state of English music in 1945, critic Eric Blom looked negatively at developments in popular music over the first four decades of the century:

> the popular aspects of music in our days. They are not pleasing. Operetta has steadily degenerated since Sullivan's time, and although Lionel Monckton, Howard Talbot and others – we must disregard the vogue of Viennese purveyors like Léhar, Leo Fall and Oscar Straus – still managed to whip up some pleasant froth, the English modern musical comedy falls quite flat.[2]

Blom noted that the American musical stage of the time was superior to the British. His review is a strange and highly opinionated picture that (certainly in terms of its discussion of "serious" music) now seems highly eccentric, but most likely embodied a certain conservative and elitist view of musical activity.[3]

The European (largely Austrian) tradition of operetta had a significant impact in Britain as elsewhere. Its most notable indigenous manifestations were the comic operas of Gilbert and Sullivan, which were comedies with a sprinkling of rousing, comic songs. The earliest adaptation of Gilbert and Sullivan to the film was *The Mikado* (1938), directed by Victor Schertzinger. It was produced by the D'Oyly Carte company, which had been formed by theatre manager Richard D'Oyly Carte, who had done much to keep Gilbert and Sullivan's collaboration together at the time and had developed theatres on the back of the musicals's success. The biographical aspect of the pairing was emphasized in Launder and Gilliat's *The Story of Gilbert and Sullivan* (1953) and Mike Leigh's *Topsy-Turvy* (1999), which also included extensive on-stage performance sequences, concerning the production of *The Mikado*. However, it is worth noting that the perennial favourites of Gilbert and Sullivan translated rather less to the screen that might have been expected.

British cinema had a good hunting ground for its material on the British stage, where successful stage musicals were often relatively quickly adapted for the screen. Ivor Novello was not only a successful actor and writer but a tremendously successful songwriter. Among other songs which he wrote, *Keep the Home Fires Burning* became massively popular during the First World War. Novello wrote exotic and escapist musicals during the 1930s, such as *Glamorous Nights* (1935), *Careless Rapture* and *The Dancing Years* (1939), the latter of which had an extended run throughout the Second World War. *The Dancing Years* had something of the operetta about it in that it started in early 1900s Vienna, but was still essentially a play with songs.

Chu Chin Chow debuted on stage in London in 1916 and ran for a number of years. It was a fine example of the popular desire for exotic Orientalism, being inspired by the story of Ali Baba and the Forty Thieves from the *Arabian Nights* and set in Baghdad. It included Westerners under the spell of inscrutable and treacherous Easterners and included the song *Any Time's Kissing Time*. It had some large-scale musical numbers with dances and flamboyant costumes, which were translated into the film version of *Chu Chin Chow* (1934), directed by Walter Forde and featuring George Robey, Fritz Kortner and Sino-American actress Anna May Wong. It had derived its production pretty much straight from the stage version of the time, a clear option for film production the world over. Probably, the most successful British stage musical of the 1930s was *Me and My Girl*, which debuted in 1937. Its success inspired a rapid adaptation to celluloid, and it was made into the film *The Lambeth Walk* (1939). *Me and My Girl* had been one of the most successful West End musicals of all time. It was written by L. Arthur Rose and Douglas Furber, and had music by Noel Gay (who had been born Reginald Armitage but took a *nom de plume* that conflated Noel Coward and singer Maisie Gay). Lupino Lane produced and starred in the play, about a Cockney who learns that he is really a lord and goes to live at a country hall. *The Lambeth Walk* took its name from the most famous song in the play, and reduced the number of songs in the film to only two (*The Lambeth Walk* and *Me and My Girl*).[4]

British stage musicals had been popular at home, but in the late 1940s and early 1950s they were increasingly marginalized by imports from Broadway. Rodgers and Hammerstein's earliest collaboration *Oklahoma!* came onto the British stage in 1947. According to Dominic Shellard, it "recast the template of the musical".[5] It broke the form's convention of starting with a big number, included a murder and was extremely simple in terms of set and song melody. This led to a welter of American musicals hitting London, although there were still home-grown musicals, such as *Bless the Bride* (1947, at the Adelphi) written by Vivian Ellis, *King's Rhapsody* (1949, Palace) and *Call Me Madam* (1952, Coliseum). Discussing the period from the end of the Second World War to the mid-1950s, Shellard notes that

> The appeal of the musicals for British audiences was matched only by the appeal of their profitability for theatre producers.... Whether a license to print money or not (adumbrating the West End in the 1980s and 1990s), the sheer proliferation of the genre on the London stage at this time does refute the notion that this was a glamour-starved period for the London stage.[6]

Some significant British productions of the time included *The Boy Friend*, first staged in 1953 and written by Sandy Wilson. It was a pastiche of musical comedy from the 1920s and made its lead Julie Andrews into a star. This was made into a film by Ken Russell in 1971, starring the model Twiggy. Another notable production was *Salad Days*, debuting in 1954 and written by Julian Slade and Dorothy Reynolds, which was about a magic piano that caused people to start dancing. Other British stage musicals included Sandy Wilson's *Divorce Me, Darling* (1964, including the songs *No Harm Done* and *Out of Step*), *Phil the Fluter* (1969, about Irish entertainer Percy French and including songs he made famous such as *That's Why the Poor Man's Dead* and *Abdul Abulbul Ameer*), *Twang!* (including the song *Dreamchild*) and *Grab Me a Gondola* (1956, including the songs *I Want a Man not a Mouse* and *That's My Biography*). None were made into films.

J.B. Priestley's *The Good Companions* (1956) was remade with little added to the version 20 years earlier (1937), which also stood close to the stage adaptation from 1929 of the original novel. This backstage musical had all songs performed on stage (using the performance mode) and set up a solid divide between backstage drama with the music hall company and their on-stage musical activities.[7] There were two adaptations of Ivor Novello stage plays with songs *Wonderful Things* (1957) and *Let's be Happy* (1957), both of which I mentioned briefly earlier, starred Errol Flynn. Both films were directed by Herbert Wilcox and also featured his wife Anna Neagle. Another stage production to find rapid adaptation to the screen was *Expresso Bongo* in 1958, released as a film in 1959, starring Cliff Richard and Laurence Harvey.

Lionel Bart's successful career as stage songwriter began with *Lock Up Your Daughters* and *Fings Ain't Wot They Used t'Be* (both in 1959), the latter of which was one of the most successful musicals of the turn of the 1960s. Its depictions of the working class showed something of what was to come from that decade, where polite middle-class plays (musicals included) receded dramatically. Bart started out writing songs for rock'n'roll singer Tommy Steele, and later for Shane Fenton and Anthony Newley. He wrote the massive hit *Little White Bull* for Steele, which had appeared in *Tommy the Toreador* (1959). In the same year, his stage musical *Fings Ain't Wot They Used t'Be* was staged by Joan Littlewood at the Theatre Workshop in Stratford, east London. It was full of lowlifes and criminals and looked back decidedly to John Gay's *The Beggar's Opera* two centuries earlier. In 1960, Bart's *Oliver!*, derived from Charles Dickens's *Oliver Twist*, opened and was a significant success. This was made into a film in 1968, directed by Carol Reed. It retained some of the rough and ready aspects of Bart's stage original. Reed's hell raising nephew Oliver Reed played Bill Sykes while the lead role was played by newcomer Mark Lester, a charming child who was unable to pitch anywhere near what the songs required. The crucial role of Fagin was taken by Ron Moody on stage and screen, and rewrote the role from Dickens's original and Alec Guinness's film version (1948), with Jewish writer and actor removing the anti-Semitic edge. Bart went on to write *Blitz* (1962), about a family during the Second World War, and the Liverpool-set *Maggie May* (1964), although his career went into hiatus later in the decade.

The 1960s saw regular adaptations of stage musicals as films. Anthony Newley's *Stop the World I Want to Get Off* opened on stage in 1961 and was made into a film in 1966. *Oh What a Lovely War!* also opened on stage in 1961, a politicized play developed at the Theatre Workshop, and was made into a film in 1969. It was an extraordinary re-enactment of events of the First World War accompanied by popular songs of the time. The film concludes with a startling crane shot that moves outwards and upwards to reveal a gigantic field war graves. There was a British–American co-production of *Half a Sixpence* (1963), which had been adapted for the stage by Beverley Cross and composer David Heneker from H.G. Wells's *Kipps*. Rock'n'roll singer-turned all-round entertainer Tommy Steele starred both on stage and on screen. A successful stage play was *Something Funny Happened on the Way to the Forum*, which quickly was made into a film and released in 1966 as a British–American co-production. The songs by Stephen Sondheim took a back seat to the comedy, with the film featuring American comedians Phil Silvers and Zero Mostel. Other notable stage musicals from the middle of the decade included *The Canterbury Tales* (1969), which attempted to update Chaucer with pop music, and *Charlie Girl* (1965), which was about a class divide and starred Joe Brown and Anna Neagle. However, these were not adapted for the screen, as film musicals became something of a rarity, not only in British film production but also in the output of Hollywood.

The 1970s began with a financial "crisis" for British film production. The loss of American investment forced the industry to tighten its belt and make films less frequently and with substantially lower budgets. The British stage was not notably affected, producing hit musicals including Anthony Newley and Lesley Bricusse's *The Good Old Bad Old Days* (1972), Andrew Lloyd Webber and Tim Rice's *Jesus Christ Superstar* (1972), which was made into an American film the following year, while there was the less-mainstream success of *The Rocky Horror Show* (1973) and children's musical *Smike* (1980), an adaptation of Nicholas Nickleby written by Simon May, one of the most successful writers of television theme music in Britain.

There were film adaptations of more upmarket musical product. For example, *The Tales of Beatrix Potter* (1971) was an adaptation of a Royal Ballet stage show that took the stage ballet and set it among Christine Edzard's sumptuous film sets. With similar upmarket credentials, Peter Schaffer's *Amadeus* was first staged in 1979. It was directed by Peter Hall, who had worked on opera at Glyndebourne, and had Mozart's music arranged by respected composer Harrison Birtwhistle.[8] It started at the National Theatre and then moved to the West End in the early 1980s. It used plenty of loud recordings of Mozart's music, often in a highly dramatic manner, most notably perhaps his *Requiem*. *Amadeus* was made into an American film in 1984, directed by Milos Forman. Ken Russell became something of a specialist director of musical films, often following art music subjects. Working for the BBC, he had made dramatized documentaries about the lives of composers including Claude Debussy, Bela Bartok and Edward Elgar. These were highly acclaimed for their drama and illustration of the composer's music. After *Billion Dollar Brain* (1968) and *Women in Love* (1969), Russell directed *The Music Lovers* (1970), starring Richard Chamberlain as Tchaikovsky, which again exploited the potential dramatization of existing classical music with visual bravura and spectacle.[9] He then went on to make more in the way of imaginative composer biopics, *Mahler* (1974) and *Lisztomania* (1975). Russell's *Tommy* had originally been developed as a stage show in 1969 emanating from The Who's concept album. It was the apogee of a cycle of "rock operas" that were definitely ambitious, some might say pretentious. Denisoff and Romanowski discuss the overblown artistic status accorded to *Tommy* and how it was performed in opera houses and legit theatres: "A Columbia Pictures advertisement was pure hype: '*Tommy* is greater than any painting, opera, piece of music, ballet or dramatic work that this century has produced.' "[10] Certainly such terms were never used for the discussion of *The Rocky Horror Picture Show*, which started as a stage production at the Royal Court Upstairs in 1973 and was made into a film in 1975, changing little. It pastiched elements of the science fiction film, the Hammer horror film and 1950s rock'n'roll, making a potent and individual mix that has retained and built on its cult status ever since.

Towards the end of the twentieth century, British musicals were not only a success on West End stages but also exported well, most notably to Broadway, at least partially reversing the trend since the 1940s of the British musical stage being dominated by American products. These productions were often characterized by a barrage of special effects, including amplified music, hydraulic set movement, pyrotechnics and special lighting effects. These musicals also tended towards the sentimental – not a trait normally associated with British culture – and contained very accessible music, written in a highly populist and quite conservative style. In many ways, they looked back at the earlier tradition of operetta.

An important figure in these developments was theatre producer and impresario Cameron Mackintosh, who rose to a pre-eminent position in London's West End, producing a startling succession of money-spinning musicals. He famously and arrogantly called Broadway "just another stop on the American tour", and has since been honoured in Britain with a knighthood. His collaboration with Andrew Lloyd Webber was an essential part of the buoyancy of London's theatre-land at this time. Lloyd Webber's musicals will be discussed in more detail later. Apart from Lloyd Webber's work, Mackintosh brought the French stage musical *Les Misérables* to London in 1985, engaging the Royal Shakespeare Company and respected director Trevor Nunn. Many other theatrical successes of the last decades of the twentieth century included Willie Russell's plays that regularly incorporated his songs, such as the stage musical *Blood Brothers* (1983), about two brothers separated at birth and adopted, who later meet and clash.[11] Other successful musicals included *Chess* (1986), written by Bjorn Ulvaeus and Benny Andersson from Abba, *Miss Saigon* (1989) and Shoenberg and Bubil's *Martin Guerre* (1995).

One highly notable aspects of the success of stage musicals at this point was the importance of merchandising, with all manner of readily identifiable logos adorning products. *Les Misérables* had a female child with hair blowing in the wind, while *Cats* had a pair of cat's eyes with the irises dancing. Marketing included soundtrack albums and singles, much as did the tradition for film musicals, glossy souvenir programmes full of photographs, T-shirts, badges, posters – in fact, these were all the trappings that had become a staple of rock concerts in the 1970s, along with a few other items, such as coffee mugs, stuffed toys and key rings. *Cats* was the likely starting point for this saturation marketing. Musicals on stage have always retained popularity in London's West End "theatre land". However, in the 1980s and 1990s, musicals became endemic on London's principal stages, driven by the increasing appeal of such theatre to a middle-class "middle brow" audience. According to Dominic Shellard,

The re-emergence of a genre popular in the 1950s was the single most noticeable feature of the West End in the 1980s, but instead of relying on American imports, London became famous for its efficient and profitable staging of home-grown musicals. Their dominance has drawn much adverse comment and they are regularly accused of vari-ously blocking the entrance of writing into the West End, restricting choice, driving up prices and being intellectually light-weight, but their enduring popularity testifies to their ability to entertain on a grand scale (often marrying impressive technical feats with soaring melodies), their capacity to reach beyond the normal pool of theatre-goers, and the ingenuity with which they are marketed.[12]

A catalyst in this development were the musicals of (later Sir) Andrew Lloyd Webber and later international dancing show successes such as *Riverdance* and *Lord of the Dance*, both of which were derived at least partially from Irish folk music and dance. There were some isolated successes that translated well to screen. For example, the stage success of *Little Voice* led to a film adaptation in 1998. This was in some ways much more traditional than many other stage musicals of the time, utilizing established showtunes. These are performed in a club by reluctant singer "Little Voice" (Jane Horrocks) at the behest of a hustling manager (Michael Caine), who sings Roy Orbison's *It's Over* on a karaoke machine at the film's conclusion.

The British stage has always had a healthy appetite for musicals, which have been perennial successes. Screen musicals have not always been so successful and since their heyday in the 1930s have become increasingly only an occasional occurrence in British cinema. This is despite the fact that adaptation is often easy and that a massive stage success is almost a guarantee of cinema audiences. Furthermore, the film musical is a cinematic form that has a closer relationship to its stage parent than perhaps any other. However, some notable stage phenomena have failed to make the transition to film.[13]

Three individuals: Coward, Newley and Lloyd Webber

Across this historical backdrop of broad developments, painted in bold brushstrokes, the careers of a handful of noteworthy individuals play in an uneven fashion. These personages I will discuss are Noel Coward (1899–1973), Anthony Newley (1931–1999) and Andrew Lloyd Webber (1948–).

Noel Coward's career started from being a child prodigy for the stage to being a morale-boosting cheerleader during the Second World War. After the war, his position was more ambiguous, with his plays appearing quickly outmoded and he reinvented himself as a cabaret turn in places like Las Vegas and on American television, repackaging himself as the consummate Englishman for the American market. Alongside and as a part of this, he increasingly made cameos in films, perhaps the most notable being *Our Man in Havana* (1959) and *The Italian Job* (1969), the latter of which was directed by Peter Collinson, a protégé of Coward's.

Noel Coward had a mixed career as a playwright, actor and songwriter (and even wrote the musical score for a few films). His stage career was at its peak in the 1920s and 1930s, with him reaching celebrity status with *The Vortex* in 1924, which he wrote and starred in, and where no punches were pulled in a drama of drugs and sex. Coward had and projected a highly distinct persona, which made him a more public face than many others in the world of the London stage. This included a very self-conscious sense of sophistication and only a thin veil over his homosexuality. Rather than writing musicals, Coward created plays with songs, bringing energy, speed and wit and sophistication to London's West End theatres.

In 1916, Coward appeared in a stage musical with Cicely Courtneidge and written by her husband Jack Hulbert, called *The Light Blues*. Later, he wrote songs for stage reviews such as *London Calling* in 1923 (where Gertrude Lawrence sang *Parisian Pierrot*), *On With the Dance* in 1925 (which included *Poor Little Rich Girl*) and *This Year of Grace* in 1928 (which starred Jessie Matthews and Sonny Hale and included the song *A Room With a View*). In 1929, Coward's *Bitter Sweet* made its debut. It was a "nostalgia musical" that looked back to Viennese operettas of the turn of the century and was about an heiress who falls in love with her music teacher, and included the song *I'll See You Again*.

In 1930, *Private Lives* was a massive success, and Coward starred in it opposite Gertrude Lawrence, with whom he had a very close personal and official relationship. The play concerned a divorced couple who meet up again on holiday in Switzerland with new spouses, and was made into a Hollywood film in 1931, starring Robert Montgomery and Norma Shearer. He went on to write *Cavalcade*, which opened in 1931 and celebrated moments in British history using an ordinary family to unify events. It was a large-scale extravaganza, which included a massive set with hydraulic movements. Coward then went back to reviews with *Words and Music* in 1932 (which included *Mad About the Boy* and *Mad Dogs and Englishmen*). *Bitter Sweet* concerned a woman marrying a musician and then being wooed by a rich man. It was made into a film directed by Herbert Wilcox in 1933, and made a star of Anna Neagle. It contained some memorable song sequences, including a notably static camera for *I'll See You Again* and 360° pans for another song. *Bitter Sweet* was also adapted into a film by Hollywood in 1940, starring the highly successful musical pairing of Jeanette MacDonald and Nelson Eddy, who were famed for a series of lucrative film operettas. In 1934, he wrote, directed and acted in *Conversation Piece*, which was more of a turn back towards the Victorian operetta. In 1936, *Tonight at 8.30* had an innovative format of being nine short plays that would be performed on successive nights and in random order. Four of these were musicals. One of the short plays, *Still Life*, was extended to make the film *Brief Encounter* (1946), directed by David Lean.

During the Second World War, Coward worked tirelessly for the war effort, writing, producing, directing and starring in *In Which We Serve* (1942), about the crew of a sunken British ship. He also wrote and acted in *This Happy Breed* (1944), and wrote the adaptations of his plays *Blithe Spirit* (1945) and *Brief Encounter* (1945). For *In Which We Serve*, Coward even wrote the incidental music, in collaboration with Ray Douglas and Clifton Parker.

Coward wrote a succession of stage plays with music, including *Operette* (1938), an attempt at a Viennese-style operetta, *Sigh No More* in 1945, starring Cyril Ritchard and Joyce Grenfell, *Pacific 1860* (1946), *Ace of Clubs* (1950), *After the Ball* (1954) (an adaptation of Oscar Wilde's *Lady Windermere's Fan*) and *Sail Away* in 1961 (starring Elaine Stritch and set on a luxurious ocean liner). These were not filmed and, in fact, only a few of his stage plays were adapted for the screen.

Noel Coward's film career began as an extra pushing a wheelbarrow in a street scene in D.W. Griffith's British-made film *Hearts of the World* (1918). He acted in the American film *The Scoundrel* (1935), and then in *This Happy Breed* (1944) which was adapted from his play of 1939. *Blithe Spirit* (1945) was adapted by David Lean from Coward's stage play of 1941, including Margaret Rutherford, repeating her stage success as the clairvoyant. Coward starred in *The Astonished Heart* (1949), directed by Anthony Darnborough and Terence Fisher, which was derived from a short play of Coward's. This Gainsborough production also starred Celia Johnson and Margaret Leighton, while Coward also wrote the film's musical score. For CBS Television, he wrote and appeared in *Together With Music* (1955), a revue with a cast of two (Coward and Mary Martin). His filmed plays included *The Vortex* (1928), *Easy Virtue* (1928), *Cavalcade* (1933 US) and *Design for Living* (1933).[14] Coward's extraordinary *Cavalcade*, which followed an English family from the turn of century to the 1930s, included the song *Twentieth Century Blues*, and the Warner Brothers film, starring Clive Brook and Diane Wynard, won an Oscar for best picture.

It is something of an enigma as to why Coward's plays and songs did not make a string of successful films. His reputation was established and retained largely by the stage rather than film, or television, which he once suggested was something "one appeared on rather than watched."

Yet his foray into films was also limited. He wrote to his mother, "I'm not very keen on Hollywood...I'd rather have a nice up of cocoa."[15]

Coward was a key figure of the British stage and popular music in the twentieth century, although he often did not tie the two in traditional stage musical formats, the plays being more like plays with occasional song interludes. According to Cole Lesley, Coward's assistant, he did not learn from the innovations brought about by *Oklahoma!* and its integration of songs to further plot development.[16] While there were some attempts to use Coward as a power for the British cinema in the late 1920s, these failed.[17] Coward was at his peak just around the time that sound cinema was beginning and later he certainly failed to endeavour with a musical contribution to British cinema in the 1930s, as his life took on more of the character of a celebrity that he retained until his final years.

Anthony Newley was another remarkable figure in British music, stage and film. He wrote musicals and songs, sang and recorded songs, directed for stage, film and television, and acted. His career started at a tender age, as one of the principal child leads, as "the Artful Dodger" in David Lean's adaptation of Charles Dickens's *Oliver Twist* (1948). By the mid-1950s, he was appearing in West End plays such as *Cranks* and *NY*, while also appearing in small parts in films. By the end of the decade, he was prominent in films such as *Idle on Parade* (1959) and *Jazz Boat* (1960).

Newley starred in ATV's *The Strange World of Gurney Slade* in 1960, a remarkable television serial that prefigured the post-modern techniques of over 20 years later. He also had a short life as a chart-topping pop singer with songs like *Strawberry Fayre* and *Pop Goes the Weasel* in the early 1960s. He utilized a very distinctive cockney-style singing voice, which later was influential on British pop singers who wanted to adopt an indigenous voice, most clearly David Bowie. Newley's first play was very successful. *Stop the World I Want to Get Off* (opened in 1961), which was about ruthless ambition, starred Newley as "littlechap" and featured the later hit song *What Kind of Fool Am I?* This became a theme song for Newley. The show also included the songs *Once in a Lifetime* and *Gonna Build a Mountain*, and the show was a notable success in London and then on Broadway. This success led to a film adaptation released in 1966, directed by Philip Saville and starring Tony Tanner in the part originally played by Newley.

Newley wrote songs and appeared in *Doctor Dolittle* (1967 US) with Rex Harrison in the title role. He wrote, directed, wrote music for and acted in *Can Hieronymous Merkin Ever Forget Mercy Humppe and Find True Happiness?* (1969), a highly singular project that demonstrated the degree of risk that was being taken with films at the time. While the film was certainly highly personal to Newley, this white elephant film made certain that a career as film director did not beckon. Instead, he followed the lead of Noel Coward, and went into cabaret in Las Vegas. An impressively varied career finished with a short run (certainly shorter than had been planned) in the BBC's flagship soap opera *EastEnders* in the late 1990s.

Overall, Newley completed a remarkable career spanning the stage, films, records and involving writing, song-writing and directing. Indeed, if any single person can claim to have crossed all the boundaries of popular culture, it is surely Newley. No other individual can claim the range of successes that he managed, and this includes the adoption of experimental procedures in *The Strange World of Gurney Slade* and *Can Hieronymous Merkin...* He was an absolute rarity in his ability to excel in multiple fields, although he was erratic in veering from massive popular success to experiment and self-indulgent obscurity. Probably the best example of this was his trajectory from number one hit *Strawberry Fayre* to *Moogies Bloogies*, his collaboration with electronic musician and experimentalist Delia Derbyshire, who arranged and realized the *Doctor Who* theme for BBC television.

Andrew Lloyd Webber has been one of the most successful composer of stage musicals and undoubtedly the most successful British composer of musicals since Arthur Sullivan. Testament to his prodigious success is that he has been recognized by the British establishment, being knighted in 1992 and then made a Lord in 1997. Most of his productions, particularly the earlier ones, are collaborations with lyricist Tim Rice. Lloyd Webber made his debut with *Joseph and his Amazing Technicolor Dreamcoat* in 1968, which was written for schools production, with lyrics by Tim Rice. This has been a perennial favourite, with a television version of the successful British stage production made in 1991, starring Australian pop singer and actor Jason Donovan. There was another version on screen in 1999, starring 1970s teenybopper Donny Osmond in the lead role. In 1971, again in collaboration with Rice, his *Jesus Christ Superstar* opened. It began as a studio recording before it was a stage show. This was probably the first rock opera, with all the dialogue sung rather than a distinct divide between songs and acted scenes. *Jesus Christ Superstar's* startling success and long run in London started off a halcyon period for London's West End and home-made productions. It was made into a film in 1973, an American production directed by Canadian director Norman Jewison, who had directed the highly successful musical *Fiddler on the Roof* (1971 US).

Lloyd Webber has made a remarkable series of successful stage plays. *Tell Me on a Sunday* (1979) was also staged for television in 1979. *Evita* (1976), co-written with Tim Rice, was about the wife of Argentina's post-War dictator Juan Peron. It spawned three hit singles (Julie Covington's *Don't Cry For Me, Argentina*, Barbara Dickson's *Another Suitcase in Another Hall* and David Essex's *Oh What a Circus*). *Cats* (1981) was based on T.S. Eliot's *Old Possum's Book of Practical Cats*, included a hit for Elaine Page (*Memory*) and was staged by Trevor Nunn and thus had the patina of legit culture to it. There was a television programme that filmed the stage production in 1998.

Starlight Express (1984) was a spectacle involving a roller-skating cast and hydraulic stage (lyrics by Richard Stilgoe), and *Phantom of the Opera* (1986) (with Stilgoe and Charles Hart, after Gaston Leroux's novel) had a hit single for Michael Crawford with *The Music of the Night*. *Aspects of Love* (1989) had lyrics by Don Black and Charles Hart and was developed from a novel by David Garnett. It was adapted for television in 1993, and directed by Lloyd Webber himself. It starred Michael Ball as the soldier who falls in love with an actress. *Sunset Boulevard* (1993), *Whistle Down the Wind* (1997) in collaboration with rock singer songwriter Jim Steinman, *The Beautiful Game* (2000) in collaboration with comedian Ben Elton, *Bombay Dreams* (2002) and *The Woman in White* (2004) after Wilkie Collins's novel. Lloyd Webber cemented his critical position in relation to the success of London's West End theatreland. After setting up the Really Useful Theatre Company, at the turn of the Millennium, he bought 10 London theatres to add to those he already owned.

Lloyd Webber has also worked with Alan Parker, who is something of a specialist with film musicals. *Evita* (1996) was a British–American co-production, starring Madonna, Antonio Banderas and Jimmy Nail.[18] *Phantom of the Opera*, which opened in 1988, starring Michael Crawford and Sarah Brightman, Lloyd Webber's wife at the time, was made into an American film in 2004, directed by Joel Schumacher, and starring Gerard Butler.[19] Films *Aspects of Love* and *Sunset Boulevard* are due to be released in the future. There is certainly a cinematic possibility for his plays. Indeed, *Sunset Boulevard* and *Whistle Down the Wind* were both based on existing films, while *Bombay Dreams* was premised upon the production of a Bollywood film.[20]

Some have declared Lloyd Webber's work to be well-crafted but not very creative. Indeed, there is a tendency to rely on only one or two melodies per show. In *Cats*, for example, the melody for *Memory* keeps reappearing as a reassuring refrain that holds the rest of the musical enterprise together. Some of his composition has been dismissed as pastiche by music specialists, although this is irrelevant to the hordes of paying fans who have made his musicals among the most popular ever. He has also been criticized for lacking the craft of American musical composers such as Rodgers and Hammerstein or Stephen Sondheim, in that his shows rely on spectacle and pyrotechnics rather than dynamics and formal development and integration. However, it cannot be denied that he produces highly successful stage shows that consistently have wrested the initiative away from the United States to Britain, in terms of dominance of the world musical stage.

Conclusion

In Britain, the stage has been particularly virile and successful but the overwhelming majority of British stage musical successes have not translated to the screen. However, by the mid-2000s, successful stage musicals such as *Summer Holiday, Sunset Boulevard* or *Footloose* were derived from film originals. This appeared to be a turn around in the dominant way of thinking about the relationship between stage and screen, which traditionally saw the stage as the originator and the screen as the adaptor. The successful film *Billy Elliot* (2000), about a young boy from a mining community who wants to be a ballet dancer, was transported to the London stage as *Billy Elliot: The Musical*. The film was a notable success both home and abroad, receiving three Academy Award nominations. The stage version was created by many of the same team who had made the film, including director Stephen Daldry, choreographer Peter Darling and even film producers Working Title. One significant addition was a full score of songs and music by (Sir) Elton John. Similarly, *Chitty Chitty Bang Bang* was produced very successfully on stage in 2002, and derived directly from the film of 1968 (and the original book by Ian Fleming, published in 1964).

At times, there has been an extremely close relationship between the British musical stage and the musical films, most notably in the 1930s. Since that time, the two have drifted apart to a situation in recent years where London's West End theatres are full of successful musicals, many of which have a British origin, while the British film industry has made only a handful of musicals in the last decade. Stephen Guy, discussing the 1930s, has pointed out

> The notion of cinema as a branch of musical theatre was also signalled by the friendly attitude of the variety profession towards it (unlike radio, which it saw as a menace killing off theatre audiences and

offering a paucity of poorly paid work by compensation). For variety artists the cinema was seen as a good potential source of employment, as well as being genuinely beneficial for the profession.[21]

In more recent years, the buoyant state of the musical stage in Britain has begun to engulf the tradition of film musicals, and even led to respected film actors onto the stage. Significant individuals such as those I have discussed – Coward, Newley and Lloyd Webber, and others (also Novello and Bart) – have had differing and often indifferent relationships with the screen and often more consistent ones with the British stage. Indeed, their careers are testaments to the strength of the British musical stage. Coward's key work was for the stage and his career peaked too early for synchronized sound. Newley was eclectic and iconoclastic, but managed a remarkable career on stage, recording, film and television; indeed, one that has not been duplicated. Lloyd Webber, on the other hand, found his principal successes with the stage and has remained loyal to it despite the more recent adaptations of his massively successful musicals. His plays seem suited to big budget adaptations, and thus have not only been slow to be adapted but also have tended to be American or American–British co-productions. The success of a handful of American-made musicals in the late 1990s (such as Baz Luhrman's films and *Chicago* [2002]) has inspired further investment in screen versions of Lloyd Webber's musicals.

9
The Perpetual Busman's Holiday: Sir Cliff Richard and the British Pop Musical

Theodor Adorno's assertion that "popular music for the masses is a perpetual busman's holiday"[1] suggests to me the Cliff Richard film *Summer Holiday* (1963). In the film, Cliff Richard plays a mechanic who with some co-workers borrows a bus from their workplace and drives across Europe, serving up a number of wholesome songs along the way. Adorno's rather catchy phrase underlines what he saw as the conservative nature and function of popular music, and Cliff Richard's career perhaps has substantiated Adorno's observation. Starting as a rock'n'roll singer, Cliff (as he is fondly known in Britain) developed into a unique British cultural institution. He became a born-again Christian and spoke in favour of censorship, represented Britain in the Eurovision Song Contest, and sang spontaneously to the rain-drenched crowd at the Wimbledon Tennis Championship in the mid-1990s. His status as a key icon of Britain since the 1950s was confirmed by his knighthood in 1996, which was an almost unprecedented acknowledgment of the power of pop music and a confirmation of Cliff's cultural status. In the light of his popularity, it seems timely to reassess the earliest period of his career and the part that films played in his conversion from a rock'n'rolling Elvis look-alike to a mainstream youth figure. The conversion directly reflected the changes in pop music culture, the British negotiation of American youth culture and the addition of rock'n'roll to the traditional musical film.

Cliff Richard held a pre-eminent position in British pop music from 1959 until the appearance of the Beatles in 1963, producing 22 top-10 records.[2] He went straight from the pop chart to the cinema screen, making an inauspicious film debut in *Serious Charge* (1958), going on to costar in *Expresso Bongo* (1959), and then starring in three musical vehicles, *The Young Ones* (1961), *Summer Holiday* (1963) and *Wonderful*

Life (1964). I will focus on these films because after 1964 his film career waned, although he continued to appear in the occasional (unsuccessful) musical vehicle while his recording career proceeded without impediment.

Cliff's films illustrate the change from representing rock'n'rollers as delinquents (as in his first film) to representing them as "good kids" (in his later films). This duplicates the subsuming of rock'n'roll into established modes of popular music, something that is made highly apparent in the three musicals of the early 1960s. Cliff's films are also a part of the process, marking a hybridization of rock'n'roll with established modes of entertainment, both in terms of styles of music and in terms of the images. In *Sounds of the City*, Charlie Gillett cites Cliff as one of the major figures in the transformation of rock'n'roll into pop music,[3] and Dick Bradley refers to "rock-pop" as the musical form that emerged from the confluence of rock'n'roll and the desire of the record industry to sell to more than teenaged audiences.[4] Cliff's films not only manifest this but dramatize it – they act out the process.

In the late 1950s, there were rumblings in the British trade press about the possibilities of popular music working for British films. *Kinematograph Weekly* speculated that "the adage 'Trade follows the film' could become 'Box-office follows the record.'. . . [British] talent can do the most good for the British film industry in the vein of popular music: the vein that could carry the life-blood of British films to the heart of the American market."[5] Cliff's films looked like they might make an impression on the international cinematic body, but they failed, and it was left to The Beatles to bring British films to the US market as a part of the large-scale British record invasion of the US charts in the mid-1960s.

Icons: The coffee bar, the rock'n'roller

British rock'n'roll was pioneered in London's 2Is coffee bar in Soho, where Tommy Steele was discovered and Cliff played.[6] Around that time, a number of cafes became spaces that allowed the flowering of an organic pop music culture in Britain. They served as meeting places for the subculture youth and the only testing ground for people with musical ambitions. The 2Is care regularly had performances from what was to become the new generation of popular musicians, performers who were inspired by American rock'n'roll and who established an indigenous brand of the new form.

By the late 1950s and early 1960s, this culture as well as the national consciousness of the rock'n'roll coffee bar had been translated into a metonymic icon in British films. *Monthly Film Bulletin*'s review of *She Knows Y'Know* (1961) noted that the film has "a pop singer and a coffee bar thrown in to prove that the film's makers are bang up to date"[7]; the same publication's review of *Mix Me a Person* (1962) declared "*Mix Me A Person* has been done up contemporary – which roughly means that the nightclub of a few years ago has been replaced by guitars and espresso in Battersea".[8] By 1960, five films had already located rock'n'roll solidly in coffee bars: *The Tommy Steele Story* (1957), *Serious Charge* (1958), *The Golden Disc* (1958), *Beat Girl* (1959) and *Expresso Bongo* (1959). *The Tommy Steele Story* establishes through biography the coffee bar culture that was the centre of British rock'n'roll. It replayed Steele's "discovery" in the 2Is cafe and allowed him the rare and highly privileged position of playing himself in his own biographical film. *Expresso Bongo* is perhaps the film that documents the culture most fully. It not only satirizes the new breed of manipulative managers that grew up around the new musical culture but firmly sets the music's origin in coffee bars, situating rock'n'roller figures as a central component of the cinematic coffee bar.

Britain imported the figure of the rock'n'roller directly (lock, stock and barrel) from the United States. It was inspired largely by the startling image of Elvis Presley.[9] According to Cliff, the media decided he was "England's answer to Elvis, and that's what I became. . . . I was fodder. I looked right. I sang rock'n'roll. . ."[10] *Serious Charge*'s producer Mickey Delamar approached Lionel Bart for songs for the film. Bart said, "[T]hey wanted a delinquent kid who sounded a bit like Presley. . .",[11] so he recommended Cliff for the part that director Terence Young had added solely to draw a younger audience.[12] Young Cliff's part in the film did not escape notice: *Kinematograph Weekly* noted that the "songs, logically introduced by Cliff Richards [*sic*], a popular teenage singer, widen [the film's] scope."[13]

Serious Charge focuses on juvenile delinquents, for which it uses rock'n'roll as a sign,[14] siting the intertwined discourses of youth, delinquency and rock'n'roll in a coffee bar. It is primarily a drama, with an established star (Anthony Quayle), focusing on juvenile delinquents and associating pop music with them. Cliff sings along to his own records that are played on the jukebox. *Beat Girl* (1959) similarly equates rock'n'roll with delinquency and is also like *Serious Charge* in terms of the film's articulation of songs, as Adam Faith sings along with the jukebox. Both films seem unsure how to integrate pop songs and dramatic performances, with the result that they attempt to contain the pop song performances within a vaguely believable diegetic scenario.

In the *Serious Charge* sequence in which Cliff performs *Living Doll*, the camera focuses on Cliff sitting in a chair, with his leg slung over its arm, as he sings adjacent to a hand-jiving woman. After a few bars of his performance, the camera moves away from him, and the music recedes in volume as dialogue takes place between two of the other "delinquent" characters in the coffee bar. This sequence seems to have a dual and contradictory function; it denotes "delinquency" for the adult audience, and on the flip side it provides enjoyment for the teenage audiences who like Cliff and rock'n'roll.

This emphasis on delinquency changed after *Serious Charge*. Cliff's next three musical vehicles show the young as benign. Indeed *The Young Ones* and *Wonderful Life* show the older generation as ignorant and, in viewing the younger generation as hoodlums, generally malign. This was a central structural principle of all of Cliff's films up to 1964. Indeed, the liner notes for the soundtrack of *The Young Ones* states that the youth club gives teenagers "a chance to let off steam with their rock'n'roll music and also acts as a retreat where they can escape the narrow and disapproving world of the adult".[15] This portrayal of the young as misrepresented can be seen as easing the entry of rock'n'roll performers to more adult, traditional modes of entertainment, specifically to the lucrative cabaret and variety circuit, where they catered to an audience who wanted slow and old standard songs rather than purely rock'n'roll songs. In terms of television and career, this presented Cliff Richard with the possibility of moving from *Oh Boy!* to Val Parnell's show and *Sunday Night at the London Palladium*.

Cliff later said, "When we sang 'Rock'n'roll is here to stay' we didn't know it would turn out to be true."[16] His career changed quickly, from rocker to family entertainer, much as had that of his British rock'n'roll predecessor Tommy Steele. Steele had moved into films immediately, starring in his own biopic, and had then made films with ever-decreasing rock'n'roll content. In 1959, *Kinematograph Weekly* reported ABC's collaboration with national tie-ins for Steele's third film, *Tommy the Toreador*,[17] which included a Decca Extended Play (EP), *Little White Bull*, sheet music, woollen toy, toreador outfit, knitting patterns, bath mat, holiday competition and a hand puppet (although it does not clarify whether the puppet is of the bull or of Steele!).

The recuperation of rock'n'roll

Rock'n'roll's recuperation by established popular music can be equated with the symbolic acceptance of teens in those films. Cliff's three musicals of the early 1960s exhibit traditional popular music and rock'n'roll as profoundly different discourses, side by side; yet at certain points in the films the hybridization of the forms is also apparent. Dick Bradley sees rock'n'roll's emergence in 1954–1958 as manifesting a "codal fusion"[18] between European musical codes and African-originated musical codes. The musical state of flux that ensued led to a refolding in of the codes and the subsuming of rock'n'roll styles by the new pop music from around 1958. In fact, 1959 was a critical year for rock'n'roll. It looked to have disintegrated, with Elvis having joined the army the previous year, Little Richard punching the Bible as much as the piano, Chuck Berry's underage-sex charge, Jerry Lee Lewis's scandal about his teenage bride and Buddy Holly's death. The rise to prominence of other musical forms, like calypso, suggested that rock'n'roll may have passed.

The trajectory of Cliff Richard's film career dramatized the current of eliding into more traditional forms of entertainment. Cliff's film debut in *Serious Charge* (1957) features him singing in a coffee bar, rock'n'roll being equated with youth and delinquency; by the time of *Wonderful Life* (1964), rock'n'roll songs are just about having "good clean fun" on the beach. As part of a larger trend, Cliff Richard's songs in the films become increasingly inflected by (if not explicitly originating in) the style of Tin Pan Alley – "rock" is replaced by ballads. Richard's three films of the early 1960s can be seen to encapsulate the conflict between rock songs and more traditional popular music, which appear in the films most blatantly as uneasy bedfellows.

Cliff's breakthrough hit *Move It*, the first big British-written rock'n'roll hit in the United Kingdom, had reached Number 2 in the charts in September 1958. In April 1959, Cliff recorded the songs from *Serious Charge* for an EP, as stipulated by the film's contract.[19] *Living Doll* was slowed down and rearranged "country style". It became a massive hit, "redefined him as a singer",[20] and "helped Cliff to cross the divide between the rock world and the entertainment universe"[21] and to collect the money of adults as well as their offspring. Charlie Gillett sees rock'n'roll as having "petered out" around 1958, partly because of the industry's recuperation of rock'n'roll.[22] *Expresso Bongo* suggests that rock'n'roll musicians inevitably move into the mainstream, manifesting what Bradley noted as the "emergence of 'smooth' rock singers".[23] George Melly stated, "Richard is the key figure in relation to the castration of the first British pop explosion. Steele may have abandoned pop for show biz but Richard dragged pop into show biz."[24] However, the changes in musical form mark a folding back of musical codes, the mutation of existing forms of rock'n'roll and popular music rather than the simple "selling out" of which Cliff was accused.

Cliff said about *Living Doll*: "It wasn't an all-out rocker...rock'n'roll seemed to be fairly limited as a beaty form of music because the public weren't buying it in their hundreds of thousands. We were the first teenagers and ten year olds [who] had no money to spend so in the end records like *Living Doll* sold because they appealed to parents who had money."[25] Gillett sums up the recuperation of rock'n'roll:

> Having failed to rival any of the first generation of American rock'n'roll stars, the British music industry recovered its ground as the Americans replaced the originals with a new generation of more conventional entertainers, under the canny guidance of publishers who were keen to supply the right kind of teen-romance material. Once the focus was back to songs, rather than mysteriously indefinable concepts such as rhythmic feel and authenticity, the British industry was able to deliver the goods again: singers with the appropriate qualities of vulnerability (to their audience) and malleability (to their managers).[26]

Lionel Bart, who had originally been in Tommy Steele's rock group "the Cavemen" but rapidly became a notable stage musicals personality, had written the song as precisely a "rock'n'roll song", yet the rock'n'rollers had turned it back, towards the mainstream, towards Tin Pan Alley.

This melding of musical styles is evident in *Expresso Bongo*, as is the explicit charting of the submerging of rock'n'roll into popular music and established structures of entertainment. In his second film in 1959, Cliff plays young rock'n'roll singer Bongo Herbert to Laurence Harvey's slick drummer turned agent. A review noted that *Expresso Bongo* "breaks out of the rut of wishy-washy gentility....It is loud, brash and vulgar."[27]

Although the association of coffee bars and rock with delinquency had become something of a standard for British films of the late 1950s and early 1960s, *Expresso Bongo*, a more prestigious film than the earlier rock'n'roll "exploitation" films, integrated pop music with a mainstream dramatic narrative set in the world of popular music. *Expresso Bongo* seemingly reenacted the music industry's discovery of Cliff Richard in the 2Is cafe, much as *The Tommy Steele Story* had with the discovery of Steele. However, it grafted this onto a very traditional narrative, that of the naive artist being exploited by the managerial hustler. It was based on Wolf Mankowitz's stage play and used the songs from the stage production, yet it was primarily a dramatic film that was set in the musical, and specifically pop musical, milieu rather than a traditional film musical.

The musical narrative of the film certainly suggests the submerging of rock'n'roll. The film's succession of songs provides both a career and a musical progression: from the first song in the coffee bar, *Love*, which has a wild beat matched by kinetic fast cutting, to the static and relatively lifeless but more emotionally coded song set in the theatre as part of a variety show (*The Shrine on the Second Floor*), which is shown in a very sedate alternation of medium shot and close-up. Between these extremes there is Cliff's hit from the film *Voice in the Wilderness*, a slow ballad that he performs to please the record company boss Mayer and television pundit Gilbert Harding.[28] Although this is also performed in a coffee bar, the tempo and musical movement of the song cause its visual rendering to be relatively static and undynamic.

The film proved a great success, and Cliff's abilities were noted: "*Expresso Bongo*...is easily the number one release. Thanks partly to the popularity of Cliff Richard, the teenagers' idol. Come what may, *Expresso Bongo* is certain to be in the year's top half-dozen."[29] Cliff, like his character in the film, Bongo Herbert, became a pioneer of melding rock'n'roll with traditional popular music, allowing him an extended career as more than simply a rock'n'roll singer, as his successive films demonstrate.

The Young Ones

Cliff said later, "We knew that mums and dads had the money. *Living Doll* got me a mum and dad audience. *The Young Ones* movie moved me very solidly into it."[30] *The Young Ones* was Cliff's next cinematic venture, and it received critical acclaim for both the film and the music, although some reviewers were happier with certain aspects more than others:

> The freshness and enthusiasm of the young cast and the crisp performance of the Associated British Orchestra under Stanley Black compensate for the thin tones of Cliff Richard, the twangy guitar of the Shadows, and the sub-standard rock numbers that mix uneasily with the tuneful work of Peter Myers and Ronald Cass.[31]

The division between the Myers/Cass songs and rock'n'roll-based pop music is highly evident in the film. Added to this, *The Young Ones* constructs Cliff as schizophrenic, as alternately a respectable "suit" and a teen rock'n'roller. This seems to reflect Cliff's career at that point, when he was still doing rock'n'roll songs but was also famed for more traditionally styled ballads and variety performances. The music in the film reflects this position precisely, interpolating rockabilly and mellow show tunes. The difference between the genres of music is startling: Within a short space of time, the film interposes music such as the full-blooded rock'n'roll of *Got a Funny Feeling* with a music hall routine that includes old songs like *Algy the Piccadilly Johnny* ("with the little glass eye"!). Indeed, the music hall sequence functions to propose a continuity between the music in this film, and thus the film itself, and traditional "adult" forms of musical entertainment. *Kinematograph Weekly* said of the music hall sequence, "[T]he artful tinge of nostalgia widens the film's scope and appeal."[32]

The naiveté of perceptions about the film's array of music are reflected in *Kinematograph Weekly*'s review: "[T]here are fourteen song numbers and at least two, *What Do You Know We've Got a Show* and *Nothing's Impossible*, are bound to figure in the hit parade."[33] The songs might have done 10 years earlier, but it was the pop songs rather than the show tunes that had a life outside of the context of the film.[34]

The song *The Young Ones* has a pivotal position in terms of musical style. Although it has a rock'n'roll-derived instrumentation, it conspicuously includes the Norrie Paramor Strings, providing a soaring answer to each sung line of the verse. The film version differs from the single release in that it loses the impressive guitar and tom-tom introduction. The expressed purpose of ditching the fanfare-like introduction is that of bonding the song to the film through segueing it with the film's non-diegetic score. In fact, Stanley Black's score asserts its power over Cliff, by playing around with the melody before he starts singing.[35]

The form of the song *The Young Ones* suggests a stylistic divide, with the singing in the first section being more sedate than the variation section, which has more rock'n'roll singing. *The Young Ones* has a sparse and clean sound (unlike the two rockabilly songs that appear in the film), with a soaring and melodic vocal line that only occasionally contains the gruff inflections and exuberant melismas that seemingly characterized the rock'n'roll vocal style. Indeed, the vocal delivery is extremely pedestrian, with the strings providing an extra dimension of space to the piece. Although the film dramatizes the generation gap both lyrically and formally, the words to the song contemplate continuity rather than difference between the youth and the adult worlds: "One day, when the years have flown, then we'll teach the young ones of our own."

The film *The Young Ones* has an obvious Hollywood genealogy, namely the "puttin' on a show" musicals, the most famous of which are those starring Mickey Rooney and Judy Garland.[36] Following directly the tradition of that subgenre, the climactic show aims to solve the youth community's immediate problems,[37] while Cliff's pirate radio broadcast as "the mystery singer" manages to unify both the young and the old.

British pop musicals

Cliff was now solidly installed in a particularly traditional form of cinematic entertainment, the film musical. The Hollywood musical style had never really been successfully imported into British filmmaking. In 1947, John Huntley wrote, "We have not the right temperament for the 'all-singing, all-dancing' stuff and now we have realized our weakness, we avoid them. We can't do big Hollywood musicals and we don't try."[38]

Though this was rather dismissive of British musicals, *The Young Ones, Summer Holiday* and *Wonderful Life* can certainly be seen as attempts to use the style of the Hollywood musicals, underlined by the importing of US choreographer Herbert Ross to work on the productions. *The Young Ones* signals its antecedents and intentions from the start, commencing with a big set piece with continuous music and a succession of singers. *The Young Ones, Summer Holiday* and *Wonderful Life* are prestige productions, especially for rock'n'roll star vehicles. They use colour and wide-screen format. All are built around a skeleton of songs written by Peter Myers and Ronald Cass that betray the genealogy of the films as mainstream musical comedies. They emulate the Hollywood tradition with energetic dances, choreographed songs and duet interactions between the male and female leads. Each film even contains a hyper-traditional, big medley-set piece section – *The Young Ones*'s music hall medley, *Summer Holiday*'s mime in the courtroom and *Wonderful Life*'s *We Love the Movies*, with its succession of film references – yet significantly each film also reserves a showcase for at least one rock'n'roll song.

In the 1950s, *Kinematograph Weekly* asked rhetorically why there were no British musicals:

Can Britain make a successful musical? Yes, as soon as we make one which is essentially British. We cannot make musicals like *On the Town* because we haven't the same mentality and outlook as the Americans and no amount of talent, technical know-how and facilities will compensate for this. We are capable of money-making musicals and not on such a high budget as some people seem to think.[39]

The Young Ones and Summer Holiday proved this to be correct. Kenneth Harper, the producer of Cliff's three musicals, said, "We hadn't had proper musicals in the UK before and no one believed we could."[40] In the light of the universally perceived British weakness in musical film production, Monthly Film Bulletin heaped praise on The Young Ones, calling it a "rare and robust shot at a British musical."[41]

Summer Holiday and Wonderful Life

Summer Holiday is seen by Cliff as the apogee of his film career. Its treatment of music is particularly interesting, displaying the process of Cliff's transplantation into more traditional popular music. It is a musical cornucopia, dense by the standards of any musical film. It contains 11 song-and-dance sequences, music for the opening and end titles, music and dance sequences tied to a Yugoslavian wedding and a courtroom mime and 3 Shadows instrumentals – a total of 18 musical sections.

Seven of the songs were written by Myers and Cass and follow the stage musical tradition, both in their materialization on screen and in their musical form. They primarily use orchestral accompaniment – the A.B.S. Orchestra again – and thus form part of the orchestral fabric that runs through the film, songs cued easily from Stanley Black's underscore in what Rick Altman calls audio dissolves.[42] The instrumental homogeneity of the songs is lessened by some arrangements that draw on the jazz-group tradition; for example, the duet A Swingin' Affair has a jazz drum beat with prominent, tuned percussion and a jazz-style flute obligato. This song displays most emphatically the union between styles: Cliff (as Don) has a smooth and understated pop voice to Barbara's show-style voice, which is replete with vibrato.

Indeed, A Swingin' Affair provides something of a stylistic bridge between the songs written by Myers and Cass and the Shadows songs. Its instrumental consistency breaks with the use of orchestral resources, moving the discourse away from the realm of the stage musical towards a small ensemble sound. A Swingin' Affair may hold more similarity to the songs of the Shadows than the others written by Myers and Cass, yet some of the Shadows songs are arranged in an instrumental format that diverges from the "classic" rock sound of guitars and drum. Summer Holiday's penultimate song is the slow ballad The Next Time, written by Kaye and Springer, the only song imported to the film and belonging neither to the Myers and Cass songs nor to the Shadows songs. However, Cliff Richard's singing is supported by the Shadows and the Norrie Paramor Strings. The song's arrangement bears little relation to rock'n'roll or to the established sound of the Shadows and consists of strings, a piano with a walking bass and a slow jazz drum beat. Much like *A Swingin' Affair* the song is more reminiscent of jazz ballads rather than the pop songs and instrumentals that appear in the film performed by the Shadows alone.

Apart from *The Next Time*, the Shadows appear on seven musical pieces in the film. All bar one were written by the Shadows and bear the hallmarks of pop song form and instrumentation. In fact, the difference between the two musical discourses is quite pronounced, with the pieces that feature the Shadows having pronounced guitar and drum-based dance beats. The Shadows have their own particular, but rather curtailed, showcase within the film. They are seen performing in a club, but the image track drifts away from concentrating on the group to focus on the audience dancing to the music. Also, *Foot Tapper*, later a number one hit, is glossed over, heard as only a snatch of music on the radio. This suggests the group's marginalization, as does their losing their instruments to perform what Bruce Welch of the Shadows called "a real wally dance"[43] for Cliff's prescient song *Bachelor Boy*.

Cliff sees his film career as declining after *Summer Holiday*,[44] and his next film was a critical and financial failure compared with its predecessors. In *Wonderful Life*, rock'n'roll-based pop music has been almost fully displaced, and the aesthetic and the music are firmly derived from the traditional film musical. The style of the song sequences reflect the film's stylistic origins in the traditional musical in which dances and interactions is given more emphasis than the actual musical performance by Cliff with the Shadows. *Wonderful Life* sees Cliff and his pals involved in making a film. It has large-scale dances (*To Make This Old World Go Round*) and sexually based interactions in terms of the duets between Cliff and Susan Hampshire (*In a Matter of Moments, With a Little Imagination*).

Although these techniques were solidly in evidence in *The Young Ones* and *Summer Holiday*, they reach a degree of plenitude in *Wonderful Life*, and although the three films seem initially to be homogeneous in their aesthetic approaches, *Wonderful Life* can be seen as the logical conclusion of the process. In the film, rock'n'roll or pop music has been displaced and the aesthetic is derived comprehensively from the Hollywood and the stage musical. *Wonderful Life* demonstrates a full repertoire of techniques characteristic of the Hollywood film musical: large-scale choreographed dance sequences, songs that interpolate dances, duets and extended medley song sequences. A prime example is Cliff and the Shadows's dance on a boat on the Thames, which is choreographed into a troupe formation and also seems to be unrelated to the film's narrative.

Many of the song sequences are used in a fashion that corresponds with the narrative patterns of the Hollywood musical, with duets and dances functioning for the sexual interaction of the principal couple. The film has not only substituted the more traditional, misunderstood youngster figure for the rock'n'roller but has concomitantly displaced rock'n'roll music with more traditional popular music. In fact, only four songs out of the 12 in the film have the appearance of pop songs rather than show songs. Those four songs (*On the Beach, What Have I Got to Do, Do You Remember?* and *In a Matter of Moments*) use a pop or rock'n'roll instrumentation – all played by the Shadows, although augmented by some orchestral instruments – rather than the purely orchestral backing that the other songs receive.

Wonderful Life was Cliff Richard's fifth film and was on release at around the same time as *A Hard Day's Night*. The contrast between the two films could not be more stark, with The Beatles espousing action, cinematic kinesis and a foregrounding of pop songs, while Cliff Richard and his cohorts from his last two films attempt to construct a highly traditional musical for the cameras in the well-worn manner of Hollywood musicals. (See this comparison in the detailed analysis of *A Hard Day's Night* in Chapter 10.)

Cliff's later films never reached the heights of his first two musicals of the early 1960s. In *Two a Penny* (1966), Cliff stars as a drug dealer who sees the error of his ways. The film also features American evangelist Billy Graham. It was described by *Monthly Film Bulletin* as a "Sunday school homily...a naive piece of propaganda".[45] As the film includes only three songs and no tied-in single, we can see that its concerns are elsewhere. In *Finders Keepers* (1966), Cliff looks after a missing bomb for authorities in Spain. By the 1970s, he appeared in *Take Me High* (1973), a semi-traditional film musical concerned with selling hamburgers in Birmingham.

Conclusion

Wonderful Life lost money and during the shoot Cliff "got religion".[46] News of The Beatles's triumphant tour of the United States, playing music that evinced a partial return to the styles of rock'n'roll,[47] marked the end of Cliff as Britain's leading pop star in films.

Cliff Richard's films from 1957 to 1964 represent a concerted attempt to import two specific aspects of American culture into British films. The first is the figure of the rock'n'roller and the second is the traditional Hollywood musical. The two impulses led to a hybridization in terms of music and the images of rock'n'roll and established modes of entertainment. Cliff's three films of the early 1960s can be seen to encapsulate the conflict between rock'n'roll songs and more traditional popular music, which appear in the films as essentially different discourses. Although some of the songs in Cliff's musicals demonstrate a degree of synthesis between popular music styles, others throw a musical opposition into sharp relief: rock'n'roll opposed to the traditional stage song.

A space opened for rock'n'roll music within the traditional film musical discourse; Cliff became an unthreatening youth figure who sang show tunes. On the other hand, this also marked the recuperation of rock'n'roll into the established structures of mainstream show business and particularly its submergence into its existent aesthetic formats, which are premised on a dramatization of the process. This all served Cliff's career wonderfully, giving him a longevity that is legendary in British popular music. Elvis may have been "the King", but Cliff Richard, a British Elvis look-alike, ended up knighted.

10
The Musical Revolution: The Beatles in *A Hard Day's Night*

Andrew Sarris famously called *A Hard Day's Night* (1964) "the *Citizen Kane* of Jukebox movies", and it was unique in going into massive profit before its cinematic release through the presales of soundtrack LPs.[1] *A Hard Day's Night* was the first of the two film vehicles for The Beatles and has to be seen as a significant point for the development of the relationship between music and cinema. The Beatles's film displaced the model of the classical film musical and offered a distinct alternative: rough and ready action and fast-paced excitement, all to the staunch beat of pop music rather than the smooth sophistication of show music.

Early examples of films that used rock'n'roll often set age-old narratives in a background of the pop music world as in *Kid Creole* (1958 US) and *Expresso Bongo* (1959), or they were derivations of the Hollywood musical like *Rock Around the Clock* (1956 US), *The Girl Can't Help It* (1956 US) and *The Young Ones* (1961). These precursors to *A Hard Day's Night* were content at first to attempt to dilute pop music by mixing it into traditional forms of musical entertainment. Pop stars such as Elvis Presley and Cliff Richard made successful films that took the traditional musical film form and attempted to imbue it with a teenage orientation, often endeavouring to attenuate pop songs within a body of Tin Pan Alley songs in film musicals clearly deriving their impetus from the stage. *A Hard Day's Night* broke dramatically with the previous uses of pop music in cinema in a number of significant ways. It marked a point where pop music in films was not mixed with previously established musical forms, through the jettisoning of songs apart from those by The Beatles, while the film even ridiculed the traditional modes of "family entertainment". The film's significance can also be attributed to the template that it offered for pop music in films: the film style that paralleled pop music with dynamic visual activity, and the articulation of songs as non-diegetic music. The success of the film put pop music firmly on the agenda of the cinema,[2] or at least confirmed its importance for the cinema. This chapter will provide a detailed close analysis of sections of the film, looking to its use of music and accompanying articulation of the image.

The Beatles

A Hard Day's Night is essentially a vehicle for The Beatles, its function being twofold. First, it shows The Beatles performing their songs in a form that is similar to the group's concerts, and secondly it parades The Beatles as personalities, assuaging the thirst for intimate contact on behalf of their fans. The film's story concerns The Beatles travelling to London with Paul's grandfather in order to perform on television in front of a theatre audience. They have a number of incidental adventures: they are mobbed by adoring fans, have trouble with Paul's grandfather, are interviewed, lose Ringo and only just manage to be back at the theatre in time for their performance.

The Beatles's songs are foregrounded in the film in various ways. Four songs are performed in the concert sequence near the end of the film. Two songs are performed at the rehearsals at the theatre. There is another (impromptu) performance in the guard's van of the train which is motivated as a movement from the film's established reality into a fantasy moment, while at a club, the group dance to their own hit records. Beatles songs are also utilized four times as non-diegetic music: in the opening/title sequence, in the sequence where The Beatles have "escaped" their professional confines and gambol on a field, in the "chase" sequence where they go between the theatre and the police station to retrieve Ringo in time for their concert appearance, and lastly during the end titles. Apart from these four occasions, songs appear diegetically, most using the performance mode and making a point of reproducing the group performing live, an example of which is *I Should Have Known Better* being played in the guard's van of the train on the way to London. Nine different songs appear in the film (some are repeated) and each is suitably foregrounded as a distinct object in itself married to the spectacle of performance or action, as a discrete entity or micro-narrative within the body of the film. Micro-narratives (songs, in this case) may be defined as relatively autonomous narratives within films, distinct episodes within a film that make sense without specific reference to the framing (overall) narrative.

In terms of the second primary function of the film, The Beatles are represented as distinct and individual personalities with an emphasis on their bonding together as a group. Their collective identity is channelled through their hair and dress and through the projection of a strong provincial image (Liverpudlian/northern English), bolstered by their youth, humour and their constant verbal repartee. The film provides a further dimension to The Beatles as individuals, which develops the star image circulated by magazine profiles and television interviews:

> The star's performance in a film reveals to the viewer all those particular aspects of movement and expression...The star is not performing here so much as "being". In other words, what the film performance permits is moments of pure voyeurism for the spectator, the sense of overlooking something which is not designed for the onlooker but passively allows itself to be seen.[3]

What the film offers to fans is a virtual contact with The Beatles. The ambiguity between the group acting and as non-actors "being themselves" allows *A Hard Day's Night* to function both as a dramatic film and as a succession of spectacles of the group.

This dual function of the film, showcasing the songs and displaying The Beatles, is paramount and as a consequence *A Hard Day's Night* is not geared to a complex developmental narrative but utilizes a loose narrative that meanders through a number of incidents rather than progresses in any purposeful manner. This means that the music and the spectacle of The Beatles articulate much if not all of the film, relegating narrative development to a function of simply unifying disparate songs and incidents.

The film has a strikingly visual impetus to complement the musical drive, having a consistently fast pace and using a number of self-conscious techniques.[4] An example of this is the press conference, where the moving image of photographs being taken is converted into a series of still images representing those photographs. Hand-held camera is utilized constantly and there is a simultaneity of action within the frame that gives the film an improvisational quality, suggesting a "capturing" of actual events. The film was shot very quickly, fitted into a break in The Beatles's schedule and consequently uses predominantly first (and only) takes.[5] The film's director, Richard Lester, had been successful in television and advertisement production[6] and it is probable that his experience of the latter in particular added to the sense of visual excitement in the film, achieved chiefly through its fragmenting of the Classical spatial and temporal systems. Lester, although American, had already made two films in the UK, *The Running, Jumping, Standing Still Film* (1959), an 11-minute surrealistic and Oscar-nominated short starring Peter Sellers and Spike Milligan, and *It's Trad, Dad!* (1962), a narratively framed feature length showcase for "trad" jazz and pop songs.

A Hard Day's Night established a model and standard for pop music in film, not only setting standards of quality but the means by which pop music and groups could be represented in the cinema. This is achieved chiefly through generic hybridization, blending documentary-derived techniques with the form of the dramatic fiction film, the former elements guaranteeing the pop group and their performances while the latter functions as a frame containing these elements. The visual style that *A Hard Day's Night* establishes for itself is a hybrid of the documentary conception of "recording reality" and the dramatic film form of mainstream cinema. This was a pragmatic move as it attained the principal aim of portraying The Beatles as themselves for an audience that desired a relationship of proximity to them, and it managed to sustain a feature film by taking The Beatles's repartees, activities and performances and framing them with a narrative derived from dramatic cinema. *A Hard Day's Night* created a substantial legacy: film style paralleling pop music with speed and kinesis, and a specific procedure for the articulation of pop songs in films. As John Hill has noted,

> The release of *A Hard Day's Night*...represents something of a milestone in the history of the genre....the film successfully challenged many of the old conventions of the pop film by introducing a new approach to both plot and visual presentation....the film's treatment of musical numbers represents one of its most important contributions to the genre.[7]

A Hard Day's Night's film style certainly established it as a foundation of sorts for pop music in visual culture that followed, its influence can be detected as early as *Catch Us If You Can* (1965) and American television's later virtual facsimile of The Beatles and the film style of their first two films for The Monkees.

Music appears within the film as autonomous performances, set pieces which either halt the progression of, or at least do nothing to further, the narrative, much as is the case with song and dance sequences in the backstage musical.[8] Yet at certain points songs are utilized as a replacement for the traditional cinematic non-diegetic music; that is to say they replace cinema's traditional "background music". This is of prime significance as the use of pop songs as non-diegetic music, which had become widespread by next decade, had not previously been used in feature films to any notable degree.[9] At the time of the film's release this was certainly an unprecedented situation, which is testified to by *A Hard Day's Night*'s persistence in using some orchestral incidental music, namely an instrumental arrangement of The Beatles's song *This Boy*, by The George Martin Orchestra which accompanies Ringo's lone wanderings.

Apart from the film's beginning and ending, Beatles songs are utilized twice as non-diegetic music in the body of the film: first in the playing field sequence and secondly for the "chase" sequence. On all of these occasions, the songs supplant diegetic sound almost totally and parallel the kinesis of the images and decoupage. The beat of the music becomes the principal articulator of time for the sequences and the conclusion of the sequences is signified by the conclusion of the songs themselves. This means that the images were cut to the music's demand (to the music's duration rather than rhythm[10]). The music then becomes the central agent of filmic action; not only does it articulate the image track, but it mediates between the audience and what are in effect silent cinema-type sequences, and in the case of the playing field sequence just a succession of relatively incoherent images of the members of The Beatles careering around.

The songs are differentiated from traditional culture. At the studio, there is a risible "showbiz"-style dance based on a Beatles song, while John Lennon parodies the Classical film musical by declaring, "why don't we do the show right here!". Most songs in *A Hard Day's Night* are presented as group performances, using the performance mode rather than using the lip-synch mode. The contemporaneous Cliff Richard and Elvis Presley films tend to adapt the classical musical form, utilizing the lip-synch mode, sometimes supported by minimal diegetic sources (like a guitar) but using substantial non-diegetic music as the principal form of song backing. The documentary-style format of the diegetic song sequences in *A Hard Day's Night* retains a reference to the song's actual production. They are presented as a group performance, rather than focusing purely on the singing as the anchor of the song to the diegesis, as does the lip-synch mode in many classical musicals. In other words, the film reproduces the song's performance fully rather than eliding its means of production, while the action sequences that use songs as their accompaniment completely divide the songs in the film from the origins of the songs (the group on screen). The proximity of these two modes of song representation functions to provide variation in *A Hard Day's Night*'s cornucopia of music and visuals. On a practical level, this solved the problem posed by the stardom of The Beatles as a group of recognizable individuals, rather than a single foregrounded individual. The lip-synch mode could have marginalized the group members who were not singing at a given moment, the tendency of this strategy being to focus on one person as the vocal and visual centre – and yet that option was taken up for a song in *Help!* in the following year.[11]

Opening sequence

The song *A Hard Day's Night* opens the film, as the title song, articulated non-diegetically and being accompanied by the footage of The Beatles running away from a mob of their fans. Although it is nominally a title sequence, where it was common to have non-diegetic songs, the titles are quickly dispensed with in what is essentially a dramatic spectacle driven by the music. The lone guitar chord at the start of the song marks the inauguration of the image track, with the camera remaining static for the opening shot while the titles "Walter Shenson Presents," "The Beatles" and "A Hard Day's Night" appear in succession superimposed on the image but not obscuring the action. The sequence is marked as discrete by the song, which proceeds with the action; the conclusion of the song signifies the conclusion of the title sequence, as The Beatles have boarded the departing train. This sequence may then be seen as having three principal functions: first, as an overture for the film, providing initial information, here primarily the titles themselves and the establishment of Beatles activity; secondly, as a presentation of the song itself; and lastly as a presentation of action, a spectacle that can also be seen as a micro-narrative concerning The Beatles escaping fans and boarding a train.

In terms of film style, this opening sequence functions to signify to the audience what will follow in the film: speed and kinesis, an exciting array of action and songs. The system of establishing space in this sequence (and certain other portions of the film) bears little resemblance to the spatial system of the Classical cinema. Spatial confusion ensues with classical conventions of continuity like the 180° line being totally disregarded. Space is not constructed by the classical method of starting with an establishing shot whose space is then analysed by subsequent closer shots. Instead space is presented in shots that only contain recognizable human figures to provide any continuity. Static long shots establish a space, but the succession of shots does not exploit this for the purposes of continuity or analytical spatial construction. Big close-ups of The Beatles individually and some of their pursuers do not function as an analysis of the space as there is little spatial continuity in a fast chase as it is presented. For example, the screen direction of the moving figures is not continuous but changes according to no fixed plan, bearing a distinct resemblance to the discontinuities appearing in some *Nouvelle Vague* films. There is thus almost no spatial stasis in the opening sequence. Screen space is made more chaotic by the use of fast-panning shots of running legs etc. that are indistinct images and spatially ambiguous. Space is thus articulated in terms of the visual objects (The Beatles and their fans); rather than establishing a space for action, it is the action that provides the spatial system of the sequence. The shots that make up the whole function as a succession rather than as a logical and ordered progression, a coherent construction, built around the relationship between shots. Continuity is not provided by space or editing but by the song which is the main device for continuity and unity in the sequence.

The opening sequence functions to regulate the rest of the film for the audience; it has a privileged position with respect to the following diegesis, and establishes the regime for the audience's cognition of the film. The elements that it contains – fast action, spatial confusion, "real" characters, foregrounded music – are, within broad bounds, "imprinted" on the audience and govern their expectation as to what will follow. Concerning the music itself, the song *A Hard Day's Night* confirms the film's title and functions in a similar way to an opera's overture, as a preamble to the narrative proper, a pleasurable presentation and induction into the diegesis.

A Hard Day's Night is initiated by a very distinctive image. This is a static shot of a street with three of The Beatles running along the pavement towards the camera with their fans in hot pursuit. The camera is static and "records" the action, action that takes place within the space established by the shot, much as the camera did in the tableau-based spatial system of early cinema. The integrity of the shot guarantees a reality of sorts, which is further confirmed by George Harrison and Ringo Starr falling over on the pavement in what appears to be an unrehearsed way. As the three reach and pass the camera their images become out of focus, reinforcing the action as taking place within the frame space rather than the action articulating film space. This sets up the film style as being a "recording" of action (based on the autonomy of shot space) that could be real rather than staged action in the traditional cinematic sense, constructed through traditional spatial systems.

This sequence establishes speed as a central drive (as well as a theme) of the film, with a large amount of kinetic activity and virtually no static images. After the three of The Beatles have run into the railway station (a low-angle long shot) followed by their fans, there are shots that appear to be close-ups of disembodied legs in fast motion. These shots are indistinct, blurred by the speed of activity and the large size of the image in the frame, and create a non-representational image of the speed and kinesis that is established in the title sequence and is a significant feature of the film in general. This particular process works intermittently throughout the sequence; when George Harrison, John Lennon and Ringo Starr hide from their pursuers in telephone kiosks, there is a slow pan across the three adjacent booths but with the shot or image constructed as a double plane of image and action: the booths in the background are in focus, while the fans rushing past in the foreground are out of focus and cannot be distinguished. This is a repeat of the kinetic processes already in circulation in the film, but rather than being constructed as an interjected shot, the image, of movement rather than of a specific object, is incorporated into the shot of the main initiators of the film's action (The Beatles), as a visual equivalent of noise or distortion.

Allied to the energetic movement within the frame is a tendency towards a polarity of shot types, oscillating between long shots and big close-ups, the former working as a spatial tableau for action and the latter as the dramatic interplay, their interaction abandoning the classical spatial concentration on medium shots as there is a marginalization of dialogue and the need for precise spatial articulation. This is harmonized with the use of out-of-focus images and dramatic zooms that zero in on the image, contracting space and further denying its analytical (classical) construction while reinforcing the speed, kinesis and materiality of the image.

The sequence not only functions as a spectacle and micro-narrative in its own right, but also establishes significant information for the film's framing or macro-narrative and includes some of these elements as a counterpoint to the energy of the chase. These include intermittent static shots of the band's stationary manager Norm struggling with a carton of milk which he has obtained from a vending machine.[12] This appears episodically in the main body of the action, as a counterpoint and contrast to the shots of speed and movement. The Beatle absent from the film's opening shot (Paul McCartney) is already at the station and is not part of the chase until its ultimate conclusion. He is waiting for the others with his grandfather (played by Wilfrid Brambell). This character is a significant addition to the film's main protagonists, the group members playing themselves. The grandfather functions as a device (perhaps the main impetus) for the filmic narrative's progression through a number of incidents.

Overall, the song *A Hard Day's Night* has to be seen as having a central role, in that it provides the title and the introduction for the film, as well as providing pleasure in its own right, unifying the image track and working with the images to impart a sense of energy, characteristic of pop music and its culture and, by inference, The Beatles themselves. Thus, it requires further analysis, particularly of its materiality and its relation to the image.

The song follows the traditionally established pattern for the present-ation of songs and popular music, known as song form, a format that encourages repetition as one of the prime means of comprehension.[13] This form allows the placement of material in specific relationships, governing a cyclical pattern of repetition of cells of music and a formula for the insertion of other material as a contrast to the principal material. Its succession of verses, choruses and variations are all sung but tradi-tionally almost all popular songs have a "middle eight," a section of variation that commonly is occupied by an instrumental break and is so-called because of the convention that it was eight bar long and in the middle of the piece as an aural contrast to its surrounding material. Here, The Beatles have a guitar solo, but with the other instruments repeating the song's verse material. The regimented repetition of material allows a maximized audience comprehension of form and recognition of the musical elements.

The form of the song may be tabulated like this:

Form of song: **A A B A A B C A A B**

A - Verses. ("It's been a hard day's night..."
          and "When I get home to you...").

B - Choruses. ("When I'm home everything seems to be...).

C - "Middle Eight". Guitar solo.

The succession of letters represents the temporal structure of the song, which corresponds to the song-form template – although there is, in fact, a certain ambiguity about what could be nominated as the chorus. The gestalt of the song is easily recognized by the audience, leading to an expectation of repeated musical material that provides pleasure upon its reappearance from a formal and temporal point of view. The formal breakdown demonstrates the organic unity of the song's material organization, and emphasizes the formal medium that is, to a greater or lesser degree, cognized by the audience. As Adorno has noted in his appraisal of popular music,

> The whole structure of popular music is standardized.... The whole is pre-given and pre-accepted, even before the actual experience of the music starts.... The composition hears for the listener. This is how popular music divests the listener of spontaneity and promotes conditional reflexes.... The schematic build up dictates the way in which he [*sic*] must listen....[14]

While Adorno's conclusions reflect his scorn for popular culture, it can be inferred that standard form is, to some extent, comprehended by the audience as a basis of musical language. The temporal structure of the song is the principal micro-narrative that the audience follows in the opening sequence, in that its continuity and structure of repetition and variation is, to an extent, cognized by the audience. The simplicity and ubiquity of this form allows the recognition of material and anticipation of its recurrence along with the song's section changes, a situation that would be impossible if the sequence had used music by Webern or Stockhausen that is based almost purely on the presentation of musical material alone.[15] The temporal aspect thus provides the sequence with one of its chief means of being decoded as it functions for the audience as the central organizational principal for time. Musical time thus replaces film time. Musical time is profoundly different from the time schemes of cinema. It is continuous rather than flexible and gapped like time in films; time in pop music is for the song's duration a regime of the beat's rigorous reiteration. The continuity of the beat is the marker of time, held within song form's harnessing of the block repetitions of musical material that govern pop music.

The pulse of the song, a relentless beat that does not change even for the chorus or guitar solo sections, is the only component of the sequence directly concerned with time, and the song's regulated musical time converts the dislocated succession of images into a coherent whole. The materiality of the music provides the impetus for the sequence and the music transfers its energy to the images, especially as it appears from outside the diegesis, as a replacement for film's traditional orchestral background music. Further, it is foregrounded to the point of obliterating diegetic sound, thus asserting itself as a component of central importance. The beat's continuity and temporal homogeneity function to unify the image track's visual heterogeneity and articulate time within the sequence.

Concert sequence

The narrative of the film apes the traditional trajectory of traditional films in that at *A Hard Day's Night*'s conclusion there is a climax towards which the narrative inexorably has been moving. This is the television broadcast, a performance in front of a theatre audience, which was established at the outset of the film as the central reason for The Beatles's journey to London. This is not only the finale of the narrative, but is more nakedly a reward or "pay-off" for The Beatles's fans in that it simulates the concert situation that the audience might have expected from the film.[16]

It is a substantial section within the film and involves the performance of four songs consecutively, they are *Tell Me Why, If I Fell, I Should Have Known Better* and *She Loves You*. A variety of formal strategies are used in the sequence. First, there is the traditional tableau that is used to "record" performers from the early cinema, through to the classical musical and to television coverage of pop groups, a style which the sequence reconstructs.[17] This format is a guarantee of the veracity of the performance context through the integrity of the shot as a discrete object in itself; film time corresponds to real time. In this sequence the frontal tableau of The Beatles on stage may be seen as a spatial anchor which is intermittently returned to as a grounding for the articulation of the other visual elements in space. The second formal strategy is the use of audience reaction shots, creating a reverse field spatial relationship with the group, which offers a screen surrogate for the cinema audience and facilitates a simulation of the concert experience. Thirdly, the presentation of the concert involves close-up shots of The Beatles themselves singing and playing their instruments; these shots are only on occasion static and thus involve some movement on behalf of the performers and camera movement between performers that destroys the classical organization of elements within the frame in favour of the flexibility of framing that had been a characteristic of footage from television news and documentaries, lacking the precision of image control and stability characteristic of cinema traditions.

The concluding song of the concert sequence is *She Loves You*, which had been a massive hit for The Beatles in the year before *A Hard Day's Night* was released.[18] This song appears as a culmination of The Beatles's performance, eliciting the most extreme reaction from the audience of baying fans. The visual style seems to be simultaneously a representation and a confirmation of the phenomenon of Beatlemania, through placing a focus on these fans beyond what might be expected. The Beatles's performance of the song is, for significant portions of the sequence, not the central focus of the image track which had been the situation established by the previous songs in this concert. The emphasis on The Beatles performing the songs is lessened in favour of a heightened representation of the relationship between the group and their fans. This entails losing some of the central signifiers of the music (The Beatles) and focusing on the music's effect on the audience.

The sequence opens with dramatic visuals that surpass those that have already been in circulation in the film, specifically in terms of movement and spatial chaos. The narrative elements have still been appearing intermittently during this concert sequence – in the break between *I Should Have Known Better* and *She Loves You*, for instance, there is a shot of Paul's grandfather (as noted, the disruptive element that seemingly drives the minimal narrative) sitting among the audience, handcuffed to Shake, the group's road manager. Immediately following this there are two dramatic panning shots which lack any clear focus and take place at such disorientating speed that the audience in the frame in each pan is converted to a purely homogenous mass. Spatial continuity is replaced by the kinesis of image as a technique for mapping the screen audience's hysteria within the cinema audience.

The performance of *She Loves You* utilizes a dual spatial system based largely on the reverse fields of The Beatles on stage and the audience facing them. The Beatles are initially re-established by a tableau shot of the stage and the four of them in position. Following this, whenever The Beatles are shown it is predominantly in big and medium close-ups with a focus on the singing, specifically on John Lennon who is the principal singer of the song. As a part of the performance's cinematic staging there is a third space that is pivotal between the two established spaces that constitute the scene: the television control room. It is, at least nominally, within the audience space and yet it is privileged in that via the numerous television monitors has multiple views of The Beatles on stage. It thus draws attention to the construction of the group's performance itself. The presence of the television coverage allows a movement beyond what would have remained a relatively simple spatial set up. The film's construction of the concert sequence can thus be motivated as the television reconstruction of the concert.

The most remarkable aspect of the image track in the *She Loves You* section of the concert is the amount of audience shots when compared to the number of shots that constitute the group's performance. After the inaugurating shots that establish a situation of mass audience hysteria, the film seems intent on reinforcing this.[19] The camera portrays members of the audience as individuals rather than representing the audience as a mass, zooming in on them to show their (presumably unrehearsed) reaction to The Beatles. Concentration on the audience serves first to manifest Beatlemania in the film as a document, and secondly guarantees the veracity of the performance and the film through the utilization of quasi-documentary techniques. John Caughie has described the interaction of the documentary and the dramatic narrative in the television documentary drama form:

> Within the conventions of documentary, the objectifying look is part of the support of truth and neutrality. For documentary drama, however, two looks are in play, and they come to constitute a hierarchy: the rhetoric of the drama operates an exchange of looks between the characters...[while the] rhetoric of documentary, the fixed and fixing look, constitutes its object...[20]

This description corresponds to the suturing processes in operation within *A Hard Day's Night* as a whole and, in this particular sequence, the articulation of characters within space is governed by a concept of the event itself. Here, the image ceases to be simply a guarantor of the music and becomes a guarantor of the event as relationship between The Beatles and their audience. Thus, their performance is simultaneously a "recording" and a dramatization.[21] The establishing of the diegetic audience allows shots of the group on stage to be seen as point-of-view shots, suturing the cinema viewer into the sequence, while the television cameras constitute the objects of vision as the performing Beatles and the hysterical audience.

She Loves You receives a more enthusiastic reception from the theatre audience than the previous songs, no doubt due to its status as The Beatles's biggest hit record. The on-screen audience's reaction can, in some ways, be seen as a model for the reaction of the cinema audience (as the on-screen audience can be seen as their replacement[22]). The song is familiar to them and, as such, they have a mental mapping of the patterns of the song, its changes and repetitions. Even if the cinema audience has no prior knowledge of the song, its temporal form becomes self-explanatory in that it is a structure of presentations and repetitions that govern the listener's perceptions of the song. As described above for the song *A Hard Day's Night*, the use of a fairly simple song form allows maximum coherence and cognition of musical material. It is the points of change that appear at regular intervals within the song (usually every four bars) and the anticipation of this by the listener that, allied to the continuous beat of the song's rhythm, establish it as a temporal structure that is cognized by audiences and the central engine of time in this and many other sequences that use pop songs. Beyond that, the representation of the performance context centres the song within the film's processes at this point, with the narration endeavouring to reproduce the excitement of a live concert.

Conclusion

In summary, *A Hard Day's Night* is a paramount film for the history of music in cinema, both in Britain and internationally. Its unprecedented commercial and critical success led to a qualitative change in subsequent films using pop music and ensured that many films featuring pop groups would follow.[23] The pop music in *A Hard Day's Night* is largely in the form of autonomous songs, set-pieces which interrupt narrative progression in a similar way to the set-pieces in some musicals. However, while films that use pop songs like those of Cliff Richard and Elvis Presley were dominated by the lip-synch mode as an adaptation of the Classical film musical form, *A Hard Day's Night* breaks significantly with many of the established modes of the film musical. It utilizes a minimal amount of orchestral non-diegetic music but notably, at certain points, The Beatles's songs are utilized as a replacement for it. When The Beatles's songs appear as non-diegetic music, a reversal in the relationship of the film's elements takes place: the songs marginalize and destroy diegetic sound and dominate the image track, whose function now is to "double" the musical energy with kinetic images and decoupage. The beat of the music becomes the principal articulator of time for the sequences and the songs mark off the sequences as discrete objects. The images are subordinated, cut to the music's requirements, which means that the music has become the central agent of filmic action. Not only does it articulate the image track, but it mediates between the audience and what bear more than a passing resemblance to silent cinema sequences through their lack of diegetic sound, namely the spatially chaotic succession of shots that comprises the title sequence and the procession of incoherent images in the later playing field sequence.[24] Although the rhythm of the editing does not double the song rhythms and structures, the endings of the songs cue the return to narrative-based cinema; the songs refuse to fade out and be subordinated to narrative development.

The film converted dramatic cinema from an object where, broadly speaking, music accompanied stories to one where images accompanied music. *A Hard Day's Night* was the point where pop musicals became their own form, moving away from the attempts to adapt the Classical Hollywood musical form, and thus seemingly putting one of the final nails in the coffin of the glamorous Hollywood musical. This was an instance of popular music rewriting cinema, as a part of the drive towards film audiences increasingly being youth audiences, as well as the burgeoning number of young consumers able to spend money on pop records. Furthermore, it marks a key point in the development of pop songs appearing as non-diegetic music, which since 1964 has become one of the fundamental stylistic aspects of modern cinema.

11
White Labels and Black Imports: Music, Assimilation and Commerce in *Absolute Beginners* (1985)

Film musicals, as a form, perhaps should be approached from the point of view where the images and the narrative are seen as *emanations* from the music, rather than the other way round. While music and the stylized language of "the spectacular" are able to discuss complex ideas, what is said often is not taken "seriously", and this is further compounded by the regular association of the spectacular with commercialism. *Absolute Beginners* (1985) seems interested in ebullient and uplifting songs and dances, yet it is also concerned with American and Caribbean imports to Britain, while pursuing a format of making "history" along commercial lines.

Absolute Beginners (1985) was arguably the most glossy and glamorous musical the British film industry has ever produced. It was one of the biggest risks of British cinema of this period: British musicals largely had not been popular and its budget was substantial. Yet the film was an unprecedented large-scale musical, a bold film, co-produced by the diversifying record company Virgin. Yet it was not the success its producers had hoped for, despite having one of the most expensively hyped openings in British cinema history.[1] It was a culturally ambivalent film, being audacious in the sense that it was a brave departure to make a big pop music-based musical film, but a cultural retreat in that nostalgia culture and its concomitant desire to resell back catalogues clearly was one of its central motivations. So, while it may have been courageous in filmic terms, it was largely conservative in musical terms.

Cinematic history

History has been at the forefront of some recent debates concerning film and television. Robert Rosenstone's monograph *Visions of the Past: The*

Challenge of Film to Our Idea of History and his edited anthology *Revisioning History* have elicited further research and discussion about film and television as a form of writing history.[2] Hayden White, in an earlier response to Rosenstone, referred to "historiophoty" (history as audio–visual object) to distinguish it from historiography (writing history).[3] Historian Alan Munslow in his book *Deconstructing History* distinguishes between three types of historians working today. The first he calls "reconstructionists", who believe the past can be apprehended as an ideology-free "truth" (a fully empiricist position). The second he calls "constructionists" (or "social theory school"), who believe that history is a construct, but the process of history is explicable through the imposition of a large-scale explanation that is outside history (such as Marxism). The third he calls "deconstructionists". These historians see history in terms of process and textuality, and centrally are concerned with the manipulation of knowledge as a discourse.[4] While the ascendant "new film history" is often "reconstructionist", *Absolute Beginners* could be seen as constituting a "deconstructionist" history (or a "historiophoty").

Before production, the film's director Julien Temple said "...*Absolute Beginners* won't be a movie set archaeologically in 1958, it's going to be a film about now as well...And that's important because that's when Teenage began and now it's over."[5] Two central tenets of postmodern or deconstructionist history are that first aesthetic objects constitute history as much as scholarly empirical writings, and secondly that in the absence of a guaranteed "real" and measurable standard, all histories have a distinct "cast" and can never be simply "neutral". *Absolute Beginners* is a rejoinder to a 1985 agenda that had tabled anti-black racism and momentous economic change. It dramatizes and writes "as history" a significant historical moment – the arrival and assimilation of American culture (including consumerism and rock'n'roll) as well as significant numbers of black immigrants from the Caribbean. Music is one of the main ways the film inscribes these things.

Absolute Beginners provided a "competing history" of 1958 with others in circulation in 1985. However, the language of *Absolute Beginners's* history mitigates against its potency. First, it uses the language of the audio–visual spectacular ("frivolous" music, stylization and colourful design), and secondly it has a plainly commercial motivation. In tandem, these determinants tend to delegitimize what the film is saying through eschewing a "serious" mode of discourse about the subject in hand. Furthermore, *Absolute Beginners* provides a historical perspective from the point of view of popular culture. It is a demotic history.

It speaks the argot of "light entertainment", popular culture of the time of its setting and this prestige-free level of British culture since that time. *Absolute Beginners* is not only a musical carnival of different styles and artists, but also a rich tapestry of popular culture references. It has a strongly developed esoteric discourse; it is run through with historicity, yet its points of reference pertain more to traditional light entertainment than the vast majority of films which espouse pop music culture.[6] The film featured celebrities such as Mandy Rice-Davies, one of the protagonists in the Profumo affair of the early 1960s, which was later depicted in the British film *Scandal* (1988). There were also reports that Keith Richard from the Rolling Stones was going to appear as a "music hall cheeky chappie",[7] although this evidently came to nothing. As well as pop stars like David Bowie, Sade, Ray Davies from the Kinks and Tenpole Tudor, the film culled actors from light entertainment and who readily were known to British audiences. *Absolute Beginners* features television personality and dancer Lionel Blair, who had appeared briefly in The Beatles's *A Hard Day's Night* (1964) and disc jockey Alan Freeman, who had appeared in *It's Trad, Dad!* (1962). Blair's part echoed the figure of pop music Svengali Larry Parnes. In an interview, Blair declared that his role, Harold Charms, was clearly based on Parnes,[8] who had also been the likely inspiration for the Johnny Jackson character of *Expresso Bongo* (1959). The film's design certainly owed a great deal to *Expresso Bongo's* vision of Soho and was strikingly set at the same period. Thus, *Absolute Beginners* pointedly refers back to one of the founding moments of the pop musical in Britain, the point where coffee bars were a cultural centre and a new Britain was opening, fuelled by the new popular culture based on rock'n'roll.[9]

The rebuilt pop musical

Absolute Beginners seems unique, yet it self-consciously follows – and self-consciously plays with – the relatively young traditions of the British pop musical, an indigenous rendering of an imported American film form. In the mid-1980s, it certainly was a bold move to make a large-scale big budget musical. Apart from one or two small-scale films like *Billy the Kid and the Green Baize Vampire* (1985), *Absolute Beginners* was the first big-scale adult musical attempted in a decade since *Tommy* (1975). Its screenwriter Don MacPherson commented:

> the very word "musical" would make a sane person reach for their gun after sustained assault by the Bee-Gees-*Evita*-MTV-Paul McCartney,

multi-headed monsters of a couple of decades...It didn't make sense to do it any other way than by breaking all the rules: mix it up, go pell-mell, swop vanilla for tutti-frutti with a cherry on top. After all, playing safe was bound to get you nowhere. By 1985 all the rules for making "musicals about the glamour-studded 1950s" had changed. All the traditions were up for grabs, with Prince, Brecht and Weill, Giuseppe Verdi and Gene Kelly all claiming credit where credit was due.[10]

Despite the rhetoric, *Absolute Beginners* was a very traditional musical in many ways. It espoused the tradition of film musicals, specifically those of the glossy 1950s Vincente Minnelli and Joshua Logan variety. Director Julien Temple declared before the film's production: "...*Absolute Beginners* will be a musical first and foremost and you've got to have dynamic performers. We need entertainers with...charisma. We need Gene Kellys, Fred Astaires and David Bowies. And we've got David Bowie."[11] This statement underlines the continuity between musical performers, firmly connecting *Absolute Beginners* with the film musical tradition. A further example is where Ray Davies (of The Kinks) as Colin's father sings his musical contribution to the film, *Quiet Life*, in the Berkeley-referencing cut away family house set, interspersed with dialogue from other characters and domestic activity such as vacuuming the floor. In an article about the film before it was shot, the *New Musical Express* noted the way that songs were going to be used in the film:

> Working closely with Temple, the songs are designed both to advance the plot and reinforce the characters and ideas of the film: they're for a *proper* musical.... An anachronism in the age of formulaic, anodyne dance movies such as *Flashdance, Absolute Beginners* will be looking back to such magical '50s musicals as *Guys and Dolls, An American in Paris* and *Singing in the Rain* [*sic*] for its inspiration.[12]

The pastiching of these musical classics is highly apparent in the film; the look of the film duplicates the glossily colourful musicals of the 1950s while adding the pace of action that had been commonplace for pop music and images since the proliferation of pop promos on music television. Director Julien Temple had started his career with the punk film *The Great Rock'n'Roll Swindle* (1980), then made promos for Culture Club, ABC and The Rolling Stones, and was convinced of the merits of involvement in pop promos for film makers.[13] MTV started broadcasting in the United States in August 1981,[14] and fairly quickly British bands of the "new pop" ilk, such as Duran Duran and Culture Club, enacted a "British video invasion" of the American market. This gave a great fillip to British pop music culture, and the concept of *Absolute Beginners*, as a British blockbuster musical film clearly was inspired by the success and proliferation of British acts in pop videos.

Pop musicals are premised upon assimilating the new and showcasing the modern. Thus, it is possible to trace some of the concerns of *Absolute Beginners* in a direct line of descent through British pop musicals since the late 1950s. Certain notions of ethnicity and sexuality have been tied to rock'n'roll. While rock'n'roll was seen simply as reductively "black" – both by conservative forces and even by some scholarly writers on the subject, *Absolute Beginners* similarly homogenizes black people. Rock'n'roll in British culture has only rarely been tied to black immigrants from the West Indies, although it often occupies the same cultural zone as notions of imperial degeneration and post-colonialism. Pop musicals have figured British Empire decline and decolonization, in varying terms. *Expresso Bongo* (1959) is fairly direct in its depiction of "jungle music" while displacing any black performers. *Performance* (1970) – which might well qualify as the first British post-colonial film – thematically deals with English decadence and the influx of the "foreign". *The Great Rock'n'Roll Swindle* (1980) shows off punk as a very English form of "degeneration". Finally, *Absolute Beginners* attempts to represent multiculturalism,[15] although selling musical back catalogues sets the terms of its historical representations.

US imports

In 1958 Britain, there was a fear of American cultural "swamping". Not only popular music, but also American films dominated cinemas and American shows graced television sets. Landmark book *The Uses of Literacy* by Richard Hoggart was published in 1957, and contained a section called "The Jukebox Boys" which denigrates British teenagers who adopt American culture.[16] This imported "Americanism" is represented explicitly in *Absolute Beginners*. Vendice Partners (David Bowie) sports a gloriously bogus American accent, and his agency represents the new commerce imported from the United States. This is embodied by the song *That's Motivation*, although the lyrics exhibit precisely the sort of jargon of sales culture that was infused into Britain in the 1980s. The film seems explicitly pro-American. Colin says in voice-over as he enters Harold Charms's office: " . . . Mustn't throw stones, especially not at Americans....England for the English and all that, but being anti-Yank is a sure sign of defeat."[17]

However, there is a fundamental confusion here: the teddy boys that represent conservative anti-American England sing "American" rock'n'roll! This contradiction is the centre of a fault line in the film's logic. Rock'n'roll, the music that was revolutionizing youth culture and causing social approbation in the late 1950s, to some degree is denigrated by the film. *Absolute Beginners* has a whole section that trivializes rock'n'roll through depicting the construction of a child pop star, "Baby Boom", by the manipulative middle-aged businessman Harold Charms. Perhaps rock'n'roll has been displaced from a central position in the film for an ulterior motive, perhaps for commercial purposes?

The music in the film consists of a series of old "relics" and modern music that adds a veneer of jazz style to pop songs. Furthermore, the portrayal of "jazz culture" also serves to encourage sales. In the 1970s, there was an LP of Pink Floyd music called *Relics*, which sold for a far cheaper price than regular records. This is because it was seemingly an album of old and unwanted material; it was detritus, much of it recorded before the group was internationally successful. *Absolute Beginners* is part of the "relic" culture that was developing in the 1980s, where old recordings and styles were dug out from the attic, dusted down and then sold as commodities. The film mixes music of the late 1950s with contemporary artists commissioned to write new music for the film, the latter conjoining the two periods.

While the paralleling of 1958 and 1985 bridged social concerns of Britain between the two periods, the film was perhaps more concerned with paralleling music of the two periods. Music and musical styles from the late 1950s and the mid-1980s are coexistent and intermingled. The appearance of some 1950s jazz and the rock'n'roll song *Rocking at the 2Is* in the film work as periodizing devices in the film, but its pop songs all tend to function as contemporary frames to the representation of the past. Pop music in the film constantly displays its contemporary (1980s) status while retaining aspects of historical musical forms. For instance, Tenpole Tudor (as Ed the Ted) performs his own song *Ted Ain't Dead* which, although it seems to correspond with the styles of rockabilly that were prominent in the late 1950s, owes more to the revival of the form that came out of the punk movement in the late 1970s.[18] Similarly, David Bowie's title song for the film, also the scout single and a hit, provided an entry to the 1950s from the 1980s, first in terms of its status as a contemporary hit by a contemporary pop singer and secondly in terms of its formal make up. The song uses some jazz chord changes while opening with and reprising a "doo-wop" vocal section that is self-consciously modelled on the vocal style that was prevalent in some 1950s American popular music. Other artists, like Sade, perform music that was in no way at odds with her smooth style that comprised part of the 1980s jazz revival, while Ray Davies from the Kinks sings his song cameo in the mock-1930s style that is evident on some of the Kinks's recordings such as their hit record *Sunny Afternoon* from the late 1960s. Many of the songs in *Absolute Beginners* demonstrate a concern with historicism, with rearticulating the past and integrating it with the musical present. Original Sound Entertainment, an American licensing company based in Hollywood that had dealt with old records since 1959 and worked on films such as *Stand by Me* (1986 US) and *Hairspray* (1988 US), had acquired old songs and musical pieces for use in the film.

Absolute Beginners guaranteed a certain musical pedigree for itself. Gil Evans, once Miles Davis's arranger and sometimes credited with inventing "cool jazz" in the 1940s, was secured as musical director for the film. In addition, a number of contemporary British pop artists were commissioned to write songs for inclusion in the film. A succession of tied-in hits thus publicized the film, including David Bowie's title song and The Style Council's *Have You Ever Had It Blue*,[19] which arises non-diegetically, accompanying a montage sequence of images of London in the early morning as the film's protagonist Colin wanders home. *Absolute Beginners* constituted the culmination of the jazz revival that occurred in the 1980s. This is not to say that jazz needed reviving – it had always been thriving in its own quarters that were usually specialist circles beyond the immediate view of mainstream culture. The difference was that a number of jazz-styled groups appeared that were aiming at a pop music market rather than the traditional market for jazz.[20] As early as 1981, the *New Musical Express* was starting to deem jazz *a la mode* by incorporating an unprecedented double-page spread about historical jazz musicians.[21] By 1983, the *New Musical Express* had its own weekly jazz section, while groups directly embracing jazz such as Blue Rondo a la Turk and Working Week emerged and Joe Jackson had converted from being a new wave singer into a jazz singer and band leader with his *Jumpin' Jive* LP. By the middle of the decade, artists were having a degree of success in the pop mainstream using this style, perhaps summed up by the smooth and auspiciously "sophisticated" jazz singer Sade, who appears in *Absolute Beginners*, yet who had currency purely in pop rather than jazz circles.

While one aspect of the jazz revival stressed contemporary material publicized as pop music, the "revival" itself brought with it the "rediscovery" of historical jazz recordings. While the whole tendency was arguably conservative, especially in terms of reviving moribund fashions, the opportunities afforded to the record industry by the post-modern recycling of jazz back catalogues proved to be symptomatic of the decade that would end with mass back catalogue recycling on CD.[22] As a saturated commodity, *Absolute Beginners* had a selection of directly tied-in products. Notably, it had two soundtrack albums released, one of which was a double-LP. There was also MacPherson's book, *The Beginners' Guide to Absolute Beginners*,[23] a glossy poster magazine and recordings such as the unconnected RCA Victor compilation of old jazz recordings *The Absolute Beginner's Guide to Jazz* and its inevitable sequel, *Son of Absolute Beginner's Guide to Jazz*.

This process matches the recycling that was endemic across culture in the mid-1980s. Record companies were milking musical catalogues and rosters, and a new form became prominent, where old songs – often ones that fitted the industry's reconception of jazz songs – were revived in a different context, simultaneously having a nostalgic effect while being invested with a new contextual meaning. In the same year as *Absolute Beginners* was released, there were two examples of this: the television serial *The Singing Detective* (1986), written by Dennis Potter, contained regular occurrences of 1930s and 1940s songs in unexpected song sequences, and Neil Jordan's film *Mona Lisa* (1986) used Nat King Cole's song as a flavour for the film as well as a thematic key to its narrative. *Absolute Beginners* demonstrates not only the emergent (post-modern) nostalgia for the popular culture of the past, but also the new intersection of commodities, with records, pop videos and other merchandise being sold at the nexus point of the film itself. In the same year, an advertisement for Levi's jeans summed up the power of the new form of cultural consumerism. Set in a launderette, the advertisement elevated to fame the non-speaking model who appeared, Nick Kamen, as well as causing the re-release and hit status of its soundtrack of Marvin Gaye's 1968 song *I Heard It Through the Grapevine*. This process matches the recycling that was endemic across culture in the mid-1980s. Record companies milking back catalogues for the screen was highly evident. Denisoff and Plasketes described the industrial strategy called synergy, involving the co-ordination of record releases from a film soundtrack as mutual publicity,[24] while Jean Rosenbluth pointed to the accommodation where "Studios and record companies began to work together regularly to maximize their products' financial potential."[25]

Absolute Beginners is most interesting in relation to its choice of music. As I have noted, rock'n'roll, the new and vibrant force of the late

1950s, is derided and trivialized. Skiffle, an intriguing and wholly British phenomenon, is ignored.[26] Instead, jazz is elevated as the characteristic music of the film's version of 1958. Why jazz? Is it simply because it is more directly associated with black people? While an interest in jazz may be evident in the "original" story, this is certainly no literary adaptation. The source book by Colin MacInnes is almost irrelevant in the face of the film as a multi-layered palimpsest, which is led by the music, the film musical tradition and the artists, some of whom were already "tied" to the project before the script was written.[27]

Jazz is now seen as something of a "black high art" and *Absolute Beginners* exploits jazz's relatively high cultural status. While the film welds this "high art" association with its screen "blacks", and it associates whites with rock'n'roll, this seems to be part of the film's multiculturalist agenda. Yet the status of jazz as "legit" and its valorization in the film are likely symptoms of industrial developments at the time, specifically the reorientation of the music industry towards adult consumers.

The late 1970s and early 1980s was a period of crisis for the music industry. As one journalist put it in 1982, "With the British record industry now in the depths of the severest decline it has ever known, there are real fears that rock music will never regain the lion's share of the entertainment market it held in the mid-seventies."[28] The mood of the record industry was demonstrated vividly by their central overbearing concern in the early and mid-1980s, that of piracy. The industry's campaign which united behind the slogan "Home taping is killing music", put pressure on the British government with an aim of levying a charge on blank recording tapes to "compensate" record companies for the revenue lost by illegal but endemic home taping of records. One corollary of this industrial contraction was that pop music's past glories became the basis for future sales, which is why the conservatism of the July 1985 Live Aid roster was so striking: Eric Clapton, Status Quo, even Led Zeppelin reformed in order to appear. This meant that the focus of the music was more in the 1970s than in the 1980s, more looking to the past than to the future, and reflecting marketing rather than aesthetic developments.

The atmosphere of seemingly lost revenues, heaped upon dwindling profits led to a retrenchment of the international music and recording industry, which towards the end of the decade was boosted by the CD "revolution".[29] This was the conclusion of a strategy that allowed record companies to reanimate and resell all their back catalogues as much as, if not more than, they sold contemporary artists. Record companies could thus concentrate on "Adult Oriented Rock" (AOR), aiming at adult audiences rather than the poorer youth audience. These currents are evident in the version of jazz promoted by the film. It is not the more challenging versions of jazz, nor is it the sort of "trad jazz" that had a strong following in Britain in the late 1950s. *Absolute Beginners* showcases a more vague form that in many cases simply involved pop musicians playing what they thought was "jazz". *Absolute Beginners* hedged its bets by including existing jazz recordings, along with new recordings by jazz artists, and adding a large amount of jazz-inflected pop music to the soundtrack which was made available by co-producer Virgin Records.

In musical terms, there is a resounding question that hangs over *Absolute Beginners*: Where is the West Indian music? There is a little ambient reggae in the Napoli street scenes, and in one of the club scenes the band play jazz with a soca beat. Yet both of these musical forms came to prominence later. In 1958, there was a thriving Calypso scene, which was internationally successful. Indeed, one of the leading exponents of calypso, the intriguingly named Lord Kitchener, was residing in Britain. The likely reason for calypso's non-appearance in *Absolute Beginners* is that it was not a marketable commodity in 1985, as the "world music" market was only in an embryonic state. Since that time, calypso has remained obscure, missing out on a "revival", except in the form of soca.[30] *Absolute Beginners* represents Americanism (rock'n'roll, consumerism) but is also concerned with the legacy of the British Empire, particularly immigration from the West Indies. Yet the film's musical contrivance betrays that *Absolute Beginners* is less about Caribbeans and their culture than about selling old records and generic "blacks" appearing as the "origin" of that music.

Multiculturalism

The arrival of the ship *Empire Windrush* at Tilbury, London, in 1948 is seen as the starting point of immigration to Britain from the Caribbean.[31] A decade later, there were in the region of 125,000 West Indians in Britain, and their hostile reception was embodied by the Notting Hill "riot" of the same year, which is represented as the *denoue-ment* of *Absolute Beginners*. The film explicitly is referencing and paral-leling the riots of 1985, which took place in predominantly black areas (Handsworth in Birmingham, Toxteth in Liverpool and Broadwater Farm, Tottenham in London). These were at least partly a result of Prime Minister Margaret Thatcher's domestic politics of confrontation, added to institutionalized racism, both of which provide indirectly an agenda for *Absolute Beginners*. In the film, the malignant forces are manifested by shady business interests manipulating the racist teddy boys.[32] This very British subculture, represented by Ed the Ted and Flicker, appears as "ethnic whites" – like American redneck-hillbillies – which embody the repressed aspects of the film's other white characters.

According to Walter Benjamin in his "Fifth Thesis on the Philosophy of History", history should "seize hold of a memory as it flashes up at a moment of danger"[33] However, there is an arresting ambiguity in Benjamin's statement, allowing for history to constitute a reactionary positioning against the danger of change. The riots of the 1980s certainly manifested moments of danger and the film explicitly represents rioting, which is shocking in the context of the film's previous light-hearted images. Yet these violent images proceed to transmogrify into a harmless dance representation of a riot. Arguably, the amelioration of the striking imagery undermines any political or representational potential.

The film endeavours to show a fantasy of a postcolonial multicultural utopia (under the auspices of a creative cultural explosion). Colin says, in voice-over as he introduces the audience to "Napoli" (Notting Hill), "The thing I love most about these streets was the thing that made some people positively hate them. Because here nobody cared where you came from, or what colour, what you did or who you did it with." Napoli is shown as a periphery, a "liminal space" of London, while the other film space, Soho is made into a central Foucauldian *heterotopia*, where everything and all conventions are up for grabs and redevelopment.[34] However, within these "progressive" spaces there is also racial (and gender) segregation. For example, when Suzette is at Henley's show, four flunkeys are black men. She dances and they join in, shedding their clothes. Their status as support dancers to Suzette, and obviously signalled as black and masculine in contradistinction to Suzette's white femininity, keeps them subordinate to a white. Here, the ethnic divide is doubled by a gender divide. Black men appear as stereotypical sex symbols, whereas black women simply do not figure. In fact, there are only a handful of black women in the film and, apart from Sade's appearance on stage, they are firmly at the film's margins. In another sequence, Sade goes to sing *Killer Blow* in the Soho club. All the dancers on the floor are black men, while the seated audience are white. Blacks are represented in stereotypical manner throughout, appearing almost exclusively as musicians and dancers. The principal black character, "Cool", first appears playing a trumpet in the street and constantly wears sunglasses both onstage and off, while there are copious amounts of black male dancers, who seem to embody a white notion of black masculinity as symbol of sexual prowess.

In attitude, *Absolute Beginners* is pre-multiculturalism, the concept having only started to take hold in Britain in the 1980s. The film is "essentialist" in its race relations, seeing a strict and simple divide between white and black, irrespective of culture or origin. This is not the unified heritage and culture described by Paul Gilroy's notion of the "Black Atlantic", where blacks in America, Africa and Europe are seen as a single entity.[35] Instead, this is an imposed unity from elsewhere: a conflation by white culture that sees blacks as "the same". So the film's "multiculturalism" is more what Thomas Fitzgerald describes as "romantic racialism".[36] *Absolute Beginners* is less a "multiculturalist history" than simply a history from a white paternalist (and "integrative") point of view. This is underlined by the fact that the film shows only one Asian (a Sikh) despite the fact that there were approximately 55,000 Asians in Britain at the time (nearly half the number of West Indians). The likely reason for this parsimonious portrayal is that Asians were generally considered "unhip" until later.[37] This is the opposite of the film's "blacks", who are all undifferentiated and "Americanized", stereotyped and overbearingly "hip".

Conclusion

The "white labels" of this chapter's title refers not only to records with white labels sent out to promote music, but also to the propensity for black culture to be packaged for white consumption. In the film, Ed the Ted shouts at Colin: "Go home, Yank, and take Sambo with you!" This moment conflates the two (in derogatory terms) and underlines *Absolute Beginners*'s attempts to depict US culture as West Indian. This has an immediate effect of homogenizing black cultures, converting both US and Caribbean cultures into a single item unified by an implicit white (and oddly "English") point of view.

Absolute Beginners was an astonishing attempt to reinvent British pop music culture through bypassing the dominant popular cultural heritage of the protean 1960s and The Beatles. This denial of the 1960s's effect pointedly parallels Margaret Thatcher's attempt at a renewal of Britain and desire to erase the effects of the 1960s, or at least her desire to blame the decade for the problems faced in the 1980s. Yet Colin and Suzette's rise to fame (and the film's emphasis on photography) matches the rise to stardom in the Swinging London musical *Smashing Time* (1967). There are similarities between the two films but with a significant difference: in *Smashing Time* the present is depicted as exciting, whereas in *Absolute Beginners* the present is dull and we escape to an exciting past. The film was a watershed for popular music being used by the heritage industry, speeding up a train of heritage films about pop music running into *Hours and the Times* (1991), *Back Beat* (1993), *Still Crazy* (1998) and *Velvet Goldmine* (1998).

Absolute Beginners is a peculiarly historical film. The film is "historiographic" – it is less concerned with what "really happened" than it is concerned with history as a living entity in the present, re-imagining the point of entry of American and Caribbean culture to Britain. The film's attempts to represent this multiculturalism effect a form through which musical back catalogues can be sold. Hence the specific form of representation in the film is, to a lesser or greater degree, the product of a history emanating from commercial interests. The key is to think of the film less in relation to cinematic traditions, than in relation to the music industry and pop traditions. From this perspective, *Absolute Beginners* demonstrates the new configuration of intersecting commodities, with records, pop videos, style and other merchandise being sold at the nexus point of the film itself.

Notes

1 Introduction

1 James Park, *Learning to Dream: The New British Cinema* (London: Faber, 1984), p. 13.

2 Claudia Gorbman, *Unheard Melodies: Narrative Film Music* (London: BFI, 1987), p. 3.

3 Songs were tied regularly to Hollywood films at around 1930. David Ewens, *All the Years of American Popular Music* (London: Prentice-Hall, 1977), p. 384.

4 Anon., "Merchandising keeps Disney Image in Sharp Focus" in *Kinematograph Weekly*, vol. 564, no. 2954, 14 May 1964, p. 22.

5 Most of the recordings are new ones, by Rumon Gamba and the BBC Philharmonic. They include *The Film Music of Richard Rodney Bennett* (Chan 9867), *The Film Music of Arthur Bliss* (Chan 9896), and also Richard Hickox and the London Symphony Orchestra performing *The Film Music of William Alwyn* (Chan 9243). There was also a compilation *British Film Music* (Naxos 85544577) released in 1999.

6 Alan Lovell, "British Cinema: the Known Cinema?" in Robert Murphy, ed., *The British Cinema Book* (London: BFI, 1997), p. 235.

7 Julian Petley, "The Lost Continent" in Charles Barr, ed., *All Our Yesterdays: 90 Years of British Cinema* (London: BFI, 1986), p. 98.

8 Exceptions include Leon Hunt, *British Low Culture: From Safari Suits to Sexploitation* (London: Routledge, 1998); David McGillivray, *Doing Rude Things: The History of the British Sex Film, 1957–1981* (London: Sun Tavern Fields, 1992); K.J. Donnelly, *Pop Music in British Cinema: A Chronicle* (London: BFI, 2001).

9 Cf. John Sedgwick, "The Comparative Popularity of Stars in Mid-1930s Britain" in *Journal of Popular British Cinema*, no. 2, 1999.

10 John Hill, *British Cinema of the 1980s* (Oxford: Oxford University Press, 1999), p. 77.

11 Marcia Landy, *British Genres: Cinema and Society, 1930–1960* (Oxford: Princeton University Press, 1991), p. 10.

12 Ibid., p. 18.

13 Justine Ashby and Andrew Higson, "Introduction"; John Ellis, "British Cinema as Performance Art: *Brief Encounter*, *Radio Parade of 1935* and the Circumstances of Film Exhibition"; and Jane Stokes, "Arthur Askey and the Construction of Popular Entertainment in *Band Waggon* and *Make Mine a Million*" in Justine Ashby and Andrew Higson, eds, *British Cinema: Past and Present* (London: Routledge, 2000).

14 Adrian Wootton, "Looking Back, Dropping Out, Making Sense: A History of the Rock-Concert Movie" in *Monthly Film Bulletin*, vol. 55, no. 659, 1988, p. 356.

15 Geoffrey Nowell-Smith, *Sight and Sound*, Autumn 1964, p. 191.

16 Peter Harcourt, *Sight and Sound*, vol. 3, no. 4, Autumn 1965, p. 199.

17 Rick Altman, *The American Film Musical* (London: BFI, 1989), p. 81.

18 American songwriters increasingly dominated British popular music in the 1930s. James J. Nott, *Music for the People: Popular Music and Dance in Interwar Britain* (Oxford: Oxford University Press, 2002), p. 225.

19 Cf. Lawrence Napper, "British Cinema and the Middlebrow" in Justine Ashby and Andrew Higson, eds, *British Cinema: Past and Present* (London: Routledge, 2000).

20 Rick Altman notes that the classical musical began at the height of piano sheet music sales. Op. cit., p. 356.

21 Ealing musical director Ernest Irving noted that he was surprised by his degree of recognition in art music circles, which came directly from his procuring of "serious" composers for film work. Ernest Irving, *Cue for Music* (London: Dennis Dobson, 1959), p. 182.

22 Cf. John Ellis, "Art, Culture and Quality: Terms for a Cinema of the Forties and Seventies" in *Screen*, vol. 19, no. 3, Autumn 1978.

23 Andrew Higson differentiates between strategies of direct competition with Hollywood studios/films, and making "films with distinctly indigenous attractions and a qualitatively different regime of experiences and pleasures" and on a low budget, aiming for profit from the home market alone. *Waving the Flag: Constructing a National Cinema in Britain* (Oxford: Clarendon, 1995), pp. 10–11.

24 Particularly when the object of representation is less stable. Hill, op. cit., p. 241.

25 Using precise written descriptions of the action on "cue sheets" until the advent of video.

26 Kathryn Kalinak, *Settling the Score: Music and the Classical Hollywood Film* (Madison: University of Wisconsin Press, 1992), pp. xv–xvi.

27 There is, of course, pressure on cultural products not to be seen as irredeemably at variance with the dominant norm. In some cases, there is a desire to fit as closely to the norm as possible.

28 I have also discussed the "composite" score, where there is an interest in retaining a cohesion across diverse pieces and styles. K.J. Donnelly, "*Performance* and the Composite Score" in K.J. Donnelly, ed., *Film Music: Critical Approaches* (Edinburgh: Edinburgh University Press, 2001).

29 R. Serge Denisoff and William D. Romanowski, *Risky Business: Rock on Film* (New York: Transaction, 1991), pp. 299–300.

30 Jane Feuer, "The Self-Reflexive Musical and the Myth of Entertainment" in Rick Altman, ed., *Genre: The Musical* (London: Routledge & Kegan Paul, 1981), pp. 168–169.

31 Altman, op. cit., p. 108.

32 Martin Sutton, "Patterns of Meaning in the Musical" in Rick Altman, ed., *Genre: The Musical* (London: Routledge & Kegan Paul, 1981), p. 191.

33 Altman, op. cit., p. 110.

34 K.J. Donnelly, *Pop Music in British Cinema*, p. viii.

35 Altman, op. cit., p. 129.

36 Barry Keith Grant, "The Classic Hollywood Musical and the 'Problem' of Rock 'n' Roll" in *Journal of Popular Film and Television*, vol. 18, no. 4, 1986, p. 199.

37 Altman, op. cit., p. 198.

38 Most notably periods in the mid and late 1960s and the early 1980s.

2 British Film Music

1 "English film music, unlike its American counterpart, never exhibited any split between 'serious' and 'film' music." William Darby and Jack Dubois, *American Film Music: Major Composers, Techniques, Trends, 1915–1990* (Jefferson, N.C.: Macfarland, 1991), p. 384.

2 Although one might argue that the requisitioning and co-ordination of resources during wartime constituted an effective centralization of both film music procedures and styles.

3 Hubert Bath's obituary in *Kinematograph Weekly*, no. 1985, 1945, p. 21.

4 Arnold was "outstanding for his range of musical styles", had a "skill in pastiche composition" and his "music blends brilliantly with sound effects". Also notes his precise writing to momentary film dynamics. Roger Manvell, "Malcolm Arnold" in Nicholas Thomas, ed., *The International Dictionary of Filmmakers* (London: St. James Press, 1990), p. 38.

5 See Michael Allen, " 'In the Mix': How Electrical Reproducers Facilitated the Transition to Sound in British Cinema" in K.J. Donnelly, ed., *Film Music: Critical Approaches* (Edinburgh: Edinburgh University Press, 2001).

6 Roger Manvell and John Huntley, *The Technique of Film Music* (London: Focal Press, 1957), pp. 27–28.

7 Sarah Street, *British National Cinema* (London: Routledge, 1997), p. 30.

8 According to Jan Swynnoe, Mathieson and Ernest Irving at Ealing "…deliberately led the British film score away from the stereotypes of the classical Hollywood score". Jan G. Swynnoe, *The Best Years of British Film Music, 1936–1958* (Woodbridge, Suffolk: Boydell Press, 2002), p. 35.

9 John Huntley, *British Film Music* (London: Skelton Robinson, 1947), pp. 39–40.

10 It was also released as a recording by Decca, on three 78 rpm discs (Decca K810/11) William Sneddon, "Things to Come: The World's First Soundtrack Album?" in *Film Score Monthly*, 6 June 2000.

11 Huntley, op. cit., pp. 101–103.

12 Furthermore, as Huntley notes, the final film was cut to fit Leigh's finished music, which was "…unheard of at the time." Op. cit., p. 74.

13 Particularly seeing as Mathieson was installed as musical director at the Ministry of Information, which produced almost all of the wartime documentaries.

14 For instance, Debussy's *La Mer*, Britten's *Sea Interludes* from *Peter Grimes* and Frank Bridge's *The Sea*.

15 Documentary style became a notable influence on British feature films. Tony Aldgate and Jeffrey Richards, *Britain Can Take It: The British Cinema in the Second World War* (Edinburgh: Edinburgh University Press, 1994), p. 219.

16 Huntley, op. cit., p. 190.

17 Vaughan Williams led "…the revival of Tudor music and the 'rediscovery' of English folk-song. These can be said to combine into a 'historical-pastoral' obsession, which was to characterize English music for the best part of half a century." Robert Stradling and Meirion Hughes, *The English Musical Renaissance, 1860–1940: Construction and Deconstruction* (London: Routledge, 1993), p. 61.

18 Mathieson tells of how he visited Vaughan Williams and found him desirous of doing more for the war effort. At the time his endeavours involved

collecting scrap metal in a cart, and the opportunity to provide music for the cinema's war effort proved highly attractive to him. Huntley, op. cit., pp. 56–57.

19   Hubert Clifford quoted in Huntley, op. cit., p. 74.

20   Ibid., p. 75.

21   The battle bears notable resemblance to Eisenstein's battle on the ice in *Alexander Nevsky* (1938) with its effective music by Prokofiev.

22   Walton also went on to score Olivier's *Hamlet* (1948), and was nominated for an Oscar, although he generally was not happy with film scoring and most of his original written scores are now lost.

23   Gerard Schurmann interviewed by Trevor Willsmer in *Movie Collector*, vol. 1, issue 7, July/August 1994, p. 64.

24   Louis Levy, *Music for the Movies* (London: Sampson Low, 1948), pp. 101–102.

25   Vincent Porter, "Methodism Versus the Market Place: The Rank Organisation and British Cinema" in Robert Murphy, ed., *The British Cinema Book* (London: BFI, 1997), p. 123; Robert Murphy, "Rank's Attempt at the American Market" in James Curran and Vincent Porter, eds, *British Cinema History* (London: Weidenfeld & Nicholson, 1983), pp. 166–167.

26   Famed conductor Sir Thomas Beecham conducted the ballet sequence while Easdale conducted the rest.

27   The same musical principle is evident in the main theme from horror film *Halloween* (1978).

28   Vaughan Williams did not compose to the images of the film, Huntley, op. cit., p. 178.

29   He had already utilized some unused music written for *A Flemish Farm* as part of his *Sixth Symphony*. Jeffrey Richards, *Films and British National Identity: From Dickens to Dad's Army* (Manchester: Manchester University Press, 1997), p. 299.

30   Huntley, op. cit., p. 161.

31   *Kinematograph Weekly*, vol. 1368, no. 2110, 9 October 1947, p. 22.

32   Upon the film's re-release it was noted that it was "...interlaced with good music". *Kinematograph Weekly*, vol. 431, no. 2383, 26 February 1953, p. 28.

33   Claudia Gorbman, *Unheard Melodies: Narrative Film Music* (London: BFI, 1987), p. 70; Kathryn Kalinak, *Settling the Score: Music and the Classical Hollywood Film* (Madison: University of Wisconsin Press, 1992), pp. xv–xvi.

34   The irony of these very British productions having music by a Frenchman was compounded by Ealing boss Michael Balcon's motto for his company of "Projecting Britain and the British Character". Musical Supervisor Ernest Irving followed Mathieson in setting a high standard of distinctive rather than functional music in Ealing's films.

35   Frankel has, since his death, been reclaimed as a "legitimate" concert hall composer – partly through the marginalization of his film scores. Huntley refers to him as a "one of our leading experts in the jazz and comedy score". Op. cit., p. 205.

36   This sound, known as "the guggle", was created by sound editor Mary Habberfield, although it was integrated with Frankel's score.

37   Perhaps as a consequence of this, he has been ignored. It might be argued that Black's work urgently deserves researching and rehabilitating.

38   *The Sound Barrier*'s cues became the *Rhapsody for Orchestra, Op.38.* Arnold had
served a wartime "apprenticeship" writing for documentaries as had many
of his contemporaries.

39   Indeed, Arnold was doubtless the best example of a concert hall composer
endeavouring with the craft of integrating music with film demands.

40   The film begins with *A Life on the Ocean Wave* as a march before running
into Dunn's music.

41   Further examples include *I Know Where I'm Going*, where Allan Gray was
aided by Walter Goehr and Robert Farnon as well as Schurmann's conten-
tious role as head orchestrator on *Lawrence of Arabia* (1962). In terms of
collaboration, mainstream films produced by Hollywood almost always used
(and still use) orchestrators, who may have a significant artistic input that
might not be recognized. It is worth noting that collaboration can be down-
played for copyright reasons and a sense of the plaudits heaped upon the
"author" to the detriment of associated "technicians".

42   See Chapter 3, "The Anti-Matter of Film Music" in K.J. Donnelly, *The Spectre
of Sound: Film and Television Music* (London: BFI, 2005).

43   While horror films increasingly adopted a modernist musical language,
inspired by developments in the concert hall, Bernard also wrote the main
themes for these films as songs without words, the melodic line aping the
film's title.

44   Such "transparent" processes align Bernard's music with minimalists such
as Lamont Young, Terry Riley, Steve Reich and Philip Glass.

45   Serial composition was a modernist composition technique developed by
Arnold Schoenberg, which destroyed the tone hierarchies of key as well as
fragmenting the traditional sound of orchestral music, through the use of
pre-fabricated rows of notes, all of which had to be wielded in (often) strict
order. An example of a score that uses this is Richard Rodney Bennett's music
for Joseph Losey's *Figures in a Landscape* (1970).

46   Jeffrey Kemp, "Write What the Film Needs: an Interview with Elizabeth
Lutyens" in *Sight and Sound*, vol. 43, no. 4, Autumn 1974, p. 203.

47   Gerhard primarily produced austere concert hall material, although he did
supply some stock pieces used in science fiction serial *Doctor Who* (BBC,
1963–1989).

48   The decision by United Artists to back these three films led to a flood of
American finance entering the British film industry. Robert Murphy, *Sixties
British Cinema* (London: BFI, 1992), p. 112.

49   Although the Bond theme is credited to Monty Norman, it seems that Barry
not only extensively rearranged material but provided a significant amount
of it, yet lost out under the agreement about screen credits.

50   Indeed, its popularity has devalued it. *Lara's Theme* can be heard played as
a jingle by ice cream vans and was used to epitomise banal music in *Super
Mario Brothers* (1993 US).

51   For example, *Superman* (1978) was registered as British, although it was to
all intents and purposes a Hollywood film.

52   K.J. Donnelly, "The Classical Film Score Forever?: Music in the Batman
Films" in Steve Neale and Murray Smith, eds, *Contemporary Hollywood Cinema*
(London: Routledge, 1998), pp. 143–144.

53   A whole debate that was viewed sceptically by Thomas Elsaesser in "Images For England: and Scotland, Ireland, Wales..." in *Monthly Film Bulletin*, no. 51, September 1984, p. 267. While the "renaissance" was probably overstated, Sarah Street notes the boom in film production in the early-mid 1980s. Op. cit., p. 21.

54   British Film Year was a nationwide promotional drive for the British film industry, encompassing highlighting British films that were on release and encouraging cinema attendance. Cf. Andrew Higson, "The Discourses of British Film Year" in *Screen*, vol. 27, no. 1, January/February 1986.

55   The *Chariots of Fire* soundtrack LP spent 97 weeks on the *Music Week* chart in the UK, peaking at number five.

56   A review noted *The Draughtsman's Contract* balanced "mainstream conventions" with "avant garde" and idiosyncrasy, Robert Brown, *Monthly Film Bulletin*, vol. 49, no. 586, November 1982, p. 254.

57   The music is a cerebral structure in that pieces are associated with certain views of the house and garden, while its modern take on baroque music is distantly similar to John Addison's music for some of *Tom Jones* (1963).

58   Robbins received Oscar nominations for *Howard's End* (1992) and *Remains of the Day* (1993).

59   In some ways, these soundtracks resembled the sort of CD that became a growth market in the 1980s and 1990s: the ubiquitous and cheaply produced "classics from the movies" compilations.

60   Barrington Pheloung's incidental music for television detective drama *Inspector Morse* (Granada, 1987–2000) illustrates the use of existing orchestral music as a sign of culture and the upper classes, particularly in that the programme mixed it with concert hall classics.

61   Nyman also wrote an influential book in the 1970s: *Experimental Music: Cage and Beyond* (Cambridge: Cambridge University Press, 1974).

62   Randall, D. Larson, "David Arnold Saves the World" in *Soundtrack!*, vol. 17, no. 65, March 1998, p. 31.

63   His score follows Addison's play with expectations of period music in *Tom Jones*, most notably in the dance sequence which uses music premised upon modern computerized dance beats.

64   It is notable that almost all the composers that have been under discussion were male and, indeed, it is the case that the field is heavily dominated by men, although less so than in Hollywood. Prominent British female composers who specialize in film music include Debbie Wiseman and Anne Dudley, the latter of whom has had a successful career as a string arranger on pop records, the equivalent of working in light orchestral music 50 years earlier. In the middle of the twentieth century, apart from Elisabeth Lutyens, who I have mentioned already, there was also Grace Williams (a pupil of Vaughan Williams), who became the first woman to score a feature film: *Blue Scar* (1949). This is discussed in detail in Swynnoe, op. cit., p. 110.

65   Film music should be approached as a component of a composite medium, the music has to be taken into context in order to gauge its significance. This line of inquiry suggests that the qualities of the individual films involved have some bearing on the significance conferred on the music itself and I would imagine that this is, to some degree, unavoidable as music from

films that have been instantly forgotten rarely enter any canons of film or musical scholarship.

66 Swynnoe, op. cit., pp. 39, 37.
67 Ralph Vaughan Williams, "Film Music" in *The Royal College of Music Magazine*, vol. XL, no. 1, 1944, p. 7.

3 Wicked Sounds and Magic Melodies: Music in Gainsborough Melodramas

1   Roger Manvell, "British Feature Films from 1925 to 1945" in Michael Balcon, Ernest Lindgren, F. Hardy and Roger Manvell, eds, *Twenty Years of British Films 1925–1945* (London: Falcon Press, 1947), p. 91.
2   Indeed, he was something of an evangelist for the musical possibilities offered by film composition. Ralph Vaughan Williams, "Film Music" in *The Royal College of Music Magazine*, vol. XL, no. 1, 1944, p. 7.
3   Muir Mathieson, "Aspects of Film Music" in John Huntley, *British Film Music* (London: Skelton Robinson: 1947), p. 184.
4   Gainsborough had been owned by Gaumont-British since 1928.
5   John Huntley, *British Film Music* (London: Skelton Robinson, 1947), p. 212.
6   Louis Levy, *Music for the Movies* (London: Sampson Low, 1948), p. 95.
7   Huntley, op. cit., p. 198.
8   Manvell and Huntley's pantheon of greats includes only four films from Gainsborough: *Man of Aran* (1934), *Love Story* (1944), *The Magic Bow* (1946) and *Christopher Columbus* (1948). These few appear among an extensive list of 10–20 of "the best" from each year. Manvell and Huntley, *The Technique of Film Music* (London: The Focal Press, 1957), pp. 211–224.
9   Louis Levy, "Music for Every Mood" (interview) in *Film Weekly*, vol. 15, no. 386, 7 March 1937, p. 8.
10 Huntley, op. cit., p. 212.
11 Michel Chion, "Chiffre de Destinee: Une Femme Disparait d'Alfred Hitchcock" in *Cahiers du Cinema*, vol. 358, April 1984, pp. 32–34.
12 Levy, 1948, op. cit., p. 109.
13 Manvell, op. cit., p. 91.
14 Huntley, op. cit., p. 161.
15 Mathieson, op. cit., p. 186.
16 R.J. Minney, *Talking of Films* (London: Home and Van Thal, 1947), p. 35.
17 Claudia Gorbman, *Unheard Melodies: Narrative Film Music* (London: BFI, 1983), p. 73.
18 Harold Huth, Hubert Bath's Obituary in *Kinematograph Weekly*, vol. 1985, 3 May 1945, p. 21.
19 Levy, 1937, op. cit., p. 9.
20 Huntley, op. cit., p. 194.
21 Sue Aspinall and Robert Murphy, eds, *BFI Dossier 18: Gainsborough Melodramas* (London: BFI, 1983), p. 2.
22 Thomas Elsaesser, "Tales of Sound and Fury: Observations on the Family Melodrama" in Christine Gledhill, ed., *Home is Where the Heart Is: Studies in Melodrama and the Woman's Film* (London: BFI, 1987), pp. 50–51.

23   Levy, 1937, op. cit., p. 9.
24   Huntley, op. cit., p. 209.
25   Levy, 1948, op. cit., pp. 64–65.
26   Hyden " . . . contributed music to a number of films, including one based on his famous radio programme, *Cafe Collette*, and a large-scale industrial film on rayon." Huntley, op. cit., p. 209.
27   Huntley, op. cit., p. 200.
28   Sue Harper, *Picturing the Past: The Rise and Fall of the Costume Film* (London: BFI, 1994), p. 182.
29   Stewart Granger, *Sparks Will Fly* (London: Granada, 1981), p. 92.
30   Levy, 1948, op. cit., p. 90.
31   Pam Cook, "Neither Here Nor There: National Identity in Gainsborough Costume Drama" in Andrew Higson, ed., *Dissolving Views: Key Writings on British Cinema* (London: Cassell, 1996), p. 63; Harper, op. cit., p. 168.
32   He even has a hustling manager, Germi, who would not be out of place in a pop musical. *The Magic Bow* anticipates Ken Russell's pop-inspired composer biopics, such as *The Music Lovers* (1970), *Mahler* (1974) and *Lisztomania* (1975), where Russell attempted to remove the composers from their "respectable" positions assigned to them by the art music establishment.
33   Harper, op. cit., p. 179.
34   Levy, 1948, op. cit., pp. 88–89.
35   Ibid., p. 98.
36   This concert sequence has a bewigged Bretton Byrd conducting the orchestra on stage behind Granger.
37   Huntley, op. cit., p. 206.
38   Henry Geehl also wrote religious music such as *Crimond*, a version of *The Lord's My Shepherd*.
39   Paganini's knighthood by the Pope makes it possible for him to marry Jeanne, and so the film is not about the inertia of class, but of the possibility of social mobility and the malleability of class relations which is apparent in many of the other melodramas.
40   Jack Courtnay, "Music" in *Kinematograph Weekly*, vol. 359, no. 2076, 30 January 1947, p. 47.
41   "He lived to put music to pictures" (anonymous obituary) in *Today's Cinema*, vol. 89, no. 7842, 20 August 1957, p. 6.
42   Other, less prominent composers used included Temple Abady (*Easy Money* [1948], *Miranda* [1948]), Arthur Wilkinson (*The Calendar* [1948], *Traveller's Joy* [1949]) and Lambert Williamson (*The Good-time Girl* [1947] and *Don't Ever Leave Me* [1949]).
43   Cook, op. cit., p. 53.
44   Examples include Arthur Bliss's score for *Conquest of the Air*, which appeared as a suite at the proms in 1938 before the release of that troubled film in 1940. Almost every composer with a concert hall reputation made their film music into suites, like Vaughan Williams's *A Flemish Farm* (1945) and William Alwyn's *Odd Man Out* (1946). Although 78 rpm recordings were issued of some Gainsborough music, including *Love Story* (1944), *Holiday Camp* (1947), *Miranda* (1948), *Boys in Brown* (1949), *So Long at the Fair* (1949), *Trio* (1949), *Vote for Huggett* (1949) and *Encore* (1950).

4 Did You Hear the One about the Irishman? Sound and Music, Forging Ethnicity in *Odd Man Out* (1946)

1 *Kinematograph Weekly*, vol. 360, no. 2077, 6 February 1947, p. 28.
2 Anonymous review, *What's on in London*, 31 January 1947, p. 127.
3 Arthur Vesselo, review in *Sight and Sound*, vol. 61, Spring 1947, p. 39.
4 Dai Vaughan, *Odd Man Out* (London: BFI, 1995).
5 They removed a large amount of the material from F.L. Green's novel, upon which the film was based. Green was born in Portsmouth, but had settled in Ulster during the previous decade. In his novel, he directly addressed the IRA and his strongly loyalist point of view was removed in the adaptation to screen.
6 In recent years, there has begun a tentative replacement of the "British" in British cinema with "English". Cf. Charles Barr, *English Hitchcock* (Moffat, Dumfriesshire: Cameron & Hollis, 1999) and Andrew Higson, *English Heritage, English Cinema: Costume Drama Since 1980* (Oxford: Oxford University Press, 2003). As well as being a victim of the slippage between the two terms, this chapter also will serve to stress their problematic semantic and symbolic status.
7 Robert F. Moss, *The Films of Carol Reed* (New York: Columbia University Press, 1987), p. 161.
8 In fact, there has been a significant focus on the aesthetics of *Odd Man Out*. The mill robbery sequence is examined in detail in Karel Reisz and Gavin Millar, *The Technique of Film Editing* (London: Focal Press, 1968 [first 1953]). pp. 261–269, while the music for the finale is analyzed in Roger Manvell and John Huntley, *The Technique of Film Music* (London: The Focal Press, 1957), pp. 123–133. These, as John Hill has suggested, have tended to keep attention on technique rather than meaning. John Hill, "*Odd Man Out*" in Nick Thomas, ed., *International Dictionary of Films and Filmmakers – 1: Films* (London: St. James Press, 1990b), p. 649.
9 Anon., "Writer of *Odd Man Out* scores again" in *The Belfast Telegraph*, Tuesday, 4 March 1947, p. 2.
10 Indeed, "... there was an avalanche of Irish actors who proceeded from there [*Odd Man Out*] into films..." Cyril Cusack, in Brian McIlroy, *World Cinema 4: Ireland* (London: Flicks Books, 1988), p. 106.
11 Some of these actors from the Abbey Theatre had appeared in John Ford's film of Sean O'Casey's play about the IRA, *The Plough and the Stars* (1936).
12 Moss, op. cit., p. 151.
13 James DeFelice, *Filmguide to Odd Man Out* (Bloomington: Indiana University Press, 1975), p. 29.
14 Robert J. Gregg, "The Scotch–Irish Dialect Boundaries in Ulster" in Martyn F. Wakelin, ed., *Patterns of Folk Speech in the British Isles* (London: Athlone Press, 1972), p. 114; Arthur Hughes and Peter Trudgill, *English Accents and Dialects* (London: Edward Arnold, 1987) p. 81; and Alison Henry, *Belfast English and Standard English: Dialect Variation and Parameter Setting* (Oxford: Oxford University Press, 1995), p. 7. There have been moves to reclassify what is commonly called "Ulster Scots" as a minor language within the European Union, rather than merely seeing it as a dialect of English.

15   Nicholas Wapshott, *A Man Between: A Biography of Carol Reed* (London: Chatto & Windus, 1990), p. 180.

16   There is a recent relevance for this denial of voice, including the continuation of rule of Northern Ireland from London despite elections and the constitution of a parliament.

17   Anon., op. cit., p. 2.

18   The current teaching of "RP" (received pronunciation) English to foreigners also serves to centralize English in home-counties (and middle-class) England, denying the validity of more peripheral versions of the language.

19   For a long time, the only Northern Irish accent appearing regularly on British television was that of James Ellis, playing Bert Lynch in the BBC's *Z Cars* (BBC, 1962–1966, 1967–1978). Film appearances of Northern Irish accents were nothing more than isolated examples, such as Harry Towb as McCleery in *Above Us the Waves* (1955), a warfilm about British midget submarines attacking the German battleship *Tirpitz* during Second World War.

20   Colin McArthur, "Scotland and Cinema: The Iniquity of the Fathers" in Colin McArthur, ed., *Scotch Reels: Scotland in Cinema and Television* (London: BFI, 1982), p. 40.

21   Modern ethnicity works through the manipulation of symbols. Thomas K. Fitzgerald, "Media, Ethnicity and Identity" in Paddy Scannel, Philip Schlesinger and Colin Sparks eds, *Culture and Power: A Media, Culture and Society Reader* (London: Sage, 1992), p. 116.

22   Cf. C.G. Duggan, *The Stage Irishman* (London: Benjamin Blom, 1969).

23   There is often an ulterior motive to actors putting on accents: for instance, burlesquing the French in television comedy *'Allo 'Allo* (BBC, 1982–1986), and underlining the evil of German Nazis in war films. There were dissenting voices about the dubbed accents for Japanese television programmes *Monkey* (1978–1980) and *The Water Margin* (1977), as the voices provided were ridiculous caricatures of Chinese accents.

24   Jeffrey Richards is happy to see representations of Irish people in British culture as "a cultural construction of Irishness in which the Irish themselves have collaborated" and so not directly determined by English/British hegemony. Jeffrey Richards, *Films and British National Identity: From Dickens to Dad's Army* (Manchester: Manchester University Press, 1997), p. 229. This is in contrast to scholars such as Lebow who see cultural representations as primary influences on colonial activities and discrimination. Richard Ned Lebow, *White Britain and Black Ireland: The Influence of Stereotypes on Colonial Policy* (Philadelphia: Institute for the Study of Human Issues, 1976), p. 45.

25   Brian McIlroy convincingly argued that most of the films dealing with the Northern Ireland conflict exploit a myth of "anti-imperialism". *Odd Man Out* certainly does so on the one hand but also attempts to deny it on the other. *Shooting to Kill: Filmmaking and the "Troubles" in Northern Ireland* (Trowbridge: Flicks, 1998), p. 38.

26   John Hill, "Images of Violence" in Kevin Rockett, John Hill and Luke Gibbons, eds, *Cinema and Ireland* (London: Croom Helm, 1987), p. 178.

27   Anon. op. cit., p. 2.

28   Anon. "The policing of cinema" in *The Belfast Telegraph*, Wednesday 5 March 1947, p. 5.

29 Cf. K.J. Donnelly, "The Policing of Cinema: Troubled Film Exhibition in Northern Ireland" in *Historical Journal of Film, Radio and Television*, vol. 20, no. 3, August 2000.

30 Harris Deans, "Here is a really great picture" in *The Belfast Telegraph*, Saturday 1 March 1947, p. 2.

31 Michel Chion, *Audio–Vision: Sound on Screen*, edited and translated by Claudia Gorbman (New York: Columbia University Press, 1990), p. 81.

32 Moss, op. cit., p. 142. Alwyn reused the main theme from *Odd Man Out* in the first movement of his *First Symphony*.

33 Schubert's *Unfinished Symphony* was popular in the 1940s. This was at least partially due to the widespread notion that Schubert died while writing it. In fact, he had set it aside much earlier. Theodor Adorno and Hanns Eisler, *Composing for the Films* (London: Athlone, 1994 [f.p. 1947]), pp. 15–16.

34 Indeed, tolling bells seem to be the aural icon *par excellence* for films set in Northern Ireland, as evidenced by films such as *The Boxer* (1998) and *Resurrection Man* (1998).

35 William Alwyn's journal, quoted in the sleevenotes to *Odd Man Out*, and corroborated by Moss, op. cit., p. 143.

36 John Hill, "Images of Violence", op. cit., p. 158.

37 Anon., op. cit., p. 2.

38 He connects *Odd Man Out* with Reed's *The Running Man* (1963), *The Upturned Glass* (1947), *The October Man* (1947), *The Long Memory* (1952) and *Hunted* (1952). Raymond Durgnat, *A Mirror For England: From Austerity to Affluence* (London: Praeger, 1971), p. 145.

39 Moss, op. cit., p. 166.

40 Ernest Lindgren, *The Art of Film* (London: Allen & Unwin, 1963), p. 189.

41 *Kinematograph Weekly*, op. cit. p. 28.

5 Experimenting with Film Scores, 1967–1970

1 Many disdainfully have pointed out that the BBC broadcast this colourful film first in black and white rather than colour. Yet this was due to the fact that the BBC was changing from a 405 line system to a 625 line system. BBC1 was still using the 405 line system and therefore was not able to be received in colour. *Magical Mystery Tour* was broadcast for a mass audience on BBC1. Its second broadcast was on the 625 line BBC2, where it went out in colour but to a very small number of people who owned colour 625 line television sets.

2 Arthur Marwick, "Introduction: Locating Key Texts Amid the Distinctive Landscape of the Sixties" in Anthony Aldgate, James Chapman and Arthur Marwick, eds, *Window on the Sixties: Exploring Key Texts of Media and Culture* (London: I.B. Tauris, 2000), p. xii.

3 *Time's* "London: The Swinging City" special issue, more particularly the article by Piri Halasz, "London: You Can Walk Across it on the Grass" in *Time*, no. 87, 15 April 1966, p. 32.

4 George Melly, *Revolt into Style: The Pop Arts in Britain* (London: Penguin, 1972), pp. 176–177.

5 "Barclay Warns: A Major Crisis Developing" in *Kinematograph Weekly*, vol. 629, no. 3241, 1969, p. 3.

6   These two films have scores that experimented with first-time film scorers. The radical developments in pop music that were taking place at the time led directly to pop musicians being approached.

7   At this time, Woody Allen's film *What's Up, Tiger Lily* (1967) took the image track from a Japanese film and added comic dubbed dialogue and music by The Lovin' Spoonful.

8   For instance, the mixing of Victoriana and military costumes with more contemporary clothes.

9   Ian MacDonald, *Revolution in the Head: The Beatles' Records and the Sixties* (London: Pimlico, 2005), p. 15.

10   Kathryn Kalinak, *Settling the Score: Music and the Classical Hollywood Film* (Madison: University of Wisconsin Press, 1992), pp. xv–xvi.

11   Jeff Smith, *The Sounds of Commerce: Marketing Popular Film Music* (New York: Columbia University Press, 1998), pp. 5–11.

12   Robert Neaverson, *The Beatles Movies* (London: Cassell, 1998), p. 120.

13   John Williams, CD sleevenotes to *Here We Go Round the Mulberry Bush: The Original Soundtrack* (rpm Records, 1997). In the 1980s, Napier Bell went on to manage Japan and Wham!

14   Ibid.

15   "Rock has often been taken to be problematic for film scorers – its very *presence* can swamp surrounding visual images." Simon Frith, "Mood Music" in *Screen*, vol. 25, no. 3, 1984, p. 83.

16   The film's title single was released in November 1967 on Island records; Adrienne Posta (Linda in the film) had released some singles earlier.

17   Their "psychedelic" album *As Is* was released in October 1966 and evinced an expanded musical vocabulary. All of the film's music was recorded in late October and early November 1967.

18   Mann alone also scored *Christa: Swedish Fly Girls* (1971).

19   The Manfred Mann "team" (Mann, Hugg and Klaus Voorman) wrote a jingle for a Hovis bread television advertisement. *Melody Maker*, 6 April 1968, p. 18.

20   Some of the Manfred Mann group went on to film and television work. Singer Paul Jones in Peter Watkins's *Privilege* (1967?) and television presentation work, while Mike Vickers scored films such as *Warlords of Atlantis*, *At the Earth's Core* and *Please Sir!*

21   John Williams, CD sleevenotes to *Manfred Mann go Up the Junction* (rpm Records, 1998).

22   The music received the headline "Manfred 'Junction' Brilliant" in *New Musical Express*, 2 March 1968, p. 6.

23   The film's premiere was in January but wide release came later.

24   There are some notable similarities. For example, The Beatles's instrumental *Flying* is reminiscent of some of *Wonderwall*, specifically the track *Party Secombe*.

25   Ian Peel, *The Unknown Paul McCartney: McCartney and the Avant Garde* (London: Reynolds and Hearn, 2002).

26   Derek Taylor, CD sleevenotes to George Harrison, *Wonderwall Music* (Apple Records, 1992).

27   While it was recorded in January 1968, Harrison's LP was not released until January 1969, while the film had opened in the UK in September 1968.

28 Sergei M. Eisenstein, "Rhythm and Vertical Montage" in Michael Glenny and Richard Taylor, eds, *Eisenstein, Selected Works II: Towards a Theory of Montage* (London: BFI, 1991), pp. 227–248.

29 The situation of music dictating screen dynamics is reminiscent of Disney's *Fantasia* (1940).

30 *The Committee* had its premiere at the Cameo Poly, Oxford Circus, London, on 26 September 1968, although it never received a proper distribution. Nick Hodges and Ian Priston, *Embryo: A Pink Floyd Chronology, 1966–1971* (London: Cherry Red Books/Red Oak Press, 1999), p. 129.

31 Ibid., pp. 110–111.

32 Pink Floyd drummer Nick Mason says it was completed in a morning and not worth releasing. Nick Mason in Bruno McDonald, ed., *Pink Floyd: Through the Eyes of...the Band, its Fans, Friends and Foes* (London: Da Capo, 1997), p. 200.

33 Stephen Farber, "*Performance* – The Nightmare Journey" in David Dalton, ed., *The Rolling Stones* (London: Star, 1975), p. 161; Alexander Walker, *Hollywood, England: The British Film Industry in the Sixties* (London: Harrap, 1986), pp. 417–419.

34 Rod Cooper, "Production" *Kinematograph Weekly*, vol. 629, no. 3240, 1968, p. 12; "Mick is writing the musical score and will sing one song in the film." "Mick Jagger to star in dramatic film role" [news] in *Melody Maker*, 30 July 1968, p. 2.

35 The film's music is discussed in greater detail in K.J. Donnelly, "*Performance* and the Composite Film Score" in K.J. Donnelly, ed., *Film Music: Critical Approaches* (Edinburgh: Edinburgh University Press, 2001).

36 Jonathan Romney, "Tracking Across the Widescreen" [interview with Ry Cooder], *The Wire*, vol. 138, August 1995, p. 42.

37 K.J. Donnelly, "*Performance* and the Composite Film Score" in K.J. Donnelly, ed., *Film Music: Critical Approaches* (Edinburgh: Edinburgh University Press, 2001).

38 Although his film career had started inauspiciously with bizarre youth film *Village of Giants* (1965 US), *Performance* led to the later successes of *The Exorcist* (1973 US) and *One Flew Over the Cuckoo's Nest* (1975 US).

39 The music reflects one of the film's themes, of England's degeneration related to the past of colonial glory, with the music as part of the imperial plunder and simultaneously the "foreign" culture that is swamping "Old England".

40 Michel Chion, *The Voice in Cinema* (New York: Columbia University Press, 1999), pp. 2–3.

41 Smith, op. cit., p. 11.

42 While Jeff Smith looks into changes wrought on film scoring, Kathryn Kalinak notes the importance of the "pop score" of songs at the turn of the 1970s. *Settling the Score: Music and the Classical Hollywood Film* (Madison: University of Wisconsin press, 1992), p. 186.

43 Indeed, there was a rush to have groups do music for films at this tie, but much came to nothing, although it provided pre-release profile for films. For example, The Herd sign up to score *Otley*, *Melody Maker*, 30 March 1968, p. 4 (They did not, Stanley Myers did); Spencer Davis recorded the *Magpie* TV theme, *Melody Maker*, 30 July 1968, p. 2; Pentangle were to score *Twelve Plus One* which featured Orson Welles and Vittorio Gassman (they did not), *Melody Maker*, 25 October 1969, p. 3; and The Tremeloes were signed to

score the Italian film *May Morning* (*Alba pagana* [1970]), recording six songs and working with an orchestra (they did some). *Melody Maker*, 31 January 1970, p. 4.

44 The irony is that the music and film are fairly autonomous in some of these cases, while being collaborations in a partnership potentially pursuing a more unified film object.

6   Pop Music Culture, Synergy and Songs in Films: *Hardware* (1990) and *Trainspotting* (1996)

1 Murray Smith notes that "[a]t times, with the continuous flow of pop music on the soundtrack and the various permutations of the gang in locomotion, the film seems like a pop film in which the gang have taken on the role of the pop group...", *Trainspotting* (London: BFI, 2002), p. 14.

2 A point noted in relation to a pop video maker–turned film director. Russell Mulcahy "... has worked extensively in rock videos, which is evident enough in the way *Highlander* has been made as a succession of set-pieces." Tim Pulleine, review of *Monthly Film Bulletin*, vol. 53, no. 631, August 1986, p. 237.

3 Some commentators have noted the increased status of music in contemporary films. Claudia Gorbman, *Unheard Melodies: Narrative Film Music* (London: BFI, 1987), p. 162.

4 Kathryn Kalinak, *Settling the Score: Music and the Classical Hollywood Film* (Madison: University of Wisconsin Press, 1992), pp. 186, 187.

5 Alan Jones, "The Devil and Mr. Stanley" in *Shivers*, issue 1, June 1992, p. 25.

6 For further and more detailed discussion of the film's music, cf. K.J. Donnelly, "Constructing the future through music of the past: The software in *Hardware*" in Ian Inglis, ed., *Popular Music and Film* (London: Wallflower, 2003).

7 Simon Boswell, quoted from the liner notes to the *Hardware* soundtrack CD (Milan records CDCH627, released in 1990).

8 "Composite score" – making a coherent unity from divergent pieces or styles. K.J. Donnelly, "Performance and the Composite Film Score" in K.J. Donnelly, ed., *Film Music: Critical Approaches* (Edinburgh: Edinburgh University Press, 2001), pp. 152–153.

9 Mark Kermode, review of *Hardware, Monthly Film Bulletin*, vol. 57, no. 681, October 1990, p. 297

10 Andrew Black, review of *Hardware* soundtrack album in *Samhain*, issue 26, April/May 1991, p. 31.

11 *Order of Death* reappears at the end of the film, as radio DJ "Angry Bob" tells his listeners that Mark 13 is going to be mass produced, the audience is then shown Carl McCoy walking in the Zone after which the song continues across the film's end titles.

12 From an unpublished interview with Richard Stanley by the author.

13 This is the conventional blueprint known as song form that was discussed in an earlier chapter.

14 When the author interviewed Richard Stanley, he asked him about this section. He was proud to have included footage that had been seen as problematic by censors but was sceptical about the alleged "snuff" status of the images.

15 The activities on television at times parallel with those in Jill's flat. As Mark 13 slashes Jill's bed, the film cuts to images of butchery on television.

16 Tom Gunning notes the logic of structuring films around such discrete elements. "The cinema of attractions: Early film, its spectator and the Avant-Garde" in Thomas Elsaesser with Adam Barker, eds, *Early Cinema: Space, Frame, Narrative* (London: BFI, 1990), p. 61.

17 Stanley had made the promo videos for Fields of the Nephilim's *Preacher Man* and *Blue Water* in the late 1980s and this zonetripper figure was remarkably close to McCoy's stage and video persona.

18 *Screen International* figures quoted by Sarah Street, "Popular British Cinema?", *Journal of Popular British Cinema*, no. 1, 1998, p. 14.

19 Robert Murphy, "Introduction" in Robert Murphy, ed., *British Cinema in the 90s* (London: BFI, 2000), p. 3.

20 As an index of the impact of *Trainspotting*'s music, in the wake of the film, the BBC utilized two songs that the film had used in its advertisements for itself (*Lust for Life* and *Perfect Day*).

21 Songs replacing score can have a highly important function Ken Garner, " 'Would You Like to Hear Some Music?' Music in-and-out-of-control in the Films of Quentin Tarantino" in K.J. Donnelly, ed., *Film Music: Critical Approaches* (Edinburgh: Edinburgh University Press, 2001), pp. 188–189.

22 Geoffrey McNab, "The Boys are Back in Town" (interview with the makers of *Trainspotting*) in *Sight and Sound*, vol. 6, no. 2, February 1996, p. 10.

23 *Boston Kickout* (1995) included Primal Scream and Oasis, *House of America* (1996 UK/Holland) included Blur and Primal Scream, *Velvet Goldmine* (1998 UK/US) and *The Full Monty* (1997) included Pulp, while *The Acid House* (1998) included Primal Scream and Oasis. *Lock, Stock and Two Smoking Barrels* (1998) featured a number of Britpop songs.

24 The film includes references to The Beatles, most notably the configuration of the four friends copying the cover of *Sgt. Pepper's Lonely Hearts Club Band* when standing at a train halt and *Abbey Road* when they cross the road in London.

25 The same event is shown later in the film, although shot and edited differently, and with different music.

26 For further analysis of this sequence and its music, see Smith, op. cit., pp. 67–70.

27 Despite the assertion that "music's changing", *Trainspotting* proceeds to use modern electronic dance music for a sequence that expresses the "abnormality" of Renton's cold turkey experience.

28 It also includes a hallucination of Diane sitting on his bed and singing some of New Order's *Temptation*, while the Underworld piece continues.

29 Including Underworld's *Dark & Long (Dark Train Mix)*, Sleeper's *Statuesque*, Heaven 17's *Temptation*, Ice MC's *Think About the Way* and the *Habanera* from Bizet's *Carmen*. It also includes an extended version of Leftfield's *A Final Hit*, an alternative mix of Underworld's *Born Slippy/NUXX*, by Darren Price and a remix by Baby Doc of Iggy Pop's *Nightclubbing*.

30 K.J. Donnelly, "The Classical Film Score Forever?: Music in the Batman Films" in Steve Neale and Murray Smith, eds, *Contemporary Hollywood Cinema* (London: Routledge, 1998), p. 144.

31 Bowie, along with Iggy Pop, was the clear point of reference for *Velvet Goldmine* (1998), although the film also featured none of his music.

32 Angus Finney, *The State of European Cinema* (London: Cassell, 1996), p. 180.
33 By the end of the decade, films like *Greenwich Mean Time* (1998) were based wholly on the new dance music and its attendant club culture. Another Irvine Welsh adaptation, *The Acid House* (1998), included industrial electronic group Techno Animal, German ambient group Porter Ricks and Scottish group Arab Strap alongside more mainstream but still credible alternative acts such as The Verve and The Chemical Brothers.
34 R. Serge Denisoff and George Plasketes, "Synergy in 1980s Film and Music: Formula for Success or Industry Mythology?" *Film History*, vol. 4, no. 3, 1990, p. 257.
35 Tom Gunning, "The Cinema of Attractions" in Thomas Elsaesser and Adam Barker, eds, *Early Cinema: Space, Frame, Narrative* (London: BFI, 1990), p. 61.
36 Smith notes that *Trainspotting* "...exemplifies the incorporation of the music video sequence into narrative cinema...", op. cit., p. 20.
37 The Primal Scream and Damon Albarn pieces were written especially for the film.
38 Sarah Street, "Popular British Cinema?" in *Journal of Popular British Cinema*, vol. 1, 1998, p. 14. However, this so-called "youth" audience appears to have been interested in records made a quarter of a century earlier.

7 History of British Film Musicals

1 Sarah Street, *British National Cinema* (London: Routledge, 1997), p. 9.
2 R. Serge Denisoff and George Plasketes, "Synergy in 1980s Film and Music: Formula for Success or Industry Mythology?", *Film History*, vol. 4, no. 3, p. 272.
3 Tom Vallance, "Musicals" in Brian MacFarlane, ed., *The Encyclopedia of British Film* (London: Methuen/BFI, 2005), p. 500.
4 Stephen Guy, "Calling All Stars: Musical Films in a Musical Decade" in Jeffrey Richards, ed., *The Unknown 1930s: An Alternative History of the British Cinema, 1929–1939* (London: I.B. Tauris, 1998), p. 99.
5 John Sedgwick's statistically derived top listing of British film stars in the 1930s is dominated by comics or musical stars. John Sedgwick, "Cinema-Going Preferences in Britain in the 1930s" in Jeffrey Richards, ed., *The Unknown 1930s: An Alternative History of the British Cinema, 1929–1939* (London: I.B. Tauris, 1998), p. 19.
6 Cf. Lawrence Napper, "A Despicable Tradition?: Quota quickies in the 1930s" in Robert Murphy, ed., *The British Cinema Book* (London: BFI, 1997).
7 There was pressure upon many entertainers to adopt the "neutral" "Received Pronunciation" version of English that was fostered by BBC radio and elocution classes.
8 Buchanan later hit Hollywood fame along with Fred Astaire in Vincente Minnelli's *The Band Wagon* (1953).
9 Cf. Michael Marshall, *Top Hat and Tails: The Story of Jack Buchanan* (London: Elm Tree/Hamish Hamilton, 1978).
10 According to James Park, "...her posh accent was sufficiently artificial to be laughed at, where a more natural intonation would have alienated audiences." *The British Cinema: The Lights that Failed* (London: Batsford, 1990), p. 44.

11 Sarah Street points to the art deco set design in Matthews's films such as *Evergreen* and *It's Love Again* as important embodiments of consumerism in Britain at the time. " 'Got to dance on my way to heaven': Jessie Matthews, Art Deco and the British musical of the 1930s", *Studies in European Cinema*, vol. 2, no. 1, 2005.

12 Jeffrey Richards, *The Age of the Dream Palace: Cinema and Society in Britain, 1930–1939* (London: Routledge & Kegan Paul, 1984), p. 207.

13 Her involvement with a stage production meant that she did not commit herself to films, only appearing in RKO's *Forever and a Day* (1943). Ibid., p. 223. She later made a return to the London stage in 1973 in *The Water Babies*.

14 Napper discusses the feed in to such films from music hall and working-class entertainment traditions. Op. cit., p. 42.

15 Andy Medhurst argues that Formby and Fields "...raise what I would claim to be the central problematic of the 1930s variety star film – how to accommodate such performers within existing cinematic genres". "Music hall and British cinema" in Charles Barr, ed., *All Our Yesterdays: 90 Years of British Cinema* (London: BFI, 1986), p. 174.

16 Although sometimes he also had non-diegetic support behind his voice and banjolele.

17 Formby had appeared as a child in *By the Shortest of Heads* (1915).

18 Marcia Landy notes that most of her films concentrate on her relationship with other women rather than men. "The Extraordinary Ordinariness of Gracie Fields: The Anatomy of a British Film Star" in Bruce Babington, ed., *British Stars and Stardom: From Alma Taylor to Sean Connery* (Manchester: Manchester University Press, 2001), p. 57.

19 Park, op. cit., p. 47.

20 In the late 1930s, Fields aimed for US success but Formby did not. Medhurst, op. cit., p. 176.

21 Ibid., p. 47.

22 Richards, 1984, op. cit., p. 172.

23 Park, op. cit., p. 44.

24 The film had a successful opening in New York, distributed by Gaumont-British's new US distribution wing. John Sedgwick, "Michael Balcon's Close Encounter with the American Market, 1934–1936", *Historical Journal of Film, Radio and Television*, vol. 16, no. 3, 1996, p. 337.

25 The film reduced the number of songs to only two.

26 John Huntley, *British Film Music* (London: Skelton Robinson, 1947), p. 92; James Chapman, "A Short History of the Big Band Musical" in Ian Conrich and Estella Tincknell, eds, *Musical Moments: Film and Musical Performance* (Edinburgh: Edinburgh University Press, 2006).

27 Medhurst points to *Elstree Calling*'s mixture of variety stars and more sophisticated revue stars from the West End (such as Jack Hulbert), where the former are less cinematically integrated and relate to an antiquated notion of "music hall". Op. cit., pp. 173–174.

28 Vallance notes that it was "Britain's best film musical of the 1940s..." Op. cit., p. 500.

29 Michael Powell, *A Life in the Movies: An Autobiography* (London: Faber & Faber, 2001), p. 181.

30 Andrew Spicer, "Prince Charming in a Top Hat: The Debonair Man-About-Town in British Romantic Musical Comedy" in Ian Conrich and Estella Tincknell, eds, *Musical Moments: Film and Musical Performance* (Edinburgh: Edinburgh University Press, 2006).

31 Guy, op. cit., p. 113.

32 The film had been planned earlier with Audrey Hepburn, the choice as the Susie Dean character. Her Hollywood career took off and she was replaced by teenager Janette Scott.

33 Czinner had directed *Escape Me Never* (1935), *As You Like It* (1936), *Dreaming Lips* (1937) and *A Stolen Life* (1939), all with incidental music by respected composer William Walton.

34 *Monthly Film Bulletin*, vol. 25, no. 296, September 1958, p. 113.

35 This was made by Amicus Films, who were on the verge of becoming specialists in horror films. Cf. Peter Hutchings, "The Amicus House of Horror" in Steve Chibnall and Julian Petley, eds, *British Horror Cinema* (London: Routledge, 2002).

36 Anonymous review in *Kinematograph Weekly*, vol. 559, no. 2931, 5 December 1963, p. 18.

37 Ibid., vol. 565, no. 2959, 18 June 1964, p. 21.

38 The term was coined in *Time*'s "London: The Swinging City" special issue, most notably the article Piri Halasz, "London: You Can Walk Across it on the Grass" in *Time*, no. 87, 15 April 1966, p. 32.

39 This information was suppressed for a long time. The voices were provided by Paul Angelis (Ringo), Geoffrey Hughes (Paul), John Clive (John) and Peter Batten (George). Paul Angelis, "The Real McCartney – Eddie Yates", *The Observer*, Sunday 4 September 1988, p. 34.

40 Ian McDonald, *Revolution in the Head: The Beatles Records and the Sixties* (London: Pimlico, 1995), pp. 187, 208.

41 *Yellow Submarine* regularly has been exhibited as a children's film since its release. The song upon which the film was based resembled a child's song and was sung by Ringo Starr who, more than two decades later, was to narrate top children's television show *Thomas the Tank Engine*.

42 Alexander Walker, *National Heroes: British Cinema in the Seventies and Eighties* (London: Harrap, 1985), p. 16.

43 Ernest Betts, *A History of the British Cinema, 1896–1972* (London: Allen & Unwin, 1973), p. 287.

44 Jim Hillier, *The New Hollywood* (London: Studio Vista, 1992), p. 8.

45 Betts, op. cit., p. 316; Margaret Dickinson and Sarah Street, *Cinema and State: The British Film Industry and the British Government, 1927–1984* (London: BFI, 1985), p. 239.

46 Derek Todd, "The Stable Door: After the (US) Force has Gone" (interview with John Boulting) in *Kinematograph Weekly*, vol. 630, no. 3243, 6 December 1969, p. 5.

47 A number of films were made on the back of successful British television series, examples being *Steptoe and Son* (1972) and sequel *Steptoe and Son Ride Again* (1973).

48 While I do not intend to deal with them here, rockumentaries and pop concert films might easily be seen as a direct development of the film musical. Beginning in the late 1960s, this format had virtually disappeared

from cinema screens by the late 1990s, although it was a healthy form on video and DVD, which suggests something of its closeness to the record industry.

49 The LP was released 6 years earlier in 1969.

50 There was a surge of promos that followed *Bohemian Rhapsody*, and it is not inconceivable that the prominence of *Tommy* had been of some influence in the development of the standardized format for the pop promo.

51 The theatre production began in the "Summer at the theatre upstairs" at Royal Court, Sloane Square, London. Record producer and film director Lon Adler took an interest and the film was shot just over a year later. Sarah Lewis, "I Was a Regular Frankie Fan", *Samhain*, vol. 26, April/May 1991, p. 25.

52 Andy Medhurst, "It Sort of Happened Here: The Strange Brief Life of the British Pop Film" in Jonathan Romney and Adrian Wootton, eds, *Celluloid Jukebox: Popular Music and the Movies since the 50s* (London: BFI, 1995), p. 61.

53 Andrew Higson, "A Diversity of Film Practices: Renewing British Cinema in the 1970s" in Bart Moore Gilbert, ed., *The Arts in the Seventies: Cultural Closure?* (London: Routledge, 1994), p. 224.

54 The troubled production of *The Great Rock'n'Roll Swindle* was demonstrated by the release of the soundtrack double LP well before the film (in February 1979) and then another, smaller and remodelled version as a tie-in for the film's release over a year later. Cf. K.J. Donnelly, "Entertainment and Dystopia: The British Punk Musical" in Bill Marshall and Robynn Stilwell, eds, *Musicals: Hollywood and Beyond* (Exeter: Intellect, 2000).

55 Hazel O'Connor's soundtrack LP entered the chart on 9 August 1980, peaked at Number 5 and remained on the chart for 37 weeks. In terms of singles, the tied-in single *Eighth Day* reached Number 5 in the charts after being released on 16 August 1980. *Give Me an Inch* fared less well, reaching Number 41 after release on 25 October 1980. Nearly a year after the film's release, *Will You* from the soundtrack was released and reached Number 8 in the charts, entering on 23 May 1981.

56 The film follows the LP closely, with the exception of a couple of added songs, including the versions of *In the Flesh* with Geldof singing. Neither of these were made available as recordings.

57 *Another Brick in the Wall (Part 1)* reached Number 1 in the charts. It entered the chart on 1 December 1979 and remained on the chart for 12 weeks. *The Wall* (a double LP) peaked at Number 3 in the charts, after entering on 8 December 1979 and remained on the chart for 46 weeks.

58 Ross Benson, *Paul McCartney: Behind the Myth* (London: Gollancz, 1993), p. 263.

59 *Absolute Beginners* failed at the box office despite having one of the most expensively hyped openings in British cinema history. Andrew Yule, *David Puttnam: The Story So Far* (London: Sphere, 1988), p. 292.

60 The film derived its named from an obscure song by David Bowie.

61 Hawkes's star burned out quickly. *The One and Only* reached Number 1 in the charts and stayed on the chart for 16 weeks after being released on 23 February 1991. *I'm a Man Not a Boy* was also a single, but fared less well, reaching no higher than Number 27 in the charts in the June of 1991.

62   Films increasingly traded upon British pop music nostalgia, including *The Birth of The Beatles* (1979), television drama *Hours and the Times* (1991) and Richard Lester's *Get Back* (1991), a concert tour film directed by Richard Lester, featuring Paul McCartney on tour along with old footage of The Beatles.

63   Film review by Mark Sinker in *Sight and Sound*, vol. 8, no. 2, February 1998, p. 49.

64   Kam Patel, "UK Musical Benefits from Ealing Arts" (interview with director Brian Izzard) in *Times Higher Education Supplement*, 28 June 1998, p. 21.

65   Huntley, op. cit., p. 91.

66   Yet, on a more optimistic note, Huntley speculated: "It is possible that eventually we shall evolve our own special type of musical, as they have in Russia and in France, and that then there will be the Hollywood musical and the Denham musical – two entirely different forms of cinema." Op. cit., p. 98.

8   Stage to Screen: Whatever Happened to the British Musical Adaptation?

1   Geoff Brown, "Sister of the Stage: British Films and British Theatre" in Charles Barr, ed., All *Our Yesterdays: 90 Years of British Cinema* (London: BFI, 1986). It also focuses on the adaptation of more highbrow or "legit" plays.

2   Eric Blom, *Music in England* (Harmondsworth: Penguin, 1945 [f.p. 1942]), p. 199.

3   It is striking how far modernism in British music is ignored by Blom's account.

4   Gay wrote few stage plays, but instead concentrated on songs, such as *Leaning on a Lamp Post*, written for George Formby.

5   Dominic Shellard, *British Theatre Since the War* (London: Yale University Press, 2000), p. 22.

6   Ibid., pp. 23–24.

7   It includes comedienne Joyce Grenfell, Celia Johnson and even Anthony Newley in a small part.

8   It initially starred Simon Callow and Paul Scofield.

9   I have already mentioned Russell's adaptation of Sandy Wilson's *The Boy Friend* (1971).

10   R. Serge Denisoff and William Romanowski, *Risky Business: Rock on Film* (London: Transaction, 1991), pp. 216–217.

11   Russell's stage play *Shirley Valentine* was also made into a successful film.

12   Shellard, op. cit., p. 190.

13   Although some have made a less than direct transition. For example, see my discussion of the influence of *Riverdance* in James Cameron's *Titanic* (1997). "Riverdancing as the Ship Goes Down" in Sarah Street and Tim Bergfelder, eds, *The Titanic in Myth and Memory: Representations in Visual and Literary Culture* (London: I.B. Tauris, 2004), pp. 205–214.

14   Coward wrote the songs for *The Grass is Greener* (1960), directed by Stanley Donen. This British film had a Hollywood cast, including Cary Grant, Deborah Kerr, Jean Simmons and Robert Mitchum.

15 Cole Lesley, *The Life of Noel Coward* (Harmondsworth: Penguin, 1976), p. 159.
16 Ibid., p. 220.
17 "Gainsborough production chief Michael Balcon pointed to Coward's material as a means of countering undue American influence on the content of British films." Ibid., p. 150.
18 It also featured Gary Brooker, singer in the 1960s group Procol Harum, in a small role.
19 The film was co-produced by Lloyd Webber, while in 2006 the stage musical became the longest running show on Broadway, http://news.bbc.co.uk/1/hi/entertainment/4594084.stm accessed 10 January 2006.
20 Lloyd Webber even wrote some film incidental music, for *Gumshoe* (1971) and *The Odessa File* (1974).
21 Stephen Guy, "Calling All Stars: Musical Films in a Musical Decade" in Jeffrey Richards, ed., *The Unknown 1930s: An Alternative History of the British Cinema, 1929–1939* (London: I.B. Tauris, 1998), p. 114.

9 The Perpetual Busman's Holiday: Sir Cliff Richard and the British Pop Musical

1 T.W. Adorno, "On Popular Music" in John Storey, ed., *Cultural Theory and Popular Culture: A Reader* (London: Harvester Wheatsheaf, 1994), pp. 210–211.
2 The British charts according to the *New Musical Express* charts (up to 1960) and the Record Retailer charts thereafter, quoted in Paul Gambaccini, Tim Rice and Jo Rice, *The Guinness Book of Hit Singles* (London: Guinness Publishing, 1995).
3 Charlie Gillett, *The Sound of the City: The Rise of Rock'n'Roll* (London: Souvenir, 1983), p. 257.
4 Dick Bradley, *Understanding Rock'n'Roll: Popular Music in Britain 1955–1964* (Buckingham: Open University Press, 1992), p. 71.
5 P. E., "Music Makes or Mars a Good Film," *Kinematograph Weekly*, vol. 473, no. 2563, 27 September 1956, p. 7 of Studio Review Supplement. The popular music this statement envisaged was certainly not rock'n'roll.
6 "The British rock'n'roll scene started at the 2Is in the heart of Soho. There are few who would deny that the little coffee bar at 59 Old Compton Street, with its cramped basement, was the first spawning ground for the new breed of musicians springing up, and a happy hunting ground, sometimes in both senses, for agents and managers early pursuing new talent" The Shadows with Mike Read, *The Story of the Shadows* (London: Elmtree/Hamish Hamilton, 1983), p. 34.
7 *Monthly Film Bulletin*, vol. 29, no. 343, August 1972, p. 116.
8 *Monthly Film Bulletin*, vol. 29, no. 344, September 1962, p. 127.
9 Another British singer who traded on an "Elvis" image was Terry Dene who appeared in *The Golden Disc* (1958). The image of Elvis had an impact on films worldwide. See Amrit Rai, "An American Raj in Filmistan: Images of Elvis in Indian films," *Screen*, vol. 35, no. 1, Spring 1994.
10 Jon Savage, "The Great Pretender" *Mojo*, no. 15, February 1995, p. 43.

11   David Roper, *Bart! The Unauthorized Life and Times Ins and Outs Ups and Downs of Lionel Bart* (London: Pavilion, 1994), p. 21.

12   Steve Turner, *Cliff Richard: The Biography* (Oxford: Lion, 1993), p. 140.

13   *Kinematograph Weekly*, vol. 504, no. 2695, April 1959, p. 17.

14   The film's controversial subject matter, delinquents and an accusation of the vicar having "interfered with" one of the youths earned the film an "X" certificate (for adults only).

15   Liner notes to *The Young Ones* LP.

16   Savage, op. cit., p. 44.

17   "Renters' News," *Kinematograph Weekly*, vol. 512, no. 2731, 28 January 1960, p. 17.

18   Bradley, op. cit, pp. 57–59.

19   Savage, op. cit., p. 44.

20   Turner, op. cit., p. 143.

21   Roper, op. cit., p. 23.

22   Gillett, op. cit., p. 3.

23   Bradley, op. cit., p. 142.

24   George Melly, *Revolt into Style: The Pop Arts in Britain* (London: Penguin, 1970), p. 70.

25   Turner, op. cit., p. 143.

26   Gillett, op. cit., p. 256.

27   *Monthly Film Bulletin*, vol. 27, no. 312, January 1960, p. 2.

28   The *Expresso Bongo* EP included *Love, Voice in the Wilderness* and *Bongo Blues*. It was released on 15 January 1960 as a tie-in with the film in circulation and reached number 14 in the charts. The second single from the film, *Voice in the Wilderness* (on its own this time), was released in quick succession, on 22 January 1960. It reached number two in the charts.

29   Josh Billings, "On release" in *Kinematograph Weekly*, vol. 512, no. 2730, 28 January 1960, p. 13.

30   Savage, op. cit., p. 44.

31   Tom Vallance, "Soundtrack" in *Film: The Magazine of the Federation of Film Societies*, no. 32, 1962, p. 41.

32   *Kinematograph Weekly*, vol. 535, no. 2827, 7 December 1961, p. 10.

33   Ibid., p. 10.

34   The contrast of the two musical discourses is nowhere demonstrated better than in the two versions of *Lessons in Love*. This song has elements of rock'n'roll, being based on the I-VI-IV-V chord progression like many other rock songs such as *Teenager in Love*. On the first occasion of the song's performance, Cliff sings alone backed by a classic Shadows accompaniment, while on the second occasion, Cliff duets with Sonya Cordeau (but with session singer Grazina Frame's voice-over!). This provides an example of the conflicting discourses in operation: the contrast between Cliff's voice and the group instrumentation and the female voice, who has a showtune-style voice with marked vibrato at the end of each line.

35   When the song reaches the guitar solo, the non-diegetic status of the music (not the singing) allows it to accompany images of water skiers. This is an early example of pop music being used as fully non-diegetic music.

36   Asserted by the film's director Sidney Furie in *Hollywood UK* (BBC Television series, 1992).

37 Rick Altman, *The American Film Musical* (London: BFI, 1989), p. 235.
38 John Huntley, *British Film Music* (London: Skelton Robinson, 1947), p. 93.
39 P. E., "Banging the Drum for the Music Makers," *Kinematograph Weekly*, vol. 634, no. 3279, 15 August 1970, p. 13.
40 Turner, op. cit., p. 190.
41 *Monthly Film Bulletin*, vol. 29, no. 336, January 1962, p. 15.
42 Altman, op. cit., p. 63.
43 The Shadows with Mike Read, op. cit, p. 132.
44 Cliff Richard speaking on *Hollywood UK* (BBC Television series, 1992).
45 *Monthly Film Bulletin*, vol. 35, no. 415, August 1968, p. 123.
46 The decline of Cliff's film career is demonstrated by the performance of each soundtrack LP. The soundtrack of *The Young Ones* (1961) stayed in the charts for 42 weeks; *Summer Holiday*'s (1963) stayed in the chart for 36 weeks; *Wonderful Life*'s (1964) stayed in the charts for 23 weeks; *Finders Keepers*'s (1966) stayed in the charts for 18 weeks; and *Take Me High*'s (1974) stayed in the charts for 4 weeks.
47 Nik Cohn, *A Wopbopa Loo Bop Alop Bam Boom* (London: Weidenfeld & Nicholson, 1969), p. 72.

10   The Musical Revolution: The Beatles in *A Hard Day's Night*

1 Stephen Glynn, *A Hard Day's Night* (London: I.B. Tauris, 2005), pp. 29–30. Robert Neaverson notes that producer Walter Shenson's interest in making a Beatles film was the soundtrack LP. *The Beatles Movies* (London: Cassell, 1998), p. 12.
2 The film was very successful. House records were broken at the London Pavilion. "Box Office Business" *Kinematograph Weekly*, vol. 566, no. 2963, 16 July 1964, p. 8.
3 John Ellis, *Visible Fictions* (London: Routledge, 1982), p. 99.
4 There are distinct similarities between the style of *A Hard Day's Night* and the earlier documentary of The Beatles made by the Maysles brothers (*Yeah, Yeah, Yeah*). Neaverson, op. cit., p. 16.
5 The shooting schedule was brief, from 2 March to 24 April 1964, chronicled in H.V. Fulpen, *The Beatles: An Illustrated Diary* (London: Plexus, 1983), p. 68. Lester states that mostly first takes were used in *Hollywood, UK*, no. 2, BBC Television documentary series, first broadcast in August and September 1993.
6 Lester's career included musical shows for television like Rediffusion's *Downbeat* (a jazz and pop show) and awards for his advertisements. Nicholas Thomas, ed., *The International Dictionary of Filmmakers* (London: St. James Press, 1990), p. 510.
7 John Hill, "A Hard Day's Night" in Nicholas Thomas, ed., *The International Dictionary of Films* (London: St. James Press, 1990), p. 373.
8 Rick Altman notes that classical narrative is not applicable to the analysis of the profoundly different narrative that exists in film musicals. Rick Altman, *The American Film Musical* (Bloomington: Indiana University Press, 1987), p. 20.

9   "For possibly the first time, the pop film demonstrated that it was possible to present a musical number without the illusion of actual performance." Hill, "A Hard Day's Night", op. cit., p. 374.

10 Lester states that the images "... were cut to the music" in *Hollywood, UK*.

11 The lip-synch mode is used for *Another Girl* in *Help!* and the tendency is therefore for the visuals to be articulated around the song's lead singer, Paul McCartney. Its appearance in the film is motivated by a desire for visual variation in the song presentations.

12 Norman Rossington as "Norm" is one of the elements that further removes the film from documentary. He was a relatively well-known actor, having appeared in *Saturday Night and Sunday Morning* (1960) among other films, and replaces Brian Epstein who, at this time, was not a famous appendage of The Beatles.

13 Barry Kernfeld, ed., *The New Grove Dictionary of Jazz* (London: Macmillan, 1988), p. 412.

14 Theodor Adorno, "On Popular Music" in Andrew Goodwin and Simon Frith, eds, *On Record: Rock, Pop and the Written Word* (London: Routledge, 1990), p. 306.

15 Indeed, it is possible to see music like that of Karl-Heinz Stockhausen as an aural equivalent of the dislocated succession of images that comprise the film style of the sequence. (Although such serial music is premised on forms of repetition, it is at pains to hide this to audiences and demonstrates a maximum of musical variation.

16 The film certainly has to be seen as a showcase for The Beatles and their talents; therefore, it seems reasonable to assume that its representation of the concert performance was one of the film's major attractions.

17 The sequence's overall decoupage bears little resemblance to the actual style of pop music performances on television in the late 1950s and early 1960s. The strategies for the construction of pop group performances on television in the late 1950s and early 1960s are elucidated in John Hill, "Television and Pop: The Case of he 1950s" in John Corner, ed., *Popular Television in Britain: Studies in Cultural History* (London: BFI, 1991), pp. 56–58.

18 *She Loves You* reached number 1 in the charts and remained in the charts for 21 weeks, while The Beatles' previous singles reached number 17 (*Love Me Do*) and number 2 (*Please Please Me*).

19 The hysteria generated during the production of the film was cited by cinematographer Gilbert Taylor as the reason why he did not want to be involved in The Beatles follow-up film. Alexander Walker, *Hollywood, England* (London: Harrap, 1986), p. 269.

20 John Caughie, "Progressive Television and Documentary Drama" in *Screen*, vol. 21, no. 3, 1980, p. 31.

21 Although the concert sequence as a whole functions for the film as a spectacle, having become uncoupled from the narrative drive, the narrative itself intrudes in the sequence to assert its continued existence. The central manifestation of the film's narrative disequilibrium, Wilfrid Brambell as Paul's grandfather, appears within the concert sequence among the audience. During the performance of *She Loves You*, he is inserted into the tableau of The Beatles on the stage by rising through the stage trap door. This functions

as a replacing of the dramatic within what is taken by the cinema audience to be a concert, reasserting the self-conscious aspect of the film.

22 This was a common device in the classical musical: "Long before television invented the studio audience and canned laughter, the Hollywood musical was putting audiences into the film for the purpose of shaping the responses of the movie audiences to the film." Jane Feuer, *The Hollywood Musical* (London: Macmillan, 1982), p. 26.

23 Some reviewers were, however, less than impressed with the film, such as Geoffrey Nowell-Smith in *Sight and Sound*, vol. 33, no. 4, Autumn 1964, p. 191.

24 Indeed, Lennon was absent for some of the shooting on the playing field, yet in the final sequence's fragmented form, this is not immediately apparent.

11 White Labels and Black Imports: Music, Assimilation and Commerce in *Absolute Beginners* (1985)

1 Andrew Yule, *David Puttnam: The Story So Far* (London: Sphere, 1988), p. 292.

2 Robert Rosenstone, *Visions of the Past: The Challenge of Film to Our Idea of History* (London: Harvard University Press, 1995); Robert Rosenstone, ed., *Revisioning History* (Princeton: Princeton University Press, 1994).

3 Hayden White, "Historiography and Historiophoty", *American History Review*, vol. 93, no. 5, 1988, p. 1193. However, the term is notably ocular-centric, failing to express the audio–visual character of film.

4 Alan Munslow, *Deconstructing History* (London: Routledge, 1997), pp. 18–19.

5 Nigel Matheson, "Inside the Temple of Teen" (interview with Julien Temple), *New Musical Express*, 27 April 1985, p. 8.

6 In terms of the density of its references and allusions, *Absolute Beginners* is almost like a popular culture version of T.S. Eliot's *The Waste Land*, although its character is closer to Andrew Lloyd-Webber's adaptation of Eliot's *Old Possum's Book of Practical Cats*.

7 Matheson, op. cit., p. 8.

8 Stuart Cosgrove, "The Creeping Czars of the Coffee Bars", *New Musical Express*, 22 March 1986, p. 24.

9 Despite Temple's quotation earlier, the strange fact that coffee bars are marginal to *Absolute Beginners* suggests that the film is not tremendously interested in teens and "youth" culture of the late 1950s. For the development of the British pop musical, cf. K.J. Donnelly, *Pop Music in British Cinema: A Chronicle* (London: BFI, 2001).

10 Don MacPherson, "Next Stop Napoli", *New Musical Express*, 22 March 1986, p. 23.

11 Matheson, op. cit., p. 8.

12 Ibid., p. 8.

13 Steve Jenkins, "Absolute Beginnings" (interview with Julien Temple), *Monthly Film Bulletin*, vol. 51, 1984, p. 231.

14 Euro-MTV started 6 years later, although terrestrial television shows were already showing pop videos and exhibiting the "MTV style".

15 In Britain, as distinct from the United States, rock'n'roll and music in its wake arguably invoked fearless for its association with blacks than to its threat to

the class system. While there was general xenophobia against blacks, and to a lesser degree other Americans, rock'n'roll as an uncontrolled influence threatened the rigid class structure and people "knowing their place" in it. Class appears as a discourse in *Absolute Beginners*, crassly depicting Henley as an upper-class gay stereotype, whose world is threatened by youth's vigour and innovations.

16 Richard Hoggart, *The Uses of Literacy* (London: Chatto & Windus, 1957).

17 This figures the renewal of the "special relationship" between Britain and the United States, which was much touted at the time by Premier Margaret Thatcher.

18 Tenpole Tudor (also known as Edward Tudor-Pole), apart from appearing in *The Great Rock'n'Roll Swindle* (1980), had two hit records in the early 1980s with rockabilly-influenced records *Swords of a Thousand Men* and *Wunderbar*, and later presented television game show *The Crystal Maze* on Channel Four.

19 Bowie's *Absolute Beginners* single was sandwiched between the two relatively unsuccessful film song projects for him, *When the Wind Blows* and *Labyrinth*, where he appeared as the King of the Fairies. It reached number 2 in the charts and remained on the chart for 9 weeks after entering on 15 March 1986.

20 Karen Lury rightly notes that 1950s jazz is marginalized by manufactured and contemporary pop. Karen Lury, "Here and Then: Space, Place and Nostalgia in British Youth Cinema of the 1990s" in Robert Murphy, ed., *British Cinema of the 90s* (London: BFI, 2000), p. 104.

21 Roy Carr, "Hi-De-Hi: A Lighthearted Look at the Era of Jump Jive and Jitterbug, the Honking Hornmen, Screamers and Shouters", *New Musical Express*, 18 July 1981, pp. 29–30. The same journal had another large feature over a year later, which demonstrates that it was no short-lived concern. Roy Carr and Fred Dellar, "In the Land of Oo-Bla-Dee", *New Musical Express*, 14 August 1982, pp. 18–19.

22 Later there was a successful charity LP of Cole Porter's songs recorded by a number of contemporary artists, called *Red Hot and Blue*, released in 1990.

23 *The Beginners' Guide to Absolute Beginners* (London: Corgi, 1986).

24 R. Serge Denisoff and George Plasketes, "Synergy in 1980s Film and Music: Formula for Success or Industry Mythology?", *Film History*, vol. 4, no. 3, 1990, p. 257.

25 Jean Rosenbluth, "Soundtrack Specialists: Maximizing Cross-Market Connections", *Billboard*, 16 July 1988, p. S-4.

26 Skiffle has had a striking lack of attention from scholars and popular writers alike. The only book on the subject appears to be Mike Dewe, *The Skiffle Craze* (Aberystwyth: Planet, 1998).

27 The source book may be about jazz aficionados, but the film is more interested in jazz that can be sold as pop music.

28 News article, *Sounds*, 17 July 1982, p. 2.

29 Jeremy Eckstein, ed., *Cultural Trends 19*, vol. 3, no. 3 (London: Policy Studies Institute, 1993), p. 45.

30 Soca is the pop music version, "Soul-Calypso", also associated mainly with Trinidad.

31 The BBC instituted a television season in 1998 to celebrate 50 years of West Indians in Britain, called "Windrush".

32 These could well be related to the beleaguered "Little Englanders" discussed in Darcus Howe's television series *White Tribe* (1999, Channel Four), in which he went in search of "Englishness".

33 Walter Benjamin, "Theses on the Philosophy of History", *Illuminations* (London: Fontana, 1992), p. 247.

34 Michel Foucault, "Of Other Spaces", *Diacritics*, vol. 16, no. 1, 1986, p. 24.

35 Paul Gilroy, *The Black Atlantic: Modernity and Double Consciousness* (London: Verso, 1993).

36 Thomas K. Fitzgerald, "Media, Ethnicity and Identity" from Paddy Scannel, Philip Schlesinger and Colin Sparks, eds, *Culture and Power: A Media, Culture and Society Reader* (London: Sage, 1992), p. 131.

37 "Finally, it appears that the 'coolie' has become cool." Sanjay Sharma, John Hutnyk and Ashwani Sharma, "Introduction" in Sanjay Sharma, John Hutnyk and Ashwani Sharma, eds, *Dis-Orienting Rhythms: The Politics of the New Asian Dance Music* (London: Zed, 1996), p. 1.

Bibliography

Adorno, T.W., "On Popular Music" in Andrew Goodwin and Simon Frith, eds, *On Record: Rock, Pop and the Written Word* (London: Routledge, 1990).

Aldgate, Tony and Jeffrey Richards, *Britain Can Take It: The British Cinema in the Second World War* (Edinburgh: Edinburgh University Press, 1994).

Allen, Michael, " 'In the Mix': How Electrical Reproducers Facilitated the Transition to Sound in British Cinema" in K.J. Donnelly, ed., *Film Music: Critical Approaches* (Edinburgh: Edinburgh University Press, 2001).

Altman, Rick, *The American Film Musical* (London: BFI, 1989).

Angelis, Paul, "The Real McCartney – Eddie Yates" in *The Observer*, Sunday 4 September 1988.

Anon., *The Beginners' Guide to Absolute Beginners* (London: Corgi, 1986).

Anon., "Merchandising keeps Disney Image in Sharp Focus" in *Kinematograph Weekly*, Vol. 564, no. 2954, 14 May 1964.

Armes, Roy, *A Critical History of British Cinema* (London: Secker & Warburg, 1978).

Ashby, Justine and Andrew Higson, eds, "Introduction" in *British Cinema: Past and Present* (London: Routledge, 2000).

Aspinall, Sue and Robert Murphy, eds, "Introduction" in *BFI Dossier 18: Gainsborough Melodramas* (London: BFI, 1983).

Auty, Martyn and Nick Roddick, eds, *British Cinema Now* (London: BFI, 1985).

Barr, Charles, *English Hitchcock* (Moffat, Dumfriesshire: Cameron and Hollis, 1999).

Barr, Charles, "Introduction: Amnesia and Schizophrenia" in *All Our Yesterdays: 90 Years of British Cinema* (London: BFI, 1986).

Baxter, John, *Ken Russell: An Appalling Talent* (London: Joseph, 1973).

Benjamin, Walter, "Theses on the Philosophy of History" in *Illuminations* (London: Fontana, 1992).

Benson, Ross, *Paul McCartney: Behind the Myth* (London: Gollancz, 1993).

Betts, Ernest, *A History of the British Cinema, 1896–1972* (London: Allen & Unwin, 1973).

Blom, Eric, *Music in England* (Harmondsworth: Penguin, 1945).

Bradley, Dick, *Understanding Rock'n'Roll: Popular Music in Britain 1955–1964* (Buckingham: Open University Press, 1992).

Brown, Geoff, "Sister of the Stage: British Films and British Theatre" in Charles Barr, ed., *All Our Yesterdays: 90 Years of British Cinema* (London: BFI, 1986).

Burgess, Muriel and Tommy Keen, *Gracie Fields* (London: W.H. Allen, 1980).

Carr, Roy, "Hi-De-Hi: A Lighthearted Look at the Era of Jump Jive and Jitterbug, the Honking Hornmen, Screamers and Shouters" in *New Musical Express*, 18 July 1981.

Carr, Roy and Fred Dellar, "In the Land of Oo-Bla-Dee" in *New Musical Express*, 14 August 1982.

Caughie, John, "Progressive Television and Documentary Drama" in *Screen*, Vol. 21, no. 3, 1980.

Chapman, James, "A Short History of the Big Band Musical" in Ian Conrich and Estella Tincknell, eds, *Musical Moments: Film and Musical Performance* (Edinburgh: Edinburgh University Press, 2006).

Chion, Michel, "Chiffre de Destinee: Une Femme Disparait d'Alfred Hitchcock" in *Cahiers du Cinema*, Vol. 358, April 1984.

Chion, Michel, *Audio-Vision: Sound on Screen*, edited and translated by Claudia Gorbman (New York: Columbia University Press, 1990).

Chion, Michel, *The Voice in Cinema*, translated by Claudia Gorbman (New York: Columbia University Press, 1999).

Cohn, Nik, *A Wopbopa Loo Bop Alop Bam Boom* (London: Weidenfeld & Nicholson, 1969).

Cook, Pam, "Neither Here nor There: National Identity in Gainsborough Costume Drama" in Andrew Higson, ed., *Dissolving Views: Key Writings on British Cinema* (London: Cassell, 1996).

Cosgrove, Stuart, "The Creeping Czars of the Coffee Bars" in *New Musical Express*, 22 March 1986.

Curran, James and Vincent Porter, eds, *British Cinema History* (London: Weidenfeld & Nicholson, 1983).

Darby, William and Jack Dubois, *American Film Music: Major Composers, Techniques, Trends, 1915–1990* (Jefferson, NC: Macfarland, 1991).

DeFelice, James, *Filmguide to Odd Man Out* (Bloomington: Indiana University Press, 1975).

Denisoff, R. Serge and William D. Romanowski, *Risky Business: Rock on Film* (New York: Transaction, 1991).

Denisoff, R. Serge and George Plasketes, "Synergy in 1980s Film and Music: Formula for Success or Industry Mythology?" in *Film History*, Vol. 4, no. 3, 1990.

Dewe, Mike, *The Skiffle Craze* (Aberystwyth: Planet, 1998).

Dickinson, Margaret and Sarah Street, *Cinema and State: The British Film Industry and the British Government, 1927–1984* (London: BFI, 1985).

Dixon, Wheeler Winston, ed., *Re-Viewing British Cinema, 1900–1992: Essays and Interviews* (New York: SUNY Press, 1994).

Donnelly, K.J., "The Classical Film Score Forever?: Music in the Batman Films" in Steve Neale and Murray Smith, eds, *Contemporary Hollywood Cinema* (London: Routledge, 1998).

Donnelly, K.J., "Entertainment and Dystopia: The British Punk Musical" in Bill Marshall and Robynn Stilwell, eds, *Musicals: Hollywood and Beyond* (Exeter: Intellect, 2000).

Donnelly, K.J., "The Policing of Cinema: Troubled Film Exhibition in Northern Ireland" in *Historical Journal of Film, Radio and Television*, Vol. 20, no. 3, August 2000.

Donnelly, K.J., "*Performance* and the Composite Score" in *Film Music: Critical Approaches* (Edinburgh: Edinburgh University Press, 2001).

Donnelly, K.J., *Pop Music in British Cinema: A Chronicle* (London: BFI, 2001).

Donnelly, K.J., "Constructing the Future Through Music of the Past: The Software in *Hardware*" in Ian Inglis, ed., *Popular Music and Film* (London: Wallflower, 2003).

Donnelly, K.J., "Riverdancing as the Ship Goes Down" in Sarah Street and Tim Bergfelder, eds, *The Titanic in Myth and Memory: Representations in Visual and Literary Culture* (London: I.B. Tauris, 2004).

Donnelly, K.J., *The Spectre of Sound: Film and Television Music* (London: BFI, 2005).

Duggan, C.G., *The Stage Irishman* (London: Benjamin Blom, 1969).

Durgnat, Raymond, *A Mirror for England: British Movies from Austerity to Affluence* (London: Faber & Faber, 1970).

Eckstein, Jeremy, ed., *Cultural Trends 19*, Vol. 3, no. 3 (London: Policy Studies Institute, 1993).

Eisenstein, Sergei M., "Rhythm and Vertical Montage" in Michael Glenny and Richard Taylor, eds, *Eisenstein, Selected Works II: Towards a Theory of Montage* (London: BFI, 1991).

Eisler, Hanns and T.W. Adorno, *Composing for the Films* (London: Athlone, 1994).

Ellis, John, "Art, Culture and Quality: Terms for a Cinema of the Forties and Seventies" in *Screen*, Vol. 19, no. 3, Autumn 1978.

Ellis, John, "British Cinema as Performance Art: *Brief Encounter, Radio Parade of 1935* and the Circumstances of Film Exhibition" in Justine Ashby and Andrew Higson, eds, *British Cinema: Past and Present* (London: Routledge, 2000).

Ellis, John, *Visible Fictions* (London: Routledge, 1982).

Elsaesser, Thomas, "Images for England: and Scotland, Ireland, Wales ..." in *Monthly Film Bulletin*, Vol. 269, no. 51, September 1984.

Elsaesser, Thomas, "Tales of Sound and Fury: Observations on the Family Melodrama" in Christine Gledhill, ed., *Home is Where the Heart Is: Studies in Melodrama and the Woman's Film* (London: BFI, 1987).

Ewens, David, *All the Years of American Popular Music* (London: Prentice Hall, 1977).

Farber, Stephen, "*Performance* – The Nightmare Journey" in David Dalton, ed., *The Rolling Stones* (London: Star, 1975).

Feuer, Jane, *The Hollywood Musical* (London: Macmillan, 1982).

Feuer, Jane, "The Self-Reflexive Musical and the Myth of Entertainment" in *Genre: The Musical* (London: Routledge & Kegan Paul, 1981).

Finney, Angus, *The State of European Cinema* (London: Cassell, 1996).

Fitzgerald, Thomas K., "Media, Ethnicity and Identity" in Paddy Scannel, Philip Schlesinger and Colin Sparks, eds, *Culture and Power: A Media, Culture and Society Reader* (London: Sage, 1992).

Foucault, Michel, "Of Other Spaces" in *Diacritics*, Vol. 16, no. 1, 1986.

Friedman, Lester, ed., *British Cinema and Thatcherism: Fires Were Started* (London: UCL Press, 1993).

Frith, Simon, "Mood Music" in *Screen*, Vol. 25, no. 3, 1984.

Fulpen, H.V., *The Beatles: An Illustrated Diary* (London: Plexus, 1983).

Gaenzl, Kurt, *The British Musical Theatre*, Vol. 2 (Basingstoke: Macmillan, 1986).

Gambaccini, Paul, Tim Rice and Jo Rice, *The Guinness Book of Hit Singles* (London: Guinness Publishing, 1995).

Garner, Ken, "Would You Like to Hear Some Music? Music in-and-Out-of-Control in the Films of Quentin Tarantino" in K.J. Donnelly, ed., *Film Music: Critical Approaches* (Edinburgh: Edinburgh University Press, 2001).

Gifford, Denis, *The British Film Catalogue, 1895–1970: A Guide to Entertainment Films* (Newton Abbott: David & Charles, 1983).

Gillett, Charlie, *The Sound of the City: The Rise of Rock'n'Roll* (London: Souvenir, 1983).

Gilroy, Paul, *The Black Atlantic: Modernity and Double Consciousness* (London: Verso, 1993).

Glynn, Stephen, *A Hard Day's Night* (London: I.B. Tauris, 2005).

Gorbman, Claudia, *Unheard Melodies: Narrative Film Music* (London: BFI, 1987).

Granger, Stewart, *Sparks Will Fly* (London: Granada, 1981).

Grant, Barry Keith, "The Classic Hollywood Musical and the 'Problem' of Rock'n'Roll" in *Journal of Popular Film and Television*, Vol. 18, no. 4, 1986.

Gregg, Robert J., "The Scotch–Irish Dialect Boundaries in Ulster" in Martyn F. Wakelin, ed., *Patterns of Folk Speech in the British Isles* (London: Athlone Press, 1972).

Gunning, Tom, "The Cinema of Attractions" in Thomas Elsaesser and Adam Barker, eds, *Early Cinema: Space, Frame, Narrative* (London: BFI, 1990).

Guy, Stephen, "Calling All Stars: Musical Films in a Musical Decade" in Jeffrey Richards, ed., *The Unknown 1930s: An Alternative History of the British Cinema, 1929–1939* (London: I.B. Tauris, 1998).

Halasz, Piri, "London: You Can Walk Across it on the Grass" in *Time*, Vol. 87, 15 April 1966.

Harper, Sue, *Picturing the Past: The Rise and Fall of the Costume Film* (London: BFI, 1994).

Henry, Alison, *Belfast English and Standard English: Dialect Variation and Parameter Setting* (Oxford: Oxford University Press, 1995).

Higson, Andrew, "The Discourses of British Film Year" in *Screen*, Vol. 27, no. 1, January/February 1986.

Higson, Andrew, "A Diversity of Film Practices: Renewing British Cinema in the 1970s" in Bart Moore Gilbert, ed., *The Arts in the Seventies: Cultural Closure?* (London: Routledge, 1994).

Higson, Andrew, *Waving the Flag: Constructing a National Cinema in Britain* (Oxford: Clarendon, 1995).

Higson, Andrew, *English Heritage, English Cinema: Costume Drama Since 1980* (Oxford: Oxford University Press, 2003).

Hill, John, *Sex, Class and Realism: British Cinema, 1956–1963* (London: BFI, 1986).

Hill, John, "Images of Violence" in Kevin Rockett, John Hill and Luke Gibbons, *Cinema and Ireland* (London: Croom Helm, 1987).

Hill, John, "*A Hard Day's Night*" in Nicholas Thomas, ed., *The International Dictionary of Films* (London: St. James Press, 1990.).

Hill, John, "*Odd Man Out*" in Nick Thomas, ed., *International Dictionary of Films and Filmmakers – 1: Films* (London: St. James Press, 1990).

Hill, John, "Television and Pop: the Case of the 1950s" in John Corner, ed., *Popular Television in Britain: Studies in Cultural History* (London: BFI, 1991).

Hill, John, Martin McLoone and Paul Hainsworth, eds, *Border Crossing: Film in Ireland, Britain and Europe* (Belfast: IIS/BFI, 1994).

Hill, John, *British Cinema of the 1980s* (Oxford: Oxford University Press, 1999).

Hillier, Jim, *The New Hollywood* (London: Studio Vista, 1992).

Hodges, Nick and Ian Priston, *Embryo: A Pink Floyd Chronology, 1966–1971* (London: Cherry Red Books/Red Oak Press, 1999).

Hoggart, Richard, *The Uses of Literacy* (London: Chatto & Windus, 1957).

Hughes, Arthur and Peter Trudgill, *English Accents and Dialects* (London: Edward Arnold, 1987).

Hunt, Leon, *British Low Culture: From Safari Suits to Sexploitation* (London: Routledge, 1998).

Huntley, John, *British Film Music* (London: Skelton Robinson, 1947).

Hutchings, Peter, *Hammer and Beyond: The British Horror Film* (Manchester: Manchester University Press, 1994).

Hutchings, Peter, "The Amicus House of Horror" in Steve Chibnall and Julian Petley, eds, *British Horror Cinema* (London: Routledge, 2002).

Huth, Harold, Hubert Bath's obituary in *Kinematograph Weekly*, Vol. 21, no. 1985, 3 May 1945.

Irving, Ernest, *Cue for Music* (London: Dennis Dobson, 1959).

Jenkins, Steve, "Absolute Beginnings" (interview with Julien Temple) in *Monthly Film Bulletin*, Vol. 51, 1984.

Johnson, Ian, *William Alwyn: The Art of Film Music* (Woodbridge, Suffolk: The Boydell Press, 2005).

Jones, Alan, "The Devil and Mr. Stanley" in *Shivers*, Vol. 1, June 1992.

Kalinak, Kathryn, *Settling the Score: Music and the Classical Hollywood Film* (Madison: University of Wisconsin Press, 1992).

Kemp, Jeffrey, "Write What the Film Needs: An Interview with Elizabeth Lutyens" in *Sight and Sound*, Vol. 43, no. 4, Autumn 1974.

Kernfeld, Barry, ed., *The New Grove Dictionary of Jazz* (London: Macmillan, 1988).

Kirkham, Pat, "Dress, Dance, Dreams and Desires: Fashion and Fantasy in *Dance Hall*" in *Journal of Design History*, Vol. 8, no. 3, 1995.

Landy, Marcia, *British Genres: Cinema and Society, 1930–1960* (Oxford: Princeton University Press, 1991).

Landy, Marcia, "The Extraordinary Ordinariness of Gracie Fields: The Anatomy of a British Film Star" in Bruce Babington, ed., *British Stars and Stardom: From Alma Taylor to Sean Connery* (Manchester: Manchester University Press, 2001).

Larson, Randall D., "David Arnold Saves the World" in *Soundtrack!* Vol. 17, no. 65, March 1998.

Lebow, Richard Ned, *White Britain and Black Ireland: The Influence of Stereotypes on Colonial Policy* (Philadelphia: Institute for the Study of Human Issues, 1976).

Lesley, Cole, *The Life of Noel Coward* (Harmondsworth: Penguin, 1976).

Levy, Louis, "Music for Every Mood" (interview) in *Film Weekly*, Vol. 15, no. 386, 7 March 1937.

Levy, Louis, *Music for the Movies* (London: Sampson Low, 1948).

Lewis, Sarah, "I Was a Regular Frankie Fan" in *Samhain*, Vol. 26, April/May 1991.

Lindgren, Ernest, *The Art of Film* (London: Allen & Unwin, 1963).

Lovell, Alan, "British Cinema: The Known Cinema?" in Robert Murphy, ed., *The British Cinema Book* (London: BFI, 1997).

Lury, Karen, "Here and Then: Space, Place and Nostalgia in British Youth Cinema of the 1990s" in Robert Murphy, ed., *British Cinema of the 90s* (London: BFI, 2000).

MacDonald, Ian, *Revolution in the Head: The Beatles' Records and the Sixties* (London: Pimlico, 2005).

MacPherson, Don, "Next Stop Napoli" in *New Musical Express*, 22 March 1986.

Manvell, Roger, "British Feature Films from 1925 to 1945" in Michael Balcon, Ernest Lindgren, F. Hardy and Roger Manvell, eds, *Twenty Years of British Films 1925–1945* (London: Falcon Press, 1947).

Manvell, Roger and John Huntley, *The Technique of Film Music* (London: Focal Press, 1957).

Manvell, Roger, "Malcolm Arnold" in Nicholas Thomas, ed., *The International Dictionary of Filmmakers* (London: St. James Press, 1990).

Marshall, Michael, *Top Hat and Tails: the Story of Jack Buchanan* (London: Elm Tree/Hamish Hamilton, 1978).

Marwick, Arthur, "Introduction: Locating Key Texts Amid the Distinctive Landscape of the Sixties" in Anthony Aldgate, James Chapman and Arthur Marwick, eds, *Window on the Sixties: Exploring Key Texts of Media and Culture* (London: I.B. Tauris, 2000).

Matheson, Nigel, "Inside the Temple of Teen" (Interview with Julien Temple) in *New Musical Express*, 27 April 1985.

Mathieson, Muir, "Aspects of Film Music" in John Huntley, ed., *British Film Music* (London: Skelton Robinson: 1947).

Matthews, Jessie and Muriel Burgess, *Over My Shoulder: An Autobiography* (London: W.H. Allen, 1974).

McArthur, Colin, "Scotland and Cinema: The Iniquity of the Fathers" in Colin McArthur, ed., *Scotch Reels: Scotland in Cinema and Television* (London: BFI, 1982).

McDonald, Bruno, ed., *Pink Floyd: Through the Eyes of ... the Band, its Fans, Friends and Foes* (London: Da Capo, 1997).

McFarlane, Brian, ed., *Sixty Voices: Celebrities Recall the Golden Age of British Cinema* (London: BFI, 1992).

McFarlane, Brian, ed., *An Autobiography of British Cinema by Actors and Filmmakers Who Made It* (London: Cassell, 1999).

McGillivray, David, *Doing Rude Things: The History of the British Sex Film, 1957–1981* (London: Sun Tavern Fields, 1992).

McIlroy, Brian, *World Cinema 4: Ireland* (London: Flicks Books, 1988).

McIlroy, Brian, *Shooting to Kill: Filmmaking and the "Troubles" in Northern Ireland* (Trowbridge, Wiltshire: Flicks, 1998).

McNab, Geoffrey, "The Boys are Back in Town" (interview with the makers of *Trainspotting*) in *Sight and Sound*, Vol. 6, no. 2, February 1996.

Medhurst, Andy, "It Sort of Happened Here: The Strange Brief Life of the British Pop Film" in Jonathan Romney and Adrian Wootton, eds, *Celluloid Jukebox: Popular Music and the Movies since the 50s* (London: BFI, 1995).

Medhurst, Andy, "Music Hall and British Cinema" in Charles Barr, ed., *All Our Yesterdays: 90 Years of British Cinema* (London: BFI, 1986).

Melly, George, *Revolt into Style: The Pop Arts in Britain* (London: Penguin, 1972).

Minney, R.J., *Talking of Films* (London: Home & Van Thal, 1947).

Moss, Robert F., *The Films of Carol Reed* (New York: Columbia University Press, 1987).

Munslow, Alan, *Deconstructing History* (London: Routledge, 1997).

Murphy, Robert, "Introduction" in *British Cinema in the 90s* (London: BFI, 2000).

Murphy, Robert, "Rank's Attempt at the American Market" in James Curran and Vincent Porter, eds, *British Cinema History* (London: Weidenfeld & Nicholson, 1983).

Murphy, Robert, *Realism and Tinsel: Cinema and Society in Britain, 1939–49* (London: Routledge, 1989).

Murphy, Robert, *Sixties British Cinema* (London: BFI, 1992).

Napper, Lawrence, "A Despicable Tradition?: Quota Quickies in the 1930s" in Robert Murphy, ed., *The British Cinema Book* (London: BFI, 1997).

Napper, Lawrence, "British Cinema and the Middlebrow" in Justine Ashby and Andrew Higson, eds, *British Cinema: Past and Present* (London: Routledge, 2000).

Napper, Lawrence, "The Middlebrow, 'National Culture' and British Cinema 1920–1930", PhD Thesis, University of East Anglia, 2001.

Neaverson, Robert, *The Beatles Movies* (London: Cassell, 1998).

Nott, James J., *Music for the People: Popular Music and Dance in Interwar Britain* (Oxford: Oxford University Press, 2002).

Nyman, Michael, *Experimental Music: Cage and Beyond* (Cambridge: Cambridge University Press, 1974).

Osgerby, Bill, "From the Roaring Twenties to the Swinging Sixties: Continuity and Change in British Youth Culture, 1929–1965" in Brian Brivati and Harriet Jones, eds, *What Difference did the War Make?* (Leicester: University of Leicester Press, 1993).

P.E., "Banging the Drum for the Music Makers," *Kinematograph Weekly*, Vol. 634, no. 3279, 15 August 1970.

P.E, "Music Makes or Mars a Good Film," *Kinematograph Weekly*, Vol. 473, no. 2563, 27 September 1956, p. 7 of Studio Review Supplement.

Park, James, *Learning to Dream: The New British Cinema* (London: Faber & Faber, 1984).

Park, James, *The British Cinema: The Lights that Failed* (London: Batsford, 1990).

Patel, Kam, "UK Musical Benefits from Ealing Arts" (interview with director Brian Izzard) in *Times Higher Education Supplement*, 28 June 1998.

Peel, Ian, *The Unknown Paul McCartney: McCartney and the Avant Garde* (London: Reynolds & Hearn, 2002).

Petley, Julian, "The Lost Continent" in Charles Barr, ed., *All Our Yesterdays: 90 Years of British Cinema* (London: BFI, 1986).

Phillips, G.D., *Ken Russell* (Boston: Twayne, 1979).

Porter, Vincent, "Methodism Versus the Market Place: The Rank Organisation and British Cinema" in Robert Murphy, ed., *The British Cinema Book* (London: BFI, 1997).

Powell, Michael, *A Life in the Movies: An Autobiography* (London: Faber & Faber, 2001).

Quinlan, David, *British Sound Films: The Studio Years, 1928–1959* (London: Batsford, 1984).

Rai, Amrit, "An American Raj in Filmistan: Images of Elvis in Indian Films" in *Screen*, Vol. 35, no. 1, Spring 1994.

Reisz, Karel and Gavin Millar, *The Technique of Film Editing* (London: Focal Press, 1968 [f.p.1953]).

Richards, Jeffrey, *The Age of the Dream Palace: Cinema and Society in Britain, 1930–39* (London: Routledge & Kegan Paul, 1984).

Richards, Jeffrey, *Films and British National Identity: From Dickens to Dad's Army* (Manchester: Manchester University Press, 1997).

Romney, Jonathan, "Tracking Across the Widescreen" (interview with Ry Cooder) in *The Wire*, Vol. 138, August 1995.

Roper, David, *Bart! The Unauthorized Life and Times Ins and Outs Ups and Downs of Lionel Bart* (London: Pavilion, 1994).

Rosenbluth, Jean, "Soundtrack Specialists: Maximizing Cross-Market Connections" in *Billboard*, 16 July 1988.

Rosenstone, Robert, ed., *Revisioning History* (Princeton: Princeton University Press, 1994).

Rosenstone, Robert, *Visions of the Past: The Challenge of Film to Our Idea of History* (London: Harvard University Press, 1995).

Sargeant, Amy, *British Cinema: A Critical History* (London: BFI, 2005).

Savage, Jon, "The Great Pretender" in *Mojo*, Vol. 15, February 1995.

Schafer, Stephen C., *British Popular Films, 1929–1939: The Cinema of Reassurance* (London: Routledge, 1997).

Sedgwick, John, "Michael Balcon's Close Encounter with the American Market, 1934–36" in *Historical Journal of Film, Radio and Television*, Vol. 16, no. 3, 1996.

Sedgwick, John, "Cinema-going Preferences in Britain in the 1930s" in Jeffrey Richards, ed., *The Unknown 1930s: An Alternative History of the British Cinema, 1929–1939* (London: I.B. Tauris, 1998).

Sedgwick, John, "The Comparative Popularity of Stars in Mid-1930s Britain" in *Journal of Popular British Cinema*, Vol. 2, 1999.

Shadows, Mike Read, *The Story of the Shadows* (London: Elmtree/Hamish Hamilton, 1983).

Sharma, Sanjay, John Hutnyk and Ashwani Sharma, "Introduction" in Sanjay Sharma, John Hutnyk and Ashwani Sharma, eds, *Dis-Orienting Rhythms: The Politics of the New Asian Dance Music* (London: Zed, 1996).

Shellard, Dominic, *British Theatre Since the War* (London: Yale University Press, 2000).

Smith, Jeff, *The Sounds of Commerce: Marketing Popular Film Music* (New York: Columbia University Press, 1998).

Smith, Murray, *Trainspotting* (London: BFI, 2002).

Sneddon, William, "*Things to Come*: The World's First Soundtrack Album?" in *Film Score Monthly*, 6 June 2000.

Snelson, John, "British Musical Theatre, 1935–1960" in William A. Everett and Paul B. Laird, eds, *The Cambridge Companion to the Musical* (Cambridge: Cambridge University Press, 2002).

Spicer, Andrew, "Prince Charming in a Top Hat: the Debonair Man-About-Town in British Romantic Musical Comedy" in Ian Conrich and Estella Tincknell, eds, *Musical Moments: Film and Musical Performance* (Edinburgh: Edinburgh University Press, 2006).

Stokes, Jane, "Arthur Askey and the Construction of Popular Entertainment in *Band Waggon* and *Make Mine a Million*" in Justine Ashby and Andrew Higson, eds, *British Cinema: Past and Present* (London: Routledge, 2000).

Stradling, Robert and Meirion Hughes, *The English Musical Renaissance, 1860–1940: Construction and Deconstruction* (London: Routledge, 1993).

Street, Sarah, *British National Cinema* (London: Routledge, 1997).

Street, Sarah, " 'Got to Dance on My Way to Heaven': Jessie Matthews, Art Deco and the British Musical of the 1930s" in *Studies in European Cinema*, Vol. 2, no. 1, 2005.

Street, Sarah, "Popular British Cinema?" in *Journal of Popular British Cinema*, Vol. 1, 1998.

Stubblebine, Donald J., *British Cinema Sheet Music: A Comprehensive Listing of Film Music Published in the United Kingdom, Canada and Australia, 1916 through 1994* (Jefferson, NC: McFarland, 1997).

Sutton, Martin, "Patterns of Meaning in the Musical" in Rick Altman, ed., *Genre: The Musical* (London: Routledge and Kegan Paul, 1981).

Swann, Paul, "The British Culture Industries and the Mythology of the American Market: Cultural Policy and Cultural Exporters in the 1940s and 1990s" in *Cinema Journal*, Vol. 39, no. 4, Summer 2000.

Swynnoe, Jan G., *The Best Years of British Film Music, 1936–1958* (Woodbridge, Suffolk: Boydell Press, 2002).

Thomas, Nicholas, ed., *The International Dictionary of Filmmakers* (London: St. James Press, 1990).

Todd, Derek, "The Stable Door: After the (US) Force has Gone" (interview with John Boulting) in *Kinematograph Weekly*, Vol. 630, no. 3243, 6 December 1969.

Turner, Steve, *Cliff Richard: The Biography* (Oxford: Lion, 1993).

Vallance, Tom, "Soundtrack" in *Film: The Magazine of the Federation of Film Societies*, Vol. 32, 1962.

Vallance, Tom, "Musicals" in Brian MacFarlane, ed., *The Encyclopedia of British Film* (London: Methuen/BFI, 2005).

Vaughan Williams, Ralph, "Film Music" in *The Royal College of Music Magazine*, Vol. XL, no. 1, 1944.

Vaughan, Dai, *Odd Man Out* (London: BFI, 1995).

Walker, Alexander, *National Heroes: British Cinema in the Seventies and Eighties* (London: Harrap, 1985).

Walker, Alexander, *Hollywood, England: The British Film Industry in the Sixties* (London: Harrap, 1986).

Wapshott, Nicholas, *A Man Between: A Biography of Carol Reed* (London: Chatto & Windus, 1990).

White, Hayden, "Historiography and Historiophoty" in *American History Review*, Vol. 93, no. 5, 1988.

Willsmer, Trevor, "Interview with Gerard Schurmann" in *Movie Collector*, Vol. 1, no. 7, July/August 1994.

Wootton, Adrian, "Looking Back, Dropping Out, Making Sense: A History of the Rock-Concert Movie" in *Monthly Film Bulletin*, Vol. 55, no. 659, 1988.

Yule, Andrew, *David Puttnam: The Story So Far* (London: Sphere, 1988).

Index